CW00501538

THE MOYNIHAN BROTHERS IN PEACE AND WAR

The Moynihan Brothers
in Peace and War
1908–1918

Their New Ireland

Edited and introduced by

Deirdre McMahon

Mary Immaculate College, University of Limerick

IRISH ACADEMIC PRESS
DUBLIN • PORTLAND, OR

First published in 2004 by
IRISH ACADEMIC PRESS
44, Northumberland Road, Dublin 4, Ireland

and in the United States of America by
IRISH ACADEMIC PRESS
c/o ISBS, 920 N.E. 58th Avenue, Suite 300
Portland, Oregon 97213-3786

Website: www.iap.ie

Introduction and Notes © Deirdre McMahon

Letters © Estate of Maurice Moynihan

British Library Cataloguing in Publication Data
A catalogue record of this book is available from the British Library

ISBN 0-7165-2755-3

Library of Congress Cataloging-in-Publication Data
A catalog record of this book is available from the Library of Congress

Typeset by FiSH Books, London
Printed by MPG Books Ltd., Bodmin, Cornwall

In memory of Michael and John, and of Maurice, who did not forget
'the deepening social and spiritual drama of their new Ireland'
(W.P. Ryan, The Plough and the Cross, *1910)*

Contents

Illustrations

Acknowledgements

MY FIRST thanks are to someone who did not live to see the publication of these letters, the late Dr Maurice Moynihan, the younger brother of Michael and John, who died in 1999. He expressed the wish that through these letters the memory of two gifted and much-loved brothers might live on. I hope that this volume has done justice to his wish. I know that it would have been infinitely poorer without his help. He went through the letters, making many shrewd, informative and funny comments on them, and drawing on what was still, in his 90s, a phenomenal memory. I have included him in the dedication although I know that he would have resisted it, preferring that it should be in memory of Michael and John alone. My next thanks are to Maurice's children, Anne Hayden, the late Joan Moynihan and Martin Moynihan, but especially to Anne, who, since Maurice's death, has given constant support and encouragement to the project. She has patiently answered many questions about the family's history, to the extent of drawing up family trees, which have been most useful.

The task of editing the letters was made infinitely easier by having a clear and efficiently organised list of the letters compiled by Seamus Helferty of the University College Dublin Archives Department, who coped admirably with my many queries and demands for clarification. Kate O'Donnell was indispensable in helping me with the index. Special thanks are also due to Simon Jones, Curator of the King's Regiment at the Museum of Liverpool Life, to Michael Costello and the staff of the local history section of Kerry County Library, Tralee, and to Captain Joe Hardy, Pastoral Assistant of the Church of Ireland parish of St John in Tralee, who showed me the war memorials in the parish church. My research was also greatly facilitated by the staff of the following archives and libraries: the National Library of Ireland; the British Library, St Pancras; the British Newspaper Library, Colindale; and the Public Record Office, Kew. Last, but by no means least, I would like to pay special tribute to John Power and his staff at the Library of Mary Immaculate College, who have provided it with splendid history holdings.

I would like to acknowledge with gratitude a grant from the Academic Research Committee of Mary Immaculate College, which helped me to carry out research in London and Liverpool.

    My colleagues in the History Department of Mary Immaculate College have listened patiently to my accounts of the letters. I would especially like to thank Liam Irwin and Maura Cronin, who read the letters in draft and made many valuable comments, as did Dr Diarmaid Ferriter of St Patrick's College, Drumcondra, and Dr Margaret O'Callaghan of Queen's University, Belfast. I would like to pay particular tribute to Maura, who has been so supportive since my arrival at Mary Immaculate College in 1997. I would also like to thank Angus Mitchell and Jerome Aan de Wiel for a memorable visit to the Somme battlefields in February 2003. As I cannot drive, Liam Irwin, who has an encyclopedic knowledge of Munster's local history, exceeded the bounds of duty by taking time out from his own busy schedule to drive me to search out memorials and monuments in Kerry. I owe a special debt to my undergraduate and postgraduate students, especially those in my course on Ireland and the British Empire, who have given me many stimulating avenues of research to pursue. I have enjoyed equally stimulating e-mail discussions with two friends, Professor Lucy McDiarmid of Villanova University, Philadelphia, whose research on Irish controversies in the period up to 1914 has contributed greatly to this book, and Madeleine Humphreys of Dublin and Killaloe, biographer of Edward Martyn, who has taken me on many fascinating expeditions in Clare and south Galway. Dr Laurence Geary of University College Cork answered queries about the Land War and the Plan of Campaign in Kerry; Dr Hugh Fenning OP, archivist of the Irish Dominicans, helped me with information on Fathers Hyacinth Power and Anselm Moynihan; and Professor Risteard Mulcahy advised me about trench fever. For help with other queries I would like to thank Mark Baily, John Collins, Rosemary Cullen-Owens, Marie Coleman, Pauric Dempsey, Paul Dillon, Professor Keith Jeffery of the University of Ulster, Niall Keogh, Felix Larkin, James McGeachie of Belfast, Owen McGee, Gillian McIntosh of Belfast, Tadhg Moloney, Rosemary Raughter of Greystones, Gordon Revington of Tralee and Darach Sanfey of Mary Immaculate College. In November 2000 I gave a seminar on these letters at the Institute of Irish Studies, Belfast, which was chaired by Jane Leonard of the Ulster Museum, who made many comments and suggestions. I would also like to express my gratitude to my colleagues Professor Eunan O'Halpin and Dr Michael Kennedy, co-convenors of the Contemporary Irish History Seminar at Trinity College Dublin, where I gave a paper on these letters in June 2001. Finally, I would like to thank my friend Bawn O'Beirne Ranelagh of London, who has provided hospitality and friendship over the years.

Abbreviations

AFIL	All For Ireland League
BEF	British Expeditionary Force
BIR	Board of Inland Revenue
CBS	Christian Brothers' School
CO	Colonial Office (Records)
CSR	Civil Service Rifles
CTS	Catholic Truth Society
GAA	Gaelic Athletic Association
GOC	General Officer Commanding
GPO	General Post Office
IN&P	*Irish Nation and Peasant*
IRB	Irish Republican Brotherhood
IV	Irish Volunteers
JKAHS	*Journal of the Kerry Archaeological and Historical Society*
KLR	King's (Liverpool) Regiment
KRM	King's Regiment Museum (Liverpool)
LGB	Local Government Board
MFP	Moynihan Family Papers
NAI	National Archives of Ireland
NLI	National Library of Ireland
OCB	Officers Cadet Brigade
OP	Order of Preachers (Dominican)
PRO	Public Record Office
RIC	Royal Irish Constabulary
TD	Teacha Dála (Member of the Irish Parliament)
UCC	University College Cork
UCD	University College Dublin
UCDAD	University College Dublin Archives Department
UIL	United Irish League
VC	Victoria Cross
WO	War Office (Records)
YMCA	Young Men's Christian Association

Introduction

IN SEPTEMBER 1908 Michael Moynihan left his home town of Tralee in County Kerry and arrived at University College, Dublin (UCD) to begin his first year of studies. He was accompanied by his anxious mother, Mary, who wanted to inspect his prospective lodgings, and by his friend and distant cousin James McElligott, who was also starting at UCD. Michael was the eldest of six children, five boys and one girl, and as he had not been to boarding school his departure marked the first break in the family circle. To the rest of the family, and particularly to his mother and his brother John, he was the adored eldest son and brother, but his prolonged absence, first in Dublin, then in London, followed by active service in France and Belgium during the First World War, led to this remarkable collection of letters, written over the following ten years.

While a considerable amount of new documentary material about Ireland and the First World War has become available to scholars in recent years, collections such as the Moynihan letters, which include material from the period before 1914, are quite rare. The family was not prominent nationally and, although the Moynihans were well known in Tralee, it was Cork rather than Dublin with which they had close personal, political and economic ties. At one level the letters tell something of the story of a single family, and particularly of two young men, Michael and John, who were reaching maturity in the ten years spanned by the letters. However, this story was played out against the background of growing political, social and cultural turbulence in Ireland, and of looming war in Europe. These events were to change the family irrevocably.

The bulk of the correspondence consists of letters between Michael and his mother Mary and, especially, between Michael and his brother John. Mary's letters, which kept him in touch with family events and gossip in Tralee, reveal the depth of her love for her cherished eldest son. The letters between Michael and John illustrate the encyclopaedic range of their interests and activities. The correspondence thus offers a fascinating contrast between the domestic and the familial, on the one hand,

and on the other hand discussion of weightier topics, such as the Irish language, the roles of church and state, local Kerry politics, unionism and Home Rule, the First World War and the Easter Rising. It has been amplified in this volume by items from contemporary newspapers and other relevant archives. Michael and John were voracious readers of newspapers, journals, popular and serious fiction, and philosophical and religious books, which they discussed eagerly and at length in their letters. Michael also wrote verse, the poor quality of which he would often joke about to John. As his poems can be quite revealing, some of them have been included here. Apart from the light they shed on contemporary Irish society, the letters are a historically valuable commentary, reflecting the social and political changes that had taken place in Ireland since the Famine, and of which the Moynihans were themselves a part.

Historical background

In the twenty years after the fall of Parnell in 1890, a new Catholic elite emerged that was to dominate the movement for Irish independence in the early twentieth century. It was largely the product of social and economic developments after the Famine, particularly the changes in the education system that followed such events as the passing of the Intermediate Education Act in 1878 and the creation of the Royal University in 1879. These provided opportunities for greater mobility for many Catholic children from middle- and lower-middle-class backgrounds. This in turn led on to greater political mobility in the 1880s and 1890s, associated with the widening of the franchise in 1884, the appearance of the tantalising mirage of Home Rule in 1886 and 1893, and the Local Government Act of 1898. In his illuminating novels of the period, which the Moynihan boys read, Canon Sheehan expressed anxiety that the new Ireland would be both stagnant and materialistic, ruled by the principles of *cui bono* ('whose profit') and *quieta non movere* ('undisturbed quiet').[1]

However, as Tom Garvin has observed, there were other undercurrents at work in the decades after 1890: restlessness, disillusion, political romanticism and cults of violence all over Europe.[2] In Ireland, in the aftermath of Parnell's fall, these were fuelled by an increasing sense of political impotence and frustration with the long wait for Home Rule. When the Moynihan family correspondence opens in 1908, Home Rule seems as far away as ever: the Liberals had won a landslide victory in the general election of 1906 and were thus under no compulsion to reintroduce Home

Rule. By 1918, when the correspondence ends, another landslide victory is in sight, but this time for Sinn Féin, a minor party that in 1908 had seemed to have attained the limits of its success by coming a poor second in a by-election in North Leitrim.

Kerry Fenianism and the Land War

Maurice Moynihan, the father of the two young men whose letters largely comprise this volume, did not live to see Sinn Féin's victory but, as the correspondence shows, he understood very clearly the sea change that had occurred after the Easter Rising and, as a longstanding member of the Irish Republican Brotherhood (IRB) (the Fenians), he rejoiced in it. He was born in 1864 at Tylough, Rathanny, east of Tralee, near the Stack's Mountains, and was educated at St Michael's College in Listowel, the leading Catholic secondary school in north Kerry. He intended to become a priest but later gave up the idea. His father, Michael, had been deeply involved in the Fenian movement, but Maurice's family believed that it was probably Denis McNamara, one of his teachers in Listowel and IRB head centre there, who inducted him into the Brotherhood. It was through the IRB that he met other prominent Kerry Fenians, notably Michael Power. Maurice Moynihan, Power and William Moore Stack (father of Austin Stack) founded the first Kerry GAA club in May 1885 and Moynihan remained closely involved with the organisation until his death. He served two terms as secretary of the Kerry county board and was joint secretary of the GAA's council in the early 1890s. In January 1888 he was sentenced to a month's imprisonment at the Tralee Petty Sessions for obstructing the police.

Tralee, the county town of Kerry and the richest of the Kerry Poor Law unions, had a population of more than 10,300 in 1911, according to the census of that year. It was a politically active town and, during the ten years covered in this volume, nine newspapers were published there at various times. Tralee was a long-established centre of Fenianism. Samuel Hussey, the agent of the Kenmare and other estates who was to play a prominent role in the Land War in Kerry, described the difference between the old Fenianism of the 1860s and 1870s and the new Fenians of the 1880s, many of whom came from Cork and Kerry:

> The old Fenianism was politically of little account, socially of no danger, except to a few individuals who could be easily protected, and has been grossly exaggerated, either wilfully or

through ignorance. Matters were very different after Mr
Gladstone, by successive acts of what I maintain were criminal
legislation, deliberately fostered treason and encouraged
outrage in Ireland.[3]

Although many Fenians preferred to avoid the land issue, the Tralee
Fenians pursued it with fervour. Kerry was to become a byword for
outrage during the Land War, but, as James Donnelly has observed, this
was all the more surprising to contemporaries as there had been little
agrarian crime in Kerry before 1880.[4] Hussey remarked bitterly that landlord–tenant relations in Kerry 'were as cordial as in any part of the world
... until what is virtually universal suffrage was introduced [in 1884] and
the ignoramus became the tool of every political knave'.[5]

The long-term causes of the Land War in Kerry were rising expectations and structural changes in the agrarian economy, chiefly the
dominance of pasture and the decline of agricultural labourers. The
short-term causes were rent rises and an increase in evictions over a short
period. Matters came to a head in November 1880, when Lord Kenmare,
owner of large estates near Killarney, received death threats and left
Ireland indefinitely. Before his departure he ordered the dismissal of
hundreds of his labourers and the Kenmare estates became the scene of
some of the worst violence of the Land War.[6]

Although the Land League was not founded in Kerry until the end of
1880, there had been an active tenant right society in Tralee in the 1870s.
In 1881 the Land League won a remarkable victory in the Tralee Poor
Law Union elections, when it contested seventeen seats and won thirteen.
The President of the North Kerry Land League was Timothy
Harrington, a former teacher who was one of the principal organisers of
the Land League in the southwest and was later appointed a secretary of
the National League.[7] He became MP for Westmeath in 1883 and later for
Dublin Harbour. In 1877 his brother Edward had founded the *Kerry
Sentinel*, which was the voice of the Land League and the National League
in the 1880s. The Harrington brothers were among Parnell's most trusted
lieutenants. Maurice Moynihan was particularly close to Edward
Harrington and wrote sporadically for the *Sentinel* until shortly before his
death. Along with Timothy Harrington, Michael Power was involved in
one of first prosecutions of the Land War in Kerry when, in January
1881, they were arrested for holding an illegal Land League court and
imprisoned in Tralee jail.

When the Plan of Campaign got under way in 1886, Kerry became even more disturbed, to such an extent that the *Cork Examiner* lamented in April 1888 that Kerry 'has become a scene of disorder which must make every Irishman, and every native of Kerry especially, grieve sorely for the low estate to which a respectable people have fallen'. Kerry became the focus of the Commission on Parnellism and Crime in 1888–89, during which Timothy Harrington was one of Parnell's counsel.[8] Maurice Moynihan was one of the quintessential 'hillside men', the Fenians who stood by Parnell after the split in 1890 and who remained devoted to his memory, a devotion that, in Maurice Moynihan's case, was still evident in October 1916, when, dying slowly from tuberculosis, he wrote a seven-part series on Parnell for the *Kerry Sentinel*. In it he excoriated the 'poltroons', 'sycophants' and 'placehunters' who had betrayed the Chief, and bitterly attacked the Catholic Church for acting at the behest of Gladstone and his party. Frank Callanan has noted the ironies in the relationship between Parnell and 'hillside' Fenians such as Maurice Moynihan. His 'strange rapport' with Fenianism conveyed allusive hints of both imaginative affinity and historical sympathy, but Fenianism was in disarray by 1890–91 precisely because Parnell's pursuit of a parliamentary strategy had revealed the political bankruptcy of the movement.[9]

As Paul Bew has written, the Land War was characterised by a 'rare combination of social and political forces which endowed Irish nationalism with a sense of excitement and purpose it was not to recover until after the Easter Rising of 1916'.[10] This was particularly true in Maurice Moynihan's case. Although the Land War violence gradually diminished in Kerry in the 1890s, agitation continued over the Kenmare estates and, later, the Ventry estates. He remained closely involved with the land question over the following decades and in the general election in January 1910 he played an active part in the campaign of Eugene O'Sullivan, a prominent champion of evicted tenants, who was standing in Kerry East.[11] In May 1913 he was a candidate for the post of secretary of the Agricultural Technical Committee, but was defeated.

The Moynihans and the Powers after the Parnell split

In 1890 Maurice Moynihan married Michael Power's twenty-year-old niece Mary. He worked at the Tralee branch of the Co-operative Wholesale Society and during the year after his marriage he spent several months at the Manchester headquarters of the Society before returning to Tralee. For the rest of his life he worked as the Tralee agent for Daly's and

Shanahan's, two big wholesale butter, tea and spirits merchants in Cork. The Cork Butter Exchange, as James S. Donnelly has written, was 'the linchpin in a great trading and marketing network which played a highly significant role in both the Irish agricultural economy and the international butter trade'. The strong farmers of north Kerry tried to loosen the grip of the Cork butter markets by setting up a butter market in Listowel where Maurice Moynihan and, later, his son John both frequently worked.[12] Interesting light is shed on business relationships in Tralee by the fact that, despite his Fenian background, Maurice Moynihan was on good terms with John Revington, a prominent Tralee unionist, who owned a large drapery store and woollen mills. Mary Moynihan was to describe Revington as 'a brick always' when he helped her out financially during the difficult first days of the First World War.[13]

Maurice Moynihan's job was intimately linked to his IRB activities, as was noted on his file in Dublin Castle's List of Suspects: he was reported to be

> a clerk in a butter buyer's establishment in Tralee and has within the last few years come into prominence as an active promoter of secret societies. He is the life and soul of the G.A.A. in Kerry, in which he holds the post of Secretary. He is smart and intelligent and is possessed of some ability as an organiser. His occupation as a butter buyer's assistant affords him opportunities of moving through the country and assists him in his capacity as Secret Society Agent. He is Secretary of the IRB of Kerry and of the Tralee Young Ireland Society...

In July 1892 the file stated that Maurice Moynihan 'does not now meddle in politics – is a Parnellite', although his addresses at the Manchester Martyrs commemorations in Tralee and Cork in 1893 and 1895 were duly noted on his file.[14] However, the Dublin Castle file is oddly silent about the John Twiss case in January 1895. At the Munster Winter Assizes in Cork, John Twiss was charged with the murder in April 1894 of James Donovan, a caretaker of an evicted farm. The *Kerry Sentinel* described the trial as 'one of the most remarkable murder trials ... for many years'. After his conviction Twiss 'pointed to a Crown official in court and deliberately charged him with having offered him a considerable sum of money if he would sweep away the lives of six persons he named'. Maurice Moynihan and Michael Power, his uncle by marriage, were two of those six.[15]

Maurice Moynihan came to the attention of the RIC again in November 1896 during the annual Manchester Martyrs Commemoration in Tralee, which was organised by the Young Ireland Society. He made 'a violent speech condemning constitutional agitation as useless, and advocating physical force'.[16] There are further references to him in the Crime Branch Special files when he was chairman of the 1798 Centenary Committee in Tralee, although the committee was not very active.[17] He subsequently visited the United States to raise money for the Tralee monument. While the Kerry County Inspector of the RIC dismissed these commemorative efforts in his monthly reports to Dublin Castle, he noted the opportunity that they offered for a reorganisation of the IRB.[18] In May 1899 Maurice Moynihan stood for election as Secretary of the new Kerry County Council, but was defeated by P.M. Quinlan, clerk of the Tralee Urban District Council.[19] He was subsequently appointed returning officer for elections in Tralee, a position he held until 1914 when ill health overtook him. When the Boer War broke out in 1899 Moynihan spoke regularly at anti-enlistment meetings. He was briefly involved with the United Irish League, founded by William O'Brien in 1898, but once it lost its anti-grazier *raison d'être* and effectively became the constituency organisation of the reunited Irish Party, he abandoned it. In the general election of 1900 he campaigned for Tom O'Donnell against the Healyite candidate J.E.J. Julian. O'Donnell won Kerry West and remained MP for the constituency until 1918. Although Maurice Moynihan's political relations with O'Donnell deteriorated after this, they remained, as the family correspondence shows, on good personal terms and in 1911, and again in 1916, he did not hesitate to ask for O'Donnell's political assistance in order to advance his son's career.

After the excitements of the Boer War, the first decade of the new century was politically tranquil in Kerry, not to say stagnant.[20] There were periodic alarms about a revival of secret societies, but nothing came of them. The United Irish League and the secret societies kept each other at arm's length, while the GAA also suffered its share of rifts and dissension. Although Maurice Moynihan was not as active politically as he had been in the 1880s and 1890s, he was still involved with the annual Manchester Martyrs commemorations in Tralee, campaigned for Eugene O'Sullivan in 1910 and spoke at a public meeting against the dismissal of a local national teacher in December 1912. As tuberculosis gradually weakened him, he wrote occasional items of journalism, including the seven-part series on Parnell already referred to and a book review for *New Ireland*.[21]

Maurice Moynihan is a shadowy presence in his family's correspondence.

The impression is of an affectionate but distant father, largely absorbed by politics. Looking back over his turbulent involvement in radical nationalism, one can readily understand his wife Mary's weary comment to her eldest son in 1909 – 'you know all I have suffered through politics' – and her fear that he too would become an extreme nationalist.[22] As is clear from the correspondence, Michael's political views became diametrically opposed to his father's, but there is no indication of any family arguments about this. Although Michael's political stance and his decision to join the Territorial Force in 1914 must have upset his father, Maurice deferred to his eldest son's wishes and in 1916 he even tried to advance Michael's wartime career in the army, as the correspondence reveals.

Mary's family, the Powers – especially her uncles Michael ('Mick') and Patrick ('Pat the Rock' as he was known in the family because he lived on Rock Street, Tralee), and her twin brother John – have a more dominant presence in the letters than her husband and his family. Mary's father John, a relatively prosperous cattle-dealer, died in 1907 and shortly afterwards her mother ('Grandmama' or 'Mama' in the correspondence) came to live with her. Mary had a younger brother, Patrick, but was closest to her beloved twin brother, John, who worked for the Post Office in London and was a leading light in the London Gaelic League, where he had the affectionate title of 'An Paorach' ('The Power'). He was a renowned piper at their St Patrick's Day concerts:

> The pipes ... as An Paorach and his kilted bodyguard played them, were magical in the way they filled the audience with a desire for more. At the end of the evening concert, the pipes set off down the Strand and Fleet Street like so many Orpheuses, drawing thousands after them by the tune of 'The Peeler and the Goat' and 'The Wearing of the Green' as far as Ludgate Circus.[23]

In December 1906, following a rumbustious send-off at Euston Station, John returned to Ireland for three years to work as a travelling teacher for the Gaelic League, based in Tipperary. He returned to London in 1910 to work for the London Gaelic League's new journal *An tEireannach*, but left within a year to become a freelance journalist. He worked for the *Kerry Weekly Reporter* and the *Cork Free Press*. He and his wife Lizzie were childless, which may explain the closeness between them and his sister's children. It is significant that it was he, and not his brother-in-law Maurice, who voiced the family's strenuous objections to Michael's decision to join the Territorial Force in March 1914 (discussed in more detail below).

Maurice and Mary Moynihan had six children. Michael was born in February 1891 and John in January 1892. Since their daughter Hannah ('Han'), was not born until October 1899, the two oldest boys were virtually twin brothers. After Hannah came Maurice, who was born in December 1902; Denis, born in January 1907; and Thomas, born in May 1913. There was thus a considerable gap between the two oldest boys and the four younger children. Although few of Michael's letters to his siblings other than John have survived, the tender postcard that he sent to Hannah in September 1914, when she was having problems in her new school, suggests why they adored him.

Mary's love for her eldest son emerges as one of the central relationships in the family letters. In a letter written to Michael in 1910, Brother Ryan, his former teacher at the Christian Brothers' School, praised his mother for keeping him at the Christian Brothers' School in Tralee and not moving him to a more prestigious school such as Clongowes, where his cousin John Power was studying. In fact this decision seems to have had little to do with education, and everything to do with Mary's desire to keep both Michael and John at home with her for as long as she could. Her anxiety about Michael emerges in the very first letter, when she expresses concern about the suitability of his lodgings in Dublin. From then on 'why are you not writing?' becomes a regular complaint. 'You know how anxious she has always been about you', his father wrote to him reproachfully in 1912, urging him to write to his mother. On occasion she could be firm with Michael. For example, she withstood his pleas to buy shares in the *Irish Nation and Peasant* in 1909, although she subsequently took his advice about which stocks and shares to buy with her small inheritance from her father. Again, in 1913 Mary's family pride made her determined that Michael would not be associated with the Quinlans when the Kerry County Secretaryship became vacant. She was equally firm that her daughter Hannah would complete her studies. Mary also displayed other traits stereotypically associated with Irish mothers, notably disapproval of any local belles who had the temerity to cast predatory eyes on her sons. As the letters of 1911–12 illustrate, the young men in question had to resort to laborious code names to deflect maternal suspicion. Since Michael and John disagreed strongly about women's suffrage – Michael expressed himself as 'entirely opposed' even during his brief socialist phase in 1909 – it is entertaining to discover that the object of Michael's affections in the winter of 1911–12, the mysterious 'Moss', turned out to have radical suffragette sympathies and was arrested for breaking windows in London.

UCD and the Civil Service

Michael was one of an increasing number of Catholics from small farm and trade backgrounds receiving post-primary education under the Intermediate Education Act 1878. John J. Horgan referred to the 'contagion' of the Intermediate results and the enormous importance placed on them by schools, since government capitation grants were dependent on them.[24] The examination results were eagerly scrutinised when they were published in the local and national press. Michael made his way through secondary school and university by winning a series of scholarships and exhibitions that were faithfully recorded in the Kerry press, some excerpts from which have been included in the correspondence.

By the time Michael went to UCD, in the autumn of 1908, the number of candidates presenting themselves for university examinations had almost trebled from 3,945 in 1879 to 11,900 in 1910. By then UCD was regarded, as Senia Pašeta has written, as 'the cream of ability', the place where the future leaders of Home Rule Ireland would be trained and moulded.[25] Michael arrived at a watershed in UCD's history. The golden generation of James Joyce, Thomas Kettle and Francis Sheehy-Skeffington had left, and the passing of the Irish Universities Act in 1908 saw the dissolution of the old Royal University and its absorption into the National University of Ireland, along with constituent colleges in Cork and Galway (the former Queen's Colleges). Michael's years at UCD thus included the last year of the old Royal University and the first year of the new National University. Among his contemporaries were Conor Maguire, who was to become a Fianna Fáil politician and Attorney General in the 1930s, High Court President and Chief Justice; and John A. Costello, another future Attorney General and later Taoiseach.

At the beginning of his second year at UCD Michael sat for the Home Civil Service examinations and won seventh place overall – the only Irish place, as the *Kerry Sentinel* gushingly recorded in February 1910. He left UCD without taking his degree in order to take up his appointment. Although there had been a tenfold increase in numbers in the Irish Civil Service between 1861 and 1911, largely because of the establishment of the Land Commission, the Department of Agriculture and Technical Instruction, and the National Insurance Commission, many ambitious

xxii   Introduction

Irish Catholics preferred to apply to the British Home Civil Service.[26] Promotion and prospects were better in the British departments because they were not at the mercy of the reactionary unionist rump that had dominated the upper echelons of Dublin Castle particularly since the administrations of Lord Salisbury and Arthur Balfour. (Michael's contemporary, friend and distant relative, James McElligott, passed the Indian Civil Service examinations but decided for family reasons to remain in Ireland and work for the Local Government Board, where prejudice against Catholics was particularly insidious.[27] McElligott subsequently joined the Irish Volunteers and took part in the Easter Rising, a fact which may or may not be attributed to his experiences at the LGB.) Michael worked at the Dublin offices of the Revenue Commissioners before being transferred to their Croydon office, then just outside London, in the autumn of 1913.

The generation of 1914

In one of his school essays, 'Characteristics Essential to Success in Life', the young Michael considered that character came first and foremost, followed by energy, the latter defined as 'push, a taking advantage of every opportunity which offers itself'. Energy and push were certainly features of the older Michael. Less recognisable was any evidence of adherence to a dictum from another essay, 'Contentment': 'happy is he who is contented with his lot'. Other essays – 'Benefits of Travel', 'Out of Debt, Out of Danger', and 'Seafaring Life' – strongly prefigured aspects of his later life.[28] 'I am an individualist', he once told John, and the individualism and complexity of his character are among the fascinating aspects of the letters. He could be arrogant, and sometimes indulged in intellectual bullying of his mother and John, who were, however, more than able to hold their own. John once referred to Michael's 'covenanting temperament', and one can detect this in Michael's sometimes relentless arguments about politics, religion and literature. There was also a profound restlessness in Michael. 'Heaven must be insufferably boring. Perfection means simplicity, and simplicity means dullness', he announced in 1909.[29] He loved mountaineering and sailing; he devoured Morley Roberts's sea stories about the romance of tramp steamers sailing around the world; he dabbled in stocks and shares; after a year at the Revenue Commissioners he wanted to be transferred to the Admiralty; he longed to leave Dublin; after six months in Croydon he joined the Territorial Force. This restlessness can, of course, be explained by the increasing burden of family responsibilities that fell on his shoulders as his father's health declined. It can also be seen as a chafing against the intense love of his mother.

John had a more equable temperament than the mercurial Michael. He was, as his teacher Brother Ryan told Michael in 1910, 'good and kind'. He was more deliberate but resembled Michael in being immensely well-read. There is no family explanation as to why he did not continue his education after secondary school, although there are references to his poor health. He went into the family butter business and, as his father's health declined, he provided much-needed support to his mother and the rest of the family at home. It appears that he never resented his more brilliant brother, although his jesting references to Michael's 'cold water dousing', and his attempts to deflate it in a mock-tragic tone, may perhaps suggest otherwise. The letters reveal the encyclopaedic nature of their interests and arguments when they were apart, while passing comments, such as 'the nights you kept me awake last Christmas' or 'as we agreed when I was home', testify to the intensity of their discussions when they were together again. One of the clearest early memories of their younger brother Maurice was of lying in bed listening to his two older brothers talking and arguing far into the night about everything under the sun. The letters offer vivid snapshots of the events, minor and momentous, that the family witnessed: John and Michael's love of the theatre in Dublin, Cork and Tralee; a performance by Sarah Bernhardt in London; Edward VII's funeral; the new London Underground lines; the Coronation visit to Dublin by George V and Queen Mary in 1911, and the opening of the new College of Science Buildings in Merrion Street; Mary's humorous account of the 'monster' shark in Fenit Harbour; Michael's curious glimpse of the Kerry peer, Lord Headley, who 'has turned Mahommedan [sic]'; labour unrest in Cork, Dublin and London; Asquith's crowded visit to Dublin in July 1912; inspection visits by Lord Kitchener in 1915; the Easter Rising and its aftermath in Kerry; and the conscription crisis in the spring of 1918.

Michael and John belonged to the generation of 1914. It was an age of unprecedented political, social, scientific, technological, philosophical, educational and religious developments, which created significant tensions. There was a new sense of confidence and optimism about Ireland in the new century, based on the hope that it could and would move away from the dispiriting legacy of the Famine. There was an emphasis on youth and a corresponding belief that the older generation was synonymous with weakness and degeneration. Many European intellectuals of the time complained that they had been born into a world lacking energy and fibre, and that this had led to crisis in their respective nations. They also felt a considerable ambivalence about modern commercial civilisation. All this created a profound generational restlessness in the relationship between parents and children, and particularly between fathers and sons. There was a sense of discontinuity and a tendency towards extremes: optimism, dogmatism and, ominously, the growing appeal of war as catharsis, as a form of national regeneration and renewal.[30]

These themes resonate through the Moynihan family's correspondence. In 1909 the letters discuss evolution, decadence and the degeneration of nations. There are also echoes of the scares about war and invasion that erupted sporadically during the first dozen years of the twentieth century. Michael's political views were to shift radically, from membership of the Socialist Party of Ireland and an enthusiasm for Irish Ireland to a deep-dyed conservatism founded upon a distaste for modernity and peace. 'Frankly, to me all this supercivilisation is entirely hateful', he wrote to John in July 1912, 'calamity would be preferable to it. What to you seems progress is to me all decadence and *fin de siècle*.'[31] John was impatient with his brother's 'unreasoning love of antiquity' and veneration of aristocracy. 'Live your life in your own age', he urged, 'an age that has never been lived before ... Don't pin your faith to dead customs.'[32] John remained a social-ist down to 1916, although he shared some of Michael's romanticism, together with his fear of social disintegration and anarchy. Western Europe, he wrote in March 1912, was 'coming under a cloud'.[33] The broth-ers read widely, ranging from Homer, Marcus Aurelius and Aeschylus in classical literature, to philosophers such as Burke, Emerson, Kant and that siren *fin de siècle* voice, Nietzsche, to such lighter works as the historical novels of Winston Churchill, Jeffery Farnol and F. Marion Crawford. They were particularly interested in what might loosely be termed 'coming of age' novels, such as W.P. Ryan's *The Plough and the Cross*, George Meredith's *The Ordeal of Richard Feverel*, Churchill's *The Inside of the Cup* and *The New Machiavelli* by H.G. Wells, in which young idealistic heroes struggle against a conventional, selfish and myopic older generation.

Religion and the Irish language

Religion was an especially absorbing subject for Michael and John, and their letters illuminate Irish Catholicism in the early decades of the twen-tieth century. While both were devout, practising Catholics, they also inherited the Fenian anticlericalism of their father, and were generally contemptuous of the Irish clergy and hierarchy, not to mention the 'wiliness' of Rome.[34] Other manifestations of popular Catholicism, such as the 'penny inanities' of the Catholic Truth Society, also irritated them.[35] The correspondence opens at a time of special turbulence in the Catholic Church. Modernism, which drew on new philosophical, social and political currents in France, Britain, Germany and Italy at the turn of the century, was condemned in September 1907 by Pius X in the encyclical *Pascendi*. Its leading advocates had their works put on the Index and were then variously dismissed, suspended or excommunicated. In 1910 Catholic clergy were further required to take an oath against Modernism. *Pascendi* convulsed the Church:

> The committees of vigilance set up by the encyclical were used as a specious support by simplist conservative groups to justify sweeping condemnations. Thinking and nuance were rejected in favour of polemics. Modernism became a slogan to be applied to whatever was disliked in liberal Catholic thought, theology, literature, and politics.[36]

Although the Irish Church could scarcely be described as a hotbed of Modernism, the suppression of the movement created significant ripples in Ireland.

W.P. Ryan, editor of the *Irish Peasant*, which folded in 1906 because of clerical disapproval, took a keen interest in the debate about Modernism and gave it prominence in the new journal he started in January 1909, the *Irish Nation and Peasant*, a journal that, as the letters vividly demonstrate, Michael and John read with much excitement throughout that year. Ryan was one of the most remarkable journalists of his generation. His views have been described as an eclectic mix of socialism, agrarianism, neo-Gaelicism and secularism; from 1907 he also became increasingly interested in Theosophy.[37] The *IN&P*, shortlived as it was, still conveys a sense of freshness and engagement with issues that helps to explain its attraction to the Moynihan brothers, along with others of their generation. Michael and John were acquainted with some of the *IN&P*'s journalists, including Ryan himself, Leonard Brannigan, J.W. O'Beirne and P.S. O'Hegarty, who had known their uncle John Power in the London Gaelic League.

Ryan caused particular alarm to the Church authorities by giving a platform to George Tyrrell, who had been dismissed by the Jesuits after *Pascendi* and then excommunicated. The 'Maynooth Movement', a somewhat shadowy liberalising group, features in the *IN&P* and even more prominently in Ryan's novel *The Plough and the Cross*, also read with great enthusiasm by the brothers, which was first serialised in the *IN&P*. It is difficult to gauge how much substance there was in the Maynooth Movement but, as delineated by Ryan, it emphasised the importance of an educated laity and the need for a less authoritarian church. Ryan also highlighted the generational crisis between the upper and lower clergy, a theme portrayed in several of Canon Sheehan's novels.

Many of these currents and tensions swirling around the Church were to surface in a controversy that galvanised the country in 1909: the dismissal of Dr Michael O'Hickey from the Chair of Irish in Maynooth because of his support for compulsory Irish for matriculation in the new National University. As the letters reveal, Michael and John eagerly followed every twist and turn of the crisis, and were deeply critical of the hierarchy's treatment of O'Hickey.[38] Modernism is the neglected element in any discussion of the O'Hickey controversy. While O'Hickey's theological views were completely orthodox, his challenge to episcopal power at such a sensitive time for the Church authorities stunned the Irish bishops. The fact that his strongest press support came from Ryan's *IN&P*, which was openly sympathetic to Modernism, was damning. The treatment of O'Hickey confirmed the Moynihan brothers in their anticlericalism, although their own religious views were to diverge over the following years. Michael was for a time attracted by ultramontanism, and in 1912 accused John of being a Modernist: 'your attitude is simply the Modernist one of approval to all current and shifting phases of opinion'.[39] For John, however, 'scepticism has become ... more and more a ruling principle of my life', and in March 1914 he was reading George Tyrrell's *Christianity at the Crossroads*.

Although the brothers keenly followed the O'Hickey controversy, they were not active in the Gaelic League and neither could speak Irish at the time. However, as Michael observed, 'the question of Irish is not one for argument, "fair" or otherwise ... it is purely a question of feeling'.[40] Their father was more lukewarm about the League and considered it a distraction from the more fundamental goal of Irish independence. In fact, the Tralee Gaelic League had been inactive for some years when it was revived in 1909. By 1914 Tom O'Donnell was writing to John Dillon, deputy leader of the Irish Party, that 'there was no constituency in Ireland where the poison of the Gaelic League was more extensively sown than West Kerry'.[41] John learned Irish, became a member of the League and later served on its Kerry County Committee. His siblings also took a great interest in the language: Hannah won a prize in Irish at school and was active in the Tralee Gaelic League after her return from boarding school in 1915, while Maurice learned the language at the Tralee CBS and soon became a fluent speaker.

Political views

In Britain *The New Age* fulfilled the same role as a forum for cultural and political debate as the *IN&P* did in Ireland. It was the first socialist weekly published in London and, like the *IN&P*, it appealed to a readership produced by the Education Acts of the 1870s and 1880s, which was dissatisfied with anodyne periodicals such as *Tit-Bits* or *T.P.'s Weekly*. After A.R. Orage became editor of *The New Age* in 1908 he commissioned regular contributions from Bernard Shaw, Hilaire Belloc, H.G.Wells, the Chesterton brothers (Cecil and G.K.), and Arnold Bennett, among others. He also published fiction by Tolstoy, Gorky and Chekhov.[42] Michael's enthusiastic reading of the two journals reflected his interest in socialism. He joined the Socialist Party of Ireland in June 1909, but soon became critical of its impracticality and its lack of a coherent programme.

Michael's political views underwent a decisive shift to the right and high Toryism in 1910, around the time he joined the Civil Service. His family seem to have regarded this shift as another instance of his incorrigible restlessness and to have made no comment. John jokingly referred to it in January 1912, however: 'About two years ago, you may remember, you made a sudden and unheralded change in your political opinions ... anticipating, presumably, a time when, as the reward of prudent speculation, you expect to become a millionaire.' As his letters indicate, Michael was contemptuous of Arthur Balfour's effete leadership of the Conservative Party and rejoiced in his resignation in 1911. As is also clear from letters written in 1912, he was deeply influenced by Lord Hugh Cecil's book *Conservatism*, which he marshalled to his side during his forceful exchanges with John on the evils of socialism, the role of the state and the individual. Cecil was a son of Lord Salisbury, the former Conservative Prime Minister, but, as John drily pointed out, Cecil's rowdy behaviour during the debates on the Parliament Bill could hardly be described as aristocratic.[43] Significantly, Michael, although he made some conventionally loyal comments about 'Their Majesties' when the King and Queen paid their Coronation visit to Dublin in 1911, soon became deeply ambivalent about monarchy and empire.[44] Equally significantly, he did not comment on Cecil's views about Home Rule. Home Rule was repulsive to the Tories, Cecil wrote in *Conservatism*,

because they regard it as the triumph of a movement deeply
tainted with Jacobinism ... There has been nothing more
Jacobinical in modern politics than the Land League agitation
under the leadership of Mr Parnell and Mr Davitt. The violence
and intimidation that disfigured it; the hideous crimes that
ominously coincided with it; the reckless disregard of private
property and the cruel oppression which it involved, reproduced
some of the worst features of the spirit of French terrorism.[45]

Given these comments on a movement in which his family had been intimately involved, it is not surprising that Home Rule eventually caused a
parting of the ways between Michael and the Tories, although he would
maintain that it was they who had betrayed Conservatism. By the end of
1913, when the battle for Home Rule was reaching its climax, his disillu-
sionment with party politics became complete. As the threat of war
loomed both in Ireland and in the rest of Europe, Michael, like many
others in the generation of 1914, saw it as a way out of his own political
and spiritual crisis. As the hero of *The New Machiavelli* declares: 'For my
part, since I love England as much as I detest her present lethargy of soul,
I pray for a chastening war – I wouldn't mind her flag in the dirt if only
her spirit would come out of it.'[46] Michael echoed these sentiments, but
applied them to Ireland.

Home Rule and the Civil Service Rifles

Perhaps surprisingly, the introduction of the Third Home Rule Bill in
April 1912 is barely referred to in these letters, by either John or Michael.[47]
They shared their father's contempt for the Irish Party, at both the local
and the national levels, and they feared that the proposed new Parliament
of Ireland would simply be Dublin Corporation writ large – a byword for
nepotism and corruption, 'shunned by all decent men'.[48]

This fear was widely shared and found expression in the literature of the
time. In his play *The Laying of the Foundations* (1902), Fred Ryan, one of the
secretaries of the Socialist Party that Michael joined in 1909, has his hero,
the idealistic young official Michael, proclaim that the new city of Dublin
must be laid on foundations of liberty and truth. When the corrupt
Alderman Farrelly asks him whether they are to be allies or at war, Michael
replies, as the curtain falls: 'The city of the future demands it. It can be
nothing else but war.'[49] An even more fervid tone of anxiety emerges nine

years later in Canon Sheehan's novel, *The Intellectuals* (1911), published in the year when, with the passing of the Parliament Act, Home Rule at last looked certain. One of the novel's leading characters, Dr Holden, asks:

> 'Let me suppose that you have obtained your Irish Parliament. Who will be elected thereunto? With the vast masses of the people so sunk in political apathy, totally devoid of political train-ing, the willing victims of every outrageous demagogue who has got "the gift of the gab", do you suppose that it is Constitutional "Moderates" will be elected to your Senate-Houses? No! But the wildest Socialist, the most rampant agitator – the man who will promise most to the mob, and who will most fiercely denounce property, religion and decency. You will cry out against it! Too late! the Lotus-Eaters will turn in their potato-patches, and ask: "Let us alone! What is the price of oats?"'[50]

Nevertheless, interest in Home Rule quickened perceptibly over the course of 1912. The Bishop of Kerry, Dr Mangan, was present in the House of Commons when the bill was introduced. There were meetings all over Kerry, including a big St Patrick's Day gathering in Tralee at which the Chairman of the Rural District Council, Thomas Slattery, warned that if the Home Rule Bill was not satisfactory 'they would have to adopt other methods'. Tom O'Donnell MP retorted that he was totally opposed to 'filling the minds of people with possibilities of other meth-ods'.[51] On 17 April the *Kerry Sentinel* reprinted a report from the Tory *Evening News* on the alleged composition of the first Home Rule cabinet: Redmond was to be Prime Minister, Dillon Minister for Finance and T.P. O'Connor Speaker of the new Irish Commons. In July Asquith was fêted during a brief visit to Dublin, an event that provoked humorous comment from Michael and John. In September there were pro- and anti-Home Rule meetings in Tralee, and this pattern of rival demonstrations was to continue through 1913. In May 1913 Tom O'Donnell gave a lecture to the Tralee branch of the Ancient Order of Hibernians on 'The Duties of the Irish Citizen under Home Rule'.

In August 1913 Michael was transferred from Dublin to the Inland Revenue offices at Croydon in Surrey. He had been anxious to move from Dublin for some time, but his arrival in London just as the imminent pass-ing of Home Rule was leading to predictions of civil war was to evoke a variety of complex responses in him. Edwardian London was at the peak of its social and political glamour, a glamour that radiates from novels such as *The New Machiavelli*, which he and John had both read that year. As Garvin, Pašeta and Hutchinson have all noted, many of the new Catholic elite found themselves pulled in two directions: they were designated as the future leaders of a Home Rule Ireland, while at the same time they were experiencing the increasing pull that the British imperial state exerted on Irish economic, social and cultural life. Many became resentful of the contempt and superiority displayed by the British establishment towards them, in particular, and Ireland, in general. It might be thought that Michael would be relatively immune from these resentments. After all, he had achieved his Civil Service appointment through merit, in open competition, and he had been an enthusiastic Tory for three years. Yet his reactions to the Home Rule crisis over the winter of 1913–14 marked a personal and political upheaval that had momentous repercussions.

The debate between Michael and John over Home Rule took place against a background of growing nationalist frustration, both with the unionist onslaught and with Liberal vacillation over the exclusion of Ulster (in whole or in part). John was against the coercion of Ulster into a united Ireland; Michael was firmly in favour and wrote bitterly of the 'criminal hypocrisy of both parties (of all indeed) towards the "Ulster question"'. He had not shed his Toryism, as he emphasised to John in December 1913. It was the Tories who had abandoned 'all the historic position of Toryism, ostensibly in the interest of an unruly gang in the North of Ireland. To read "Tory" speeches … anxiously quoting precedents to justify revolution, is more than I can stomach'. Michael also detected the strong vein of anti-Catholicism underlying much of the anti-Home Rule case: 'What they do fear and hate is the idea that the Catholic Church should take its rightful place in Ireland, or that the Catholic point of view should have its proper influence.' He was similarly scathing about unionist protestations about the empire: '"Loyalty" to the Empire has nothing to do with it, except that it happens to be a convenient whip with which to flog the Nationalists. It is laughable to think of these rapscallions burning with love for an Empire which exists only in name, and the component parts of which are under no sentimental illusions as to their relationships.' Failing a proper settlement, he thought that Redmond should 'stand firm, and resist any attempt at exclusion, or further restriction'.[52] John did not think that the unionists in Ulster were bluffing:

> The Protestants of Ulster are there – very much there – and
> there they will remain. (I should like to know how you propose
> to exterminate them.)…If our future history is not to be, like

our past, a record of failure and disillusion and bloodshed, we must change all that. We must draw all our parties and factions together and make them ready to sink their differences in face of the common enemy.

John thought that the Home Rule Bill was divisive and unsatisfactory to both sides. He favoured something like the aborted Councils Bill of 1907, as it would be acceptable to Ulster and 'would offer a basis for the re-union of the country'.[53]

On 2 March 1914, without telling John or the rest of his family, Michael enlisted in the Civil Service Rifles (CSR), a Territorial Force unit of the London Regiment. He did not tell John until three weeks later. A clue to his decision lies in a letter that he wrote to John on 17 November 1913: 'If the [Home Rule] Bill goes through as it stands, and the Orange crowd try their little game on, one must rely on the Irish soldiers in the British army, at any rate to obey the order to shoot.' He later told John, half-jestingly: 'I am far too much of a pessimist to hope for the felicity of war against Ulster. Perhaps it is my disbelief in the possibility of any extensive operations at any rate that has induced me to take up my latest pastime.'[54] Yet it is clear from these and other letters that operations were precisely what he was hoping for when he joined the CSR.

The Territorial Force had been set up in 1907, but, after an initial surge in recruiting numbers, it had been declining since 1910. There was hostility to it at the highest levels of the British army, which would have preferred some form of conscription. The Territorials were further handicapped by cumbersome organisation, obsolete equipment and poor training of officers and men. No units were ever established in Ireland and none was to serve there until after the outbreak of war in 1914.[55] In the wake of the Curragh incident, which occurred barely two weeks after Michael joined up, and which he and John watched with absorbed interest, it became more unlikely than ever that Territorial units would be used to deal with unrest in Ulster, since the very deployment of the regular army there had caused uproar.

The peremptory letter from Michael's uncle John Power, in which he asked his nephew to resign 'your membership of what you call the "Civil Service Rifles"', suggests the depth of family feeling that Michael's decision aroused. In a draft reply Michael defended his motives as 'neither unworthy nor inadequate'. He was joining because the only way 'of serving Ireland is fighting for it', despite the 'empty words and irresolute deeds' of nationalist Ireland, which stood in contrast to the 'strength of purpose and energy of resource' of its enemies. He also made it clear, however, that there was a strong element of spiritual crisis in his decision: 'my idea of patriotism ... has nothing in common with later ideas of ordered progress and industrial development ... Considerations such as these combined ... with a perhaps excessive distaste for peace and for modernity, have brought me to my present position which is far too bound up with my present philosophy of life to be shaken by petty criticism.'[56]

In *Ireland and the Great War* Keith Jeffery notes how the separate experiences of Redmondites, unionists and advanced nationalists actually constitute a series of 'parallel texts'.[57] This point emerges clearly in the letters of the spring of 1914. The Irish Volunteers had been founded in November 1913 and over the following six months the movement spread rapidly, the first Tralee corps being established in April 1914. Michael took a keen interest in the Volunteers and John sent him copies of their journal, the *Irish Volunteer*. The Tory papers, as he told John presciently in May 1914, treated the Volunteers with respect but more out of politeness than alarm: 'However, this English complacency *may* be mistaken. The deadening influence of the long years of peace and order and comparative prosperity is hard to shake off, but it could perhaps be done in Ireland, if soldier leaders were found.'[58] Michael seems to have relished his first experience of army life. He was 'very proud' of his Lee-Enfield; he did 'fairly well' at his first shoot; and he was looking forward to a weekend musketry camp. Yet, as he confided to John, it also 'gives you a sort of double life, in one of which you feel as near to the Mexican Rurales as in the other you are to civilised men about you'.[59]

By June 1914, with Mary's three youngest children still under eleven years old, her husband had become seriously ill with tuberculosis, and she and John were doing most of his work, both in relation to his post as electoral returning officer and in the butter agency. Mary was increasingly dependent on Michael's support and the financial help that he unstintingly gave from his Civil Service salary. Thus the outbreak of war in August had profound consequences for Mary, not only because of the possibility of a cut in Michael's salary, but, much more agonisingly, because it marked the beginning of four years of increasing anxiety about her adored eldest son. Michael, as he made clear to his mother, wished to volunteer for foreign service, but would not do so without her consent. 'Whatever my own feelings in the matter, I should take no avoidable steps which might cause you anxiety.'[60] Mary refused her consent until 1916, when matters were taken out of her hands by the passing of the Military Service Act, which left Michael with the choice of being conscripted or signing up for foreign service. His frustration at being denied the adventure of foreign service found expression in a poem he wrote during that first winter of the war.[61] The tensions in the regiment between those who signed up for foreign service and those who opted for home service are graphically revealed in the regimental history:

> It is not for anyone to comment upon the actions of others; circumstances alter cases, and during the war to act up to the dictates of one's own conscience was the duty of all. Nevertheless, the departure of the home service contingent was a matter of great relief to the 2nd Battalion. True, many good friends were lost, and many who had striven hard for the efficiency and well-being of the Battalion had to bid farewell, but for those who remained there there was that resuscitated feeling that the 2nd Battalion could some day take its proper place in the fight on the continent.[62]

Kerry and the Great War

When war broke out there was, according to the RIC County Inspector, 'extremely strong anti-German feeling' in Kerry, which was 'partly religious', but it was not translated into recruiting figures. The Volunteers were left without leaders or drill instruction, as many of their officers were called back to their regiments. In any event, few were anxious to volunteer for foreign service 'and at present none of them are of much use for home defence'.[63] When M.J. Flavin, MP for Kerry North, addressed a well-attended Volunteer rally at Ardfert on 27 September, he 'got a hint beforehand to avoid any reference to recruiting and made only a mild reference to the subject which was not well received'.[64] In Kerry the split within the Volunteers between the pro- and anti-Redmond factions caused a further weakening of the movement, as a sizeable minority, the largest in any county, sided with Eoin MacNeill's anti-Redmond group. This was despite the best efforts of Tom O'Donnell, who remained one of the staunchest pro-war MPs in the Irish Party, even though most of his colleagues had deserted the recruiting platforms by autumn 1915.[65] In the year from December 1914 to December 1915 only 3.3 per cent of Kerry Catholic males not engaged in agriculture volunteered for the British army, the lowest rate in the whole country;[66] 'very poor' and 'nil' became the monotonous refrain about recruiting in the County Inspector's monthly reports. Of Michael's immediate Tralee contemporaries, Leo

Casey, Denis Baily, James Murphy, Edmond Slattery and John Revington all joined up, and received commissions, while James McElligott joined the MacNeill Volunteers.

Michael watched the war from a distance until June 1916, when he went to France just before the Somme offensive, although Zeppelin raids on the Home Counties were to bring the front line a little closer. He believed that the war would be a long one and in his letters to John he speculated on some of its ramifications: his prediction that it would bring about the end of the Habsburg empire, and lead to 'everlasting strife' in central and eastern Europe, proved especially prescient.[67] In July 1915 he wondered what 'these myriads of men' were really fighting for:

> Few, even among the fairly intelligent, have any conception of the real spiritual forces that play with their lives, or of the real outcome of final victory or defeat ... Most of these men, then, are dying for either fictitious or secondary causes, and this perhaps adds to the tragedy of their slaughter.

Nevertheless, he concluded, 'we must not fall into the error of regarding this holocaust as useless or avoidable. The great questions must now, as always, be decided by blood'.[68]

Throughout the war Michael and John continued their extensive reading. In 1915 they had long epistolary discussions about Winston Churchill's novel *The Inside of the Cup*, which coincided with a period of spiritual crisis for John. Michael, who was reading the New Testament and the *Imitation of Christ*, dismissed Churchill as peddling a form of 'pseudo-religion' and dispensed one of his 'cold water dousings' on John's mood of spiritual elation. Given the depths of Germanophobia in Britain during the war, it is remarkable that in 1915 Michael embarked on a study of German literature and acquired a great appreciation of Goethe. He also read a considerable amount of French literature, especially Balzac. Although he was able to visit Tralee several times on leave, the imminent prospect of foreign service was both distracting and exciting. For Mary it was unmitigated misery.

The Easter Rising

Censorship meant that the brothers' previously uninhibited discussion of politics was somewhat curtailed. There was much that John could not relate about the deteriorating political situation in Ireland and how it was affecting their family.

There was considerable labour unrest in Tralee and in October 1915 there was a big labour rally in the town, which was attended by James Connolly.[69] Tom O'Donnell planned a big meeting of the United Irish League in Tralee for 31 October, with John Redmond and Joseph Devlin, but such was the lack of enthusiasm for, indeed overt hostility to, both Redmond and O'Donnell that it had to be cancelled. O'Donnell was also still organising recruiting meetings. On 15 January 1916 the *Kerry Sentinel* reported on one held at Ardfert at which Lieutenant O'Leary VC was present, but the results of which were negligible. Meanwhile, police reports throughout 1915 detailed the continued growth of what were called the Sinn Féin Volunteers, who held regular drills and route marches. The RIC Inspector General wrote in his monthly report for May 1915 that 'a spirit of disloyalty and pro-Germanism ... is spreading – particularly in Kerry'.[70] That year's Manchester Martyrs Commemoration in November was organised by the Sinn Féin (MacNeill) Volunteers.

At the end of February 1916 John was present when Patrick Pearse, who was on an inspection visit to the local Volunteers, gave a lecture at the Rink.[71] It was this speech, as John told Michael in a long letter of 21 May 1916, that made him realise that a rising was imminent. However, Michael would have been well aware that John's suspicions of an imminent rising were based on something more than intuition. Despite his ill health, their father was still deeply involved in the IRB, and Austin Stack, the IRB's head centre and commandant of the Tralee Volunteers, was a close family friend. In autumn 1915 Stack and Alf Cotton, vice-commandant, met Pearse at St Enda's in Dublin and were informed of the plans for a rising the following Easter Sunday. They had further discussions when Pearse came to Tralee at the end of February 1916 and told the Kerry leaders that a German ship carrying arms would arrive in Tralee Bay on Easter Sunday, and that until then they were 'to lay [sic] doggo and do nothing that would draw the attention of British intelligence'. In the event, the ship, the *Aud*, arrived in Tralee Bay on Holy Thursday, three days early, and was seen by many people. The result was consternation and from that moment, as a local Volunteer was to recall, 'all the years of planning started to go astray'.[72] Stack was arrested on the evening of Good Friday, following the debacle of the Casement landing earlier that day. The following day, Easter Saturday, Maurice junior, then a schoolboy of thirteen, saw a tall man surrounded by RIC men and soldiers being marched from the RIC barracks in the centre of Tralee to the railway station. He rushed home to tell his father what he had seen, but his father made no comment. Maurice realised many years later, from his memory of the expression on his father's face, that he had known that the man was Roger Casement.

After the Rising

By a deeply ironic coincidence, among the British army units rushed to Ireland after the Rising were 300 officers and men from Michael's own regiment, although Michael himself remained behind in England. They were engaged in operations in west Cork, within thirty miles of Tralee. The regimental history expresses some perplexity about this episode, while dwelling appreciatively on the beauties of the Irish countryside:

> No demonstration was made by the Irish people, and no one could understand why they should be regarded with suspicion ... The new camp on Fota Island was situated in a beautiful park ... and for the next few days the Battalion was engaged in ordinary field training and not a bloodthirsty battle as many had anticipated.

In Cork the streets

> were lined with citizens, none of whom appeared to be really warlike. The real sensation, however, was an officer of the Munsters who passed the Battalion. He wore a steel helmet, which at that time was unique and hardly seen in the United Kingdom, and the atmosphere of real war conjured up by that single steel helmet somewhat counteracted the peacefulness of Cork.

In Macroom the men besieged the shops for items that had become luxuries in England. They left Ireland on 13 May 1916. The visit to Ireland, the regimental history concludes

> soon appeared like a dream, so sudden and short had it been. The value of the 'Irish stunt', as it was commonly called, cannot be discounted even if actual warfare had not been encountered. The Battalion had learned to entrain and detrain; embark and disembark; and move its home day by day and in general to become a mobile unit. The experience was invaluable.[73]

A long letter written by John to Michael on 21–22 May, three weeks after the surrender of the rebels, is an historically valuable document, not only in its analysis of the Rising, but also because his tone of spiritual elation graphically illustrates the change of opinion that was already sweeping the country in the aftermath of the executions and the mass arrests. In 1914, after all, John had regarded the Councils Bill as a satisfactory compromise: now he poured scorn on those men 'who have led Ireland for some decades' and who wanted a 'mere semi-self-governing province'.

When we look at the letters from this point onwards we can discern a certain emotional as well as physical distance opening up between the two brothers. John was increasingly absorbed by the stirring developments in Ireland, while Michael was experiencing his own sense of elation at being sent to the front at last. As has been mentioned, Michael arrived in France at the end of June, just before the Battle of the Somme. Once he was there the grim reality of war blotted out events elsewhere. Over the summer of 1916 Mary did her best to get him out of the army, despite his deep reluctance to leave it. 'I know you want to fight for your country', she wrote to him pathetically in July 1916, 'but you know well my unfortunate circumstances ... Your father is dying. John suffering as he is from the spine & all my young children [are] wholly dependent on you.' Helped by Tom O'Donnell, Mary actually went to London to speak to Lloyd George's under-secretary, but although Michael was temporarily given a clerical post away from the front line he then remained at the front, apart from some weeks recovering from trench fever, until the beginning of 1917.

Like the vast majority of his fellow soldiers, Michael spared his family the bloody, squalid details of trench warfare, but his letters home between October and December 1916 convey gloom, and a sense of terror and death among men at the whim of vast forces. In a letter written to John on 29 November 1916 he actually apologises for sending him a depressed letter the previous week and tries to reassure him: 'It represents a mood which is not new or infrequent and certainly gives a true aspect of the catastrophic convulsions of the time, as seen by one who is taking part in them, yet it is only one of several aspects.'[74] Poignantly, he was also deeply homesick for Tralee, 'that far-off little town, with all that it contains of peace and solace for the spirit, that makes one wish passionately to pierce through the intervening spaces of time, and see the end'.[75]

In December 1916 Michael decided to apply for a commission. He returned to England the following February for officer training. He was not particularly impressed with the training, as he told John: most of the

officers and NCOs in charge had not seen active service since the beginning of the war, and their lectures were 'seldom anything more than an
unskilful rehash of the text-books'.[76] However, being back in England gave
him more opportunity to absorb news of events in Ireland, where Sinn
Féin's by-election victories in Roscommon North and Longford South had
begun to alter the political landscape. His father wrote a particularly vehe-
ment assessment of the Longford South by-election for the *Kerry Sentinel*,
published on 19 May 1917, in which he urged Sinn Féin to leave the
minor points in its platform in the background for the time being, and to
concentrate on abstention from Westminster and the repudiation of
Britain's claims on Ireland.[77] Michael also welcomed the by-election victories, correctly predicting that Lloyd George's Convention on the future of
Ireland was doomed without Sinn Féin's support. He commented to John:

> I wonder if the Government have any realisation of this.
> Probably, with their usual total misunderstanding of Irish polit-
> ical tendencies, they have not. I have never yet met any
> Englishman capable of grasping the point of view of any coun-
> try but his own. This failing will always prove the greatest
> obstacle to even the most well-meant endeavours to settle the
> Irish question.[78]

In September the death on hunger strike of Thomas Ashe, a Volunteer
leader who came from Kinard, near Dingle, further raised the political
temperature. It was John who proposed a resolution of sympathy at a
meeting of the Tralee Gaelic League.[79]

Also in September 1917, Michael was commissioned as a second lieutenant in the 8th (Irish) Battalion of the King's Liverpool Regiment. Apart
from the fact that he was Irish, Michael had no connection with the battalion, but, in any case, by this stage of the war manpower pressures meant
that such local associations had become virtually irrelevant. Even so,
Michael bought a copy of the regimental history and was impressed by
the fact that members of it had won two VCs.[80] He returned to France in
October, just in time for the Second Battle of Passchendaele, which soon
got bogged down in a sea of mud. Conditions were, if anything, even
more difficult and dangerous than they had been the year before, but he
allowed few hints of despondency or depression to emerge in his letters,
which become more factual, and are devoid of the philosophical and literary discussions that he had previously enjoyed with John. In January 1918
he was given compassionate leave after his father's death and went home

to Tralee, where his younger brother Maurice thought that he detected a feeling of fatalism in Michael. Maurice later recalled a revealing incident: 'My grandmother, she was a silly woman, told Michael how glorious it must be to fight for your country. Michael replied bitterly that there was nothing glorious about it.'

Shortly after Michael's return to the front, events moved to a climax both in Ireland and in France. On 21 March the German spring offensive started, bringing the prospect of conscription in Ireland appreciably closer. Throughout Kerry there were nightly meetings against conscription, which the RIC proved completely unable to cope with, and on 13 April a raid on Gortatlea barracks led to the deaths of two of the attackers. In May many of Sinn Féin's leaders, including Austin Stack, were arrested and interned. Michael found it difficult to focus attention on Ireland, as he wrote to John, evidently with a trace of irritation:

> Situated as I am over here, it is impossible to follow Irish affairs with the same knowledge or the same perspective as when at home. The events of world-importance amidst which we live must of necessity overshadow everything else in our minds ... The humblest private here understands and thinks more about international, than he ever did about domestic politics, so it comes about that I see Ireland through the wrong end of a telescope.[81]

Just ten days later, however, Michael made his deeper feelings about Ireland plain in a letter to his cousin Father Hyacinth Power: 'I have nothing but the fullest sympathy for the new men and the new (or "old but ever new") teachings... One does not part willingly with early loyalties or early traditions, and indeed the rolling years do but confirm them.'[82]

In May 1916 John wrote optimistically to Michael, just before his departure for the front: 'We feel, and even mother, notwithstanding her fears, feels that in any case you will be safe. I have an impression that you are not the sort of person to die young.'[83] It was not to be. To the great grief of his family, Michael was killed on 3 June, just five months before the Armistice. It is tempting to speculate on what role he would have played in the 'new Ireland', in which his brothers John and Maurice played out their own roles with distinction. Would there have been a role for an ex-serviceman such as Michael? Armistice Day was commemorated in Tralee in the 1920s and 1930s,[84] but there is no First World War memorial there, even though nearly 200 men from the town died in the war, including, among Michael's contemporaries, Denis Baily and John Revington.[85] Michael's family barely had time to mourn him before they were confronted with another war, which would bring them further sorrow.

CHAPTER ONE

University College Dublin, 1908–09

1 Michael (Dublin) to Mary (Tralee), 27 November 1908[1]

I had just written this when a telegram came asking me to write whether I was well. I am rather surprised to get this. There is no occasion for such solicitude. I am as well as usual. As there is no reason why you should suppose otherwise I did not think it necessary to reply to the telegram.

Whelan's, I suppose, is out of court. But it is as well to correct some misapprehensions of yours regarding it. Who told you that any student that ever went there from Tralee utterly failed? I refer you to Dr Molyneux of Tralee as a conspicuous example of success. He stayed at W.'s during his student days.[2] Then, you are wrong in thinking that McElligott and Enright were particularly anxious that I should go there; they would not have benefited in the way you suggest.[3] As to the place breeding idleness, I may mention the fact that McElligott can scarcely be drawn from study at all.

McElligott had an interview with Dr Coffey yesterday. I believe he got a letter of introduction from Miss Coffey. The Doctor has invited the three of us to dinner on Saturday week...[4]

2 Michael (Dublin) to John (Tralee), no date (c. February 1909)

I am glad to see that you appreciate the *Nation* so much. I think you will find it more interesting than ever this week. Read carefully 'On the People's Service', and let me know what you think of archbishops of the kind whose antics are described there, and whether you are surprised at the amount of presumptuous 'ignorance' which the 'gentleman' in question displays.[5]

The story *The Plough and the Cross* is excellent in many respects, and I hope it will be published in volume form; but I doubt whether it has the qualities which make a popular novel. It is pitched in too high a key, too overladen with thought for that; and I must confess that, however admirable the sentiments and ideas, their constant repetition has a somewhat wearying effect. Whoever the author is, he is evidently a bit of a novice at fiction-writing. Its defects, nevertheless, are merely technical, and as a piece of literature it is beyond praise.[6]

A paper, unfortunately, cannot live on appreciation; least of all, perhaps, a paper which deserves it. Money, as Bernard Shaw has told you, is the one thing needful. The *Irish Nation* must be made a financial success, or it will be at the mercy of all its enemies. You will understand, of course, that its recent appeal for more capital is not a sign of breakdown, or anything of that sort. It simply means that its present capital cannot, by itself, be used to the best advantage; many possible new departures are hindered by its inadequacy...

I hope these considerations will make you impress on mother the desirability of investing her P[ost]. O[ffice]. capital in this concern. I am sure you agree with me that it is a thoroughly sound business proposition, besides being an excellent way of helping Irish industries, Irish ideals, and progressive movements. Do not fail then to use your unequalled powers of persuasion in this regard...

3 John (Tralee) to Michael (Dublin), 21 February 1909

I see from your latest letter to mother that you have met Mr O'Beirne's wife.[7] I suppose you obtained a great deal of information about the 'Irish Ireland' and 'Maynooth Movements'.[8] Doubtless also you discovered the authorship of that splendid story *The Plough and the Cross.*

Congratulating you on your conversion and on being more or less 'behind the scenes'...

4 Michael (Dublin) to John (Tralee), 23 February 1909

Thanks for congratulations. But seeing that every day I meet two or three of the senators with whom the issue rests, and yet have no idea what they will do in the matter, I am hardly behind the scenes.[9] Who can tell how all will end? Only a very few of the senators can be trusted and the official Church is untiring and unscrupulous in its exertions. [Cardinal] Bourne of Westminster actually thanked the government for giving the new Irish university. This is significant of much, and gives some clue to what is going on at the back of the stage.

Mr and Mrs O'Beirne were here last Sunday, but we did not talk shop. The authorship of *The Plough and the Cross* will be made known in due time. And as to the Maynooth movement, if it exists (which is more than doubtful) a disclosure at this juncture would be premature, and might nip it in the bud. But you may be sure that it is all a fiction. If you remember that the Maynooth authorities have 'suppressed' Dr O'Hickey,[10] you may guess how they would deal with any display of that heinous heresy, Immanentism (*vide* Encyclical) or any suggestion of that offspring of Satan, 'practical Christianity'.[11]

I suppose you are no longer an amateur at billiards now. What is your break? I have not played any since leaving Tralee but have to find compensation in the less exciting game of bridge.

5 John (Tralee) to Michael (Dublin), 26 February 1909

You seem to me to be rather pessimistic with regard to the fate of Irish. After all, the bishops must realise by now that they cannot, without a serious loss of prestige, persevere in their present policy.

Whatever the issue may be I may safely say that clerical domination is knocked on the head. It cannot long survive the blow it received when for perhaps the first time in Irish History the all but unanimous opinion of Irishmen was against its exercise. At any rate we may expect that in future the bishops will issue *religious* pastorals and that they will have time to do so more frequently than once a year.

You seem to doubt altogether the existence of the 'Maynooth Movement' on account of the bishops' inaction. You must, however, remember that the bishops would be wary about exposing to 'Holy Ireland' and to the unholy world the existence of a heresy (I don't mean a political heresy) in Maynooth itself.

Do you still persevere in your opinion that Mr O'Beirne is the author of the serial? Is Mrs O'Beirne very like Elsie O'K.? Finally have you been to the Boyne Valley? ...[12]

6 Michael (Dublin) to John (Tralee), no date (c. 3 March 1909)

I am not exactly pessimistic about the Irish question. But you must remember that it entirely depends on the extent to which the senate think they may safely disregard the wishes of the people. That the majority are hostile there is little doubt. When Gwynn, a member of the Coiste Gnotha, and Windle, of Cork, who has always made a pretence of friendship to the Irish revival, are still openly or secretly working against Irish, you may judge of what the rest are likely to do.[13] Coffey I know to be opposed to compulsory Irish. Of Delany I need not speak.[14] You may be sure that if the senate can tire out the present agitation, their decision will be adverse. As to the bishops, you evidently have not seen the letter which Cardinal Logue wrote to the *Evening Telegraph*.[15] He lamely repudiates the charge of Roman and English interference, reiterates the conclusion of the Standing Committee, and has the presumption to say that the bishops had a right to express their opinion. We can only answer, of course, that they had no right to use the spiritual influence they possess for an entirely non-religious, and moreover, anti-national, purpose.

I am afraid so long as bishops are bishops they will continue interfering in the wrong way in politics. It is marvellous how a man's private interests, without his being conscious of it, colour his opinions on larger questions. And the interests of the Catholic Church to-day are essentially conservative. One sees it in our Jesuits here, who are reactionaries to the very marrow of their bones. At present, we are treated every Friday to a so-called religion lecture which canvasses most quaintly medieval notions about 'civil or social liberty' as the pet ecclesiastical phrase goes.

It is not O'Beirne whom I suppose to be the author of *The Plough and the Cross*, but W.P. O'Ryan, the editor of the *Nation*. Mr O'Beirne is the manager of the paper.

I know little about T.P. [O'Connor]'s latest development except what I have seen on his yellow placards. I got his paper this week for the first time for several months, and did not see an interesting page in it, except the 'review' of *Tono-Bungay* the subject of which alone contained the interest. I do not think *T.P.'s Weekly* is any longer worth getting.[16] The only English weekly which is thoroughly good is the *New Age*, which you will have seen frequently mentioned in the *Nation*. I do not suppose it reaches Tralee, however.[17]

As it is past ten o'clock, and all the house is in bed, I must close.

7 Michael (Dublin) to Mary (Tralee), 3 March 1909

I was very disappointed by your reply to my proposal re *Irish Nation*. I can only hope, at all events, that you do not mean what you say when you state that you would not be the one to keep it alive. I am not now going to discuss its claims; you can judge them as well as I from the paper itself. But

1. Mary Moynihan (mother of Michael and John)

2. John Power ('An Paorach') and his pipes

I must say that if it does die, as you expect, I hope it will be pre-deceased by its episcopal enemies, and, above all, by that clerical domination with which it is at daggers drawn.

Thinking that your reluctance to invest might arise from doubts as to its financial position, I went into the *Nation* office to-day to find out the true position of things. Mr Brannigan gave me a glowing and, to me, encouraging account of its advance, both in Ireland and across the water.[18] He will send me last year's report shortly, and I will send it for your consideration. In the meantime, you may be perfectly sure that your capital will be safe in the *Nation*.[19]

I repeat then, my former proposal to you, that you will take at least fifteen or twenty shares. You need have no conscientious scruples, for be assured that you are helping the right. I am sorry that it should be necessary to ask you a second time, and I would not do so if I did not feel confident that you will come to a wiser conclusion on second thoughts. You ask me whether there is anything you could send me. I want nothing more, or as much, as a favourable answer to this.

8 John (Tralee) to Michael (Dublin), postmarked 6 March 1909

I have read 'On the People's Service'. Need I say what I think of Dr Healy's action with regard to Dr MacEinri? Did you read his amazing reference to the 'fair discussion' farce? By the way it seems to me that Fr Crehan's action is a substantial proof of the growth of a free and independent spirit amongst the clergy.[20]

I have endeavoured to persuade Mother to agree with your proposal re the 'Irish Nation Shares', but have found [it] impossible to do so. She is rather prejudiced against the paper, so perhaps I should say that she thinks it would be sinful to be otherwise, thanks to Fr O'Quigley...[21]

9 Michael (Dublin) to John (Tralee), 14 March 1909

It looks as if Dr Healy will hear more of his recent outbreak. A piquant situation will arise if another college is established, though such an assertion of independence might have serious consequences for the Gaelic League. It is easy to think that clerical influence is dying out, when there has been no serious attack on it; but the power of vested interests can never be discovered until they have to fight for existence. Nevertheless, it is pretty clear that, sooner or later, the Gaelic League is bound to come into conflict with the church political, just as did the Fenian movement, but in a much more formidable way. You are perfectly right in remarking the growth of a liberal spirit among the younger clergy, but how far will that spirit take them? To the extent of disobeying their superiors and violating discipline? It is not likely. There is perhaps not a more patriotic priest in Ireland than Dr O'Hickey; yet how tamely he allowed himself to be suppressed by the bishops!

In John Power's last letter he told me they were going to debate the subject of compulsory Irish in Clongowes on the following Thursday; but I have not yet heard how it came off.[22] Did you see Dr O'Hickey's letters on the subject yet? If they are not on sale in Tralee, I will take them home with me.[23]

Between the Lord Mayor's procession, the Fodhla concerts, etc., there will be plenty of entertainment here on Patrick's Day. I hope to see the former at any rate...

10 John (Tralee) to Michael (Dublin), 19 March 1909

At last I have some good news for you. On the evg. of St Patrick's Day Fr Quigley OP recited the rosary in Irish and afterwards preached on the moral obligation of the Irish people to speak their own language. Imagine Fr Quigley the ultramontane member of the order of the inquisition the same who denounced the 'anticlericalism' of *The Peasant* as an anticleric!!!

Poor T.P. [O'Connor] got an awful slating in this week's *Nation*.

Let me know the result of the debate in Clongowes, and John Power's attitude with regard to the language question.

I don't think Dr O'Hickey's letters are on sale here, at all events I have not seen them.

11 Michael (Dublin) to John (Tralee), 23 March 1909

I saw Mr O'Beirne yesterday, and asked him some leading questions. The weekly issue of *The Nation* is 15,000 copies. As I thought, its editor, W.P. O'Ryan, is the writer of *The Plough and the Cross* of which two more books are coming on. Fergus O'Hagan is himself, and Maeve, not his sister, but his wife.[24]

O'Beirne was up in Belfast last week, visiting local industries, and he is going to write a series of articles on them for the paper, which he expects will result in more advertisements.[25] Later on he hopes to do the same for other centres, and if it brings in sufficient ads., he will increase the size of the paper to twelve pages.

He is also thinking of starting another paper, *The Gaelic Athlete*, which, with *The Observer*, the *Irish Nation*, and the printing business, will make a fourth source of revenue. So that, with one thing and another, we may hope to have something like a dividend next February.

Fr Quigley's sermon was interesting, but is not very surprising. *The Irish Rosary*, the organ of his order, is, I believe, in favour of compulsory Irish. And seeing that he has nothing to gain one way or another by the matter, it is natural that his opinion should be conscientious. It is only bishop-ridden priests, and self-interested Jesuits, who are opposed to Irish. Fr Quigley may seem inconsistent in his enmity to *The Peasant* and his advocacy of national-ity, and no doubt he is so, but it is futile to look for consistency in matters of emotion. The question of Irish is not one for argument, 'fair' or otherwise, with Fr Q., any more than with you or with me. It is purely a question of feeling, and it is not, therefore, surprising that Fr Q.'s patriotism should carry him one way, and his church-instinct another.

For real thoroughness you must go to the Jesuits, who act always on uniform principles, handed down to them from their famous founder. Look at Dr Delany, for instance, who is having some foolish charity meeting shortly in University College, under the patronage of Her Excellency, the Countess of Aberdeen.[26] There is a man who will not be carried away by idle sentiment, and for whom it is indeed true that 'all roads lead to Rome'.

I have had no letter from John Power since last writing to him, and do not know the result of the Clongowes debate. He is himself in favour of compulsory Irish.[27]

12 Mary (Tralee) to Michael (Dublin), postmarked 29 March 1909

I am afraid you are becoming a very extreme Nationalist & indeed I would be sorry to think so, as you know all I have suffered through politics...

13 John (Cork) to Michael (Dublin), 5 May 1909

Here I am at last in the capital of south-west Britain, my native Cork.[28] I find it more British than ever; even here in this supposed stronghold of nationalism my ears are every moment assailed by the latest music-hall ditty. Indeed last night I was carried off perforce to the Palace Theatre, where I was supposed to admire and applaud a conjuror, a ventriloquist, some performing dogs, a badly acted scene from an absurd musical comedy, which is not even comic, called *The Daughter of the Regiment*, and sundry other things.

I got the *New Age* yesterday. G.K.C[hesterton].'s shriek is brilliantly musical this week...[29]

14 Michael (Dublin) to John (Cork), 9 May 1909

I had intended to go to *An Englishman's Home*[30] yesterday, but owing to the outrageous and disloyal treatment meted out to it on Monday night by a few rowdies, I found that the management had been compelled to raise the price of the gallery to 1/-. As I thought this an excessive amount to pay, even for the privilege of helping to save the Empire, I went to the Abbey instead, where I saw *The Cross-Roads*, a strong play by a Cork author.[31]

'G.K.''s shriek is answered effectively by Cecil and by Muggeridge this week.[32] The great man is a very brilliant sophist, but no more. His nightmare ideas about the oligarchy show that he does not know what Socialism means, and knows still less what an oligarchy means. He also has a habit of going off on non-essential points, instead of following where his nose leads him. G.K.C., no doubt, would lead us back to feudalism and papal supremacy, thereby destroying all the freedom which Socialism will not only leave intact, but will greatly augment. Plutocracy is bad enough but theocracy would be infinitely worse. Religious and moral ideas are only a blessing (to the mind) when spontaneous and individual; when imposed by an outside authority they are a curse and a hindrance. Of course this in no way affects punishment for crime. The enforcement of certain laws is an unmitigated good; the enforcement of any beliefs is wrong. So Gilbert's alternative stands self-condemned. Of course he and his friend Belloc are perfectly honest; but that makes it all the more pity that they should oppose the only honest political movement of to-day.

I will send you *New Age* to-morrow.

Hoping you and Uncle Mick are well.

I got your letter on Sat. and the *New Age* this morning. C.C.'s 'For the Reassurance of G.K.C.', Muggeridge's letter and the comments on the budget are very interesting.[33]

On Thursday and Friday last a play named *The Embers* was produced by the Cork Dramatic Society. I had intended to go on the second night but the enlightened 'criticism' of the *Cork Examiner*, though couched in appreciative terms, damped my ardour.[34] *The Gondoliers*, a Sullivan opera I believe, will be produced at the Opera House to-morrow night and I hope to go.

Uncle Mick is quite well now and is going to fairs again . . .

I think it is a pity you did not go to see *The Embers*, whatever the *Examiner* might have said about it. It is the first production of the new Cork Dramatic Soc., which may have a successful future before it. When an Irish daily paper damns an Irish play with faint praise, it often means that the 'critic' is not competent to appreciate good drama, and, at the same time, has not the courage to speak his mind openly. The *Nation* has a notice this week which gives a very favourable notion of it.

The *New Age* returns to the Budget this week. Next week the opinion of its readers will be taken as to raising the price of the paper to 2d.[35]

There was a great Bung[36] meeting here last night to protest against the iniquitous proposals of the budget. By the way, our friend Archbishop Healy was one of the first to denounce the new liquor tax as a 'shameful' impost. For my part, I think the outcry about unfair treatment of Ireland is patent humbug. The new revenue is principally raised by taxes on wealth, and this, confessedly, will hit 'England' more than 'Ireland'. I use inverted commas advisedly, because the real England and Ireland will lose nothing, but gain a great deal, from taxes on property.

Hoping you enjoyed *The Gondoliers*.

P.S. I notice in this week's *Nation* the interesting announcement that a meeting will be held shortly to create a Socialist organisation in Ireland. If it attains any measure of success, it will be a very important step on the road to progress.

17 John (Cork) to Michael (Dublin), postmarked 18 May 1909

. . . The trams are running again since Sunday, the strikers having resumed work without obtaining any concessions whatever.[37]

Though not claiming to be a socialist or anything else, I hope the movement to which you refer to create a Socialist organisation in this country will succeed.

As I must hurry back to Shanahans I will now say good-bye.

18 Michael (Dublin) to John (Cork), 19 May 1909

Mother tells me that you have not been well. I hope it was nothing serious, and that you are now better. I suppose you are very busy at present.

I met Mr O'Beirne on Friday, and also on Saturday, and found him very communicative on various subjects. With regard to the proposed new Socialist organisation, he thinks that if it adopts the name Socialist it will not have a chance of success. He has an idea himself of establishing a 'Fintan Lalor Association', which would be purely Socialist in its basis, and in everything but name. At the same time he intends to be present at the forthcoming meeting, and would, of course, be delighted to see it succeed.

I was at a Socialist meeting in Phoenix Park on Sunday, which attracted an audience of about 100. It seems to have been got up by 'The Socialist Party of Ireland', a body of whose existence I was previously unaware. There were good, sound temperate speeches delivered, but, of course, few, if any, of the audience were converted. The chief good such meetings can do is to familiarise the people with the Socialist idea.

Having gathered from a previous conversation that the circulation of the *Nation* was 15,000, I was surprised to learn from O'Beirne on Saturday that it was only 4,500.

He told me a strange story about Archbishop Healy, which hardly bears repetition. If it became publicly known, it might deprive that venerable prelate of his see. It was hinted at in the *Nation* some time ago, after a public attack on the paper by his grace (he accused it, not by name, of course, of 'undermining the morals of the people'). A copy was sent to him, and he has kept a discreet silence ever since.[38]

To conclude, you may be interested to know that Mr O'Beirne has twice heard the banshee, at least once under unmistakeable circumstances. Who shall talk now about the 'superstitions' of the peasantry?

P.S. So the last of the great early Victorian Englishmen has past [sic] away in the person of George Meredith. On the whole, his chances of immortality are probably much less than those of Swinburne. He may survive as a burnt-out planet, like Macaulay, or Carlyle, or Herbert Spencer, though not at all as great a man as either of the last two.[39]

19 John (Cork) to Michael (Dublin), postmarked 20 May 1909

Mr O'Beirne may be right with regard to the Soc.[ialist] organisation still I don't think that his idea of masking the object of the Association under such a name as he proposes would avail much or for long in an island blessed with such a splendidly trained body of priest-police as ours is.

I don't think that Meredith's fame will die so soon after his body as you think probable. At least let us hope that if it does it will have a resurrection day...

20 Michael (Dublin) to John (Cork), 23 May 1909

I sent you *New Age* yesterday. I hope you got last week's all right. You will notice an article on Wells's latest development, and I enclose a humorous sketch of him by Shaw from this week's *Christian Commonwealth*.[40] Wells is after declaring his belief in the infallibility of Pope Keir Hardie & Co., and excommunicating Shaw, Blatchford, Grayson, and others.[41] Further, he has said good-bye to the Fabian Society. It is not easy to see what he is after. Anyone would judge from his writings that he is a man of insight and good-will, yet on this occasion he has made a signal blunder. It is not often that he comes down from the clouds to see what is going on on the earth, and perhaps that partly accounts for his lack of practical understanding. The root of the whole matter, passing over all the side issues, is whether there is to be a Socialist Party or a Labour Party in British politics. Wells declares for the latter, and he is wrong.

I was at the Abbey on Thursday night, and saw two of Synge's plays *Riders to the Sea* and *In the Shadow of the Glen*. They are two short, but powerful pieces, and are comparatively free from the oddities of the *Playboy*. The latter is to be revived this week, and it will be interesting to see the reception it gets.[42]

The statutes of the National University were issued yesterday. There is a most generous scheme of professorships and lectureships from metaphysics to accountancy. One wonders whether half the professors will not be idle. There is to be a special Faculty of Celtic studies, and there is no reasonable ground of complaint as to the position of Irish. The question of compulsory Irish for matriculation is not settled by the statutes. If it is not settled in the right way by the senate, it will, so far as the nation is concerned, be the same as if Irish was banished entirely. There is a grave danger, too, that philosophical subjects will fall under theological influence and that post-thirteenth century thought may be given a mute part. If this is so, it will throw a blight over the whole life of the university, and blast any claims it may have to be a modern institution, and a vehicle of progress. I sincerely hope that 'true philosophy' will be kept in its proper place, and will not swamp the less pretentious systems of later date. The prominent place given to commercial studies must be gratifying to everyone. Nothing is more desirable than the diffusion of deeper knowledge with respect to the financial foundations of society.

I suppose you have heard that the famous German airship was seen over Donnybrook a few nights ago. In well-informed quarters it is whispered that with this vessel which can travel at a prodigious rate and is capable of being in several places at once, the German government *hopes* to complete the conquest of England (with, of course, the assistance of the numerous German bands in the country already)...[43]

21 *John (Cork) to Michael (Dublin), postmarked 27 May 1909*

I got *New Age* on Sunday. It is a very good number. I have read the article on Wells also that by Shaw which you enclosed in letter.

I understand from mother that your exam is close at hand. Do you still intend to go in for Civil Service Exam this year?

I fear that the clerical will be the order of the day in the new university. Indeed such a thing appears to have been premeditated by the government.

I wish there were some truth in the 'German' airship rumours...

22 *John (Cork) to Michael (Dublin), 3 June 1909*

I got *New Age* and your letter. I thought *New Age* a particularly good number. Tonson's opinion[s] on the Victorian novelists rather astound me.[44] He can read Jane Austen for ever! In fact he likes her milk and water novels better than the strong novels of the Brontes and George Eliot.

Again he prefers Trollope to Thackeray who is an arrant, craven 'snob'! I would be strongly inclined to doubt Mr Tonson's sanity or sobriety were it not for his high opinion of Meredith. The latter I am commencing to regard as the greatest of English novelists.

The article 'Genius or Superman' is also very interesting.[45] My own ideas on the subject of this article are as follows. The goal, the object of evolution, the superman is not man at all but a race evolved from man. For surely 'tis the perfections of conceit to imagine that we, imperfect as we are, are or can be, no matter how improved upon, the ultimate object of evolution and many thousands perhaps millions of years before the consummation of the great object of evolution – perfection.

I am also inclined to believe in a divine power, directing and guiding this grand scheme and in reincarnation which alone could make it in any way compatible with justice. As to the ultimate end of the soul I am still in doubt but is it not possible that an immortal life in a perfect earth may crown and reward all its transitions? Of course, I believe in development of the soul, do you?

Apologising for this, the longest letter I have ever written . . .

23 Michael (Dublin) to John (Cork), 13 June 1909

The exams were on last week, and I could not get time to reply to you in full. I was very interested by your religious views. I am glad to see that you accept evolution. As to your idea that evolution is an intelligent process, with a definite goal, it is a good working hypothesis, but no doubt you recognise that it has no foundation in pure reason. It must be clear to you, in the first place, that decadence is as much a law of human society as progress. The whole experience of the world is that societies, after reaching a certain degree of progress, inevitably begin to decay, physically and morally. It is needless to go back to antiquity; you see the process going on to-day in Europe, and particularly in France. Beyond all question France is the most civilised country in the world today. Yet her civilisation can avail absolutely nothing to stop the secular decay in energy and vitality which must ultimately spell disruption of the whole social organism. So far as the French race is concerned, the goal of evolution is not perfection, but doom . . .

As to reincarnation, it will probably form part of the future European religion (if there is to be any), but it can hardly be said to be less of a dream than some of the dogmas that are now being abandoned. That is a finer and more beautiful dream I grant you, but that, combined with its antiquity, only shows the little progress we have made.

To conclude on this subject, I may say that I consider all religious opinion to be a matter of emotion and temperament, even of mood.

The long-expected Socialist meeting took place this evening in the Trades Hall, in a typical mean street. It was a very interesting gathering. There were about a hundred present, including many middle-class people. The most distinguished person was Sheehy-Skeffington, author of the Life of Davitt.[46] Among the speakers were two Englishmen, and one Continental, I think a German. Differences of opinion as between revolutionaries and evolutionaries manifested themselves. The general sentiment was, however, that the new organisation should combine all shades of opinion. The proposer of the main resolution was Mr Frederick Ryan.[47] The upshot was that a committee was formed to make arrangements for bringing the new society into being. You will probably see a report in the *Nation* this week . . .[48]

24 Michael (Dublin) to John (Cork), 21 June 1909

I received your letter this evening, and hasten to answer it. If you think that decadence in a society is purely material, and that it can be compared to fatigue in a horse, I can only say that you are under a misapprehension. It would be far truer to say that a nation's life is exactly similar to that of an individual. When a man reaches a certain age, he does not stand still as though tired, but he goes back, very decidedly. It is the same with a community of men. In primitive communities, the quantity of energy or vital force is an increasing factor. A time comes when it reaches a maximum, and then exhaustion begins. Intelligence continues increasing, as in an old man, until a very late period, but creative powers decline. Then the sense of social duty is weakened, things which were done quite naturally in earlier ages have to be enforced by the state, the population declines, and at length the community begins to forget the fruits of its own civilisation, like an old man in his dotage. If this was mere theory I should hestitate to weary you with it, but it is all historically true. The history of Rome is the most remarkable instance of it. That nation originally was the most energetic in the world; one small city was able to subdue all the lands around the Mediterranean, and far beyond. Then by an inevitable law of nature, that great race degenerated; it gradually lost its warlike character, and became entirely devoted to economic pursuits.

The first result was a reversion in the form of government from a republic to an autocracy. Later still, it became increasingly difficult to recruit soldiers for the armies, and such as could be had were worthless. Then men refused to take up public offices, and exemption from the magistracies was a special privilege. In the meantime literature decayed. The science which had grown up in the earlier period was forgotten, even medicine was given up, and magic took its place. The Roman state was in its dotage and fell an easy prey to the barbarians. As a consequence European civilisation fell back very far, and the Middle Ages were a much less civilised epoch than the early Roman Empire.

It is worth while noting, too, that these things which men most prize are the quickest means of bringing about decadence. It seems to be a fact that wealth and peace, superficially blessings, accelerate decline.

As to the other matter, I do not think evolutionists will bear you out in stating that eternity is contrary to evolution. Heckel says, 'The duration of the world is equally infinite and unbounded; it has no beginning and no end; it is eternity.' Any arguments against the eternity of the world apply equally to the eternity of God. No doubt eternity and creation are each inconceivable. I think the best solution of the riddle is to give it up as insoluble. It is a wearisome and a futile thing to be seeking a satisfactory answer to it.[49]

25 John (Cork) to Michael (Dublin), 22 June 1909

I received your letter and *New Age*.

You are right after a manner in saying that the life of a nation is similar to that of an individual viz: when a nation reaches an uncertain age it begins to decay (materially), when it reaches another uncertain age (corresponding to the age of 90–95 in a man) its spirit begins to chafe at prolonged and over-intimate association with its decayed and infirm body [and] from loathing it passes by a very natural transition to indifference which corresponds to the dotage of an old man. But for the spirit of a nation as for the spirit of man there is a life beyond death, a reincarnation.

But I can no longer advocate this theory of mind. As has happened before I, a shipwrecked voyager on the ocean of Life and Mystery grasped, in the darkness, at an illusion, as a man drowning on the oceans of earth grasps at a straw, I cried out in the fullness of my heart that I was saved but alas! you brought the bright and pitiless light of reason to bear on my illusions saying 'It is beautiful indeed and many there are who will grasp at it as you have done but it is still an illusion.' And lo! it forthwith vanishes.

Many a time have I tried to justify existence and God and when I have done so to my satisfaction, I rejoice, I tell you the glad tidings with what result you know.

Once more then you have reduced me to despair, once more you have made me cry out against nature and nature's God. Rejoice and be merry. I am in despair John PM.

26 Michael (Dublin) to John (Cork), 24 June 1909

I see you grant a large part of my contention, but still maintain that the spirit of a nation has a life beyond death. You mean, I suppose, that it survives in the memory of later generations. That is so in some cases, no doubt, but by no means all. The spirit of the ancient Assyrian nation, of the Peruvian nation, are in no true sense alive today. Here again the fate of the nation resembles that of the individual. For a few there is that shadowy kind of immortality which consists in the remembrance of posterity, but for the majority life indeed ends with death.

As for your despair, I hope it is only figurative. It is not essential to happiness to hold views on the origin of the universe. And I think despair at fundamental cosmic facts is incongruous. The wisest thing is to seek the truth without any desire that it should agree with this or that preconceived opinion; and above all not to go too deep. Think of the countless religions and philosophies conceived by men; and you will see the improbability of ultimate truth being ever known.

For the rest, the fact of decadence in nations is not, it seems to me, a matter for despair, but a subject of the deepest interest. Socialist though I am, the idea of a perfect state arouses no enthusiasm in me; I agree with those cynics who think heaven must be insufferably boring. Perfection means simplicity, and simplicity means dullness. To illustrate the matter, what interest would you feel in a novel in which all the characters were actuated by the loftiest motives, in which there were no misunderstandings, no quarrels, no follies, no crimes? Again, do you not feel an instinctive admiration for men like Napoleon, who are incarnations of the anti-social spirit? Such interest as human history possesses arises from its complexity, its imperfections.

Might I suggest to you, as a fruitful subject of study, the decadence of the Anglo-Saxon race all over the world, at the moment when it seems most triumphant? In England it is manifested in countless ways. The birth-rate is tumbling down, a sure sign of failing vitality. It is curious, too, to note the ever-increasing number of foreign names in English literature, business, and art. A large number of the contributors to the *New Age* are aliens. Most of the anti-German scare writers are of German origin. Again, in America, it is a matter of common repute that the old Anglo-Saxon part of the population is dying out. The birth-rate in Australia is falling at an 'alarming' rate. Mid-Victorian men looked forward to the time when English would be the universal language. It is now doubtful whether it will be spoken at all a hundred years hence. The near future will almost certainly see the destruction of England's trade, and the trans-ference of the world's exchanges to New York. This is a subject of infinite aspects, and you might do worse than give it attention.[50]

Hoping you are recovered from your despair.

27 John (Cork) to Michael (Dublin), 28 June 1909

. . . I suppose you got last week's *Irish Nation*. What do you think of the bish-ops' treatment of Dr O'Hickey? I hope time will prove that they have overreached themselves. I wonder how will Dr O'Hickey take it – in the approved saintly fashion, that is, with humility, or in a manly way, with indignation . . . [51]

28 Michael (Dublin) to John (Cork), 30 June 1909

It is impossible to say what Dr O'Hickey will do as regards his dismissal, but it is certain that, whether openly or not, he will show a spirit equal to the circumstances. The *Independent* on Friday published a report stating that Dr O'Hickey had resigned his chair of Irish of his own accord. On the follow-ing day there was a letter from him characterising that report as 'a baseless fabrication'.[52] Whether the bishops have been cutting their own throats by their action is a question which time alone can decide. At all events, it is impossible to consider any longer their motives as either honourable or clean. It is ludicrous to suppose that they would act as they are doing if they were disinterested. And the Gaelic Leaguer who still tries to separate their political from their moral authority is in a very false position. The whole issue is as closely connected with morals as it could well be, and it is needless to insist on the hopelessly immoral way in which they have decided it.

The adjourned socialist meeting was resumed on Sunday, but very little business was done. An 'immediate' programme was proposed, which included adult suffrage and secular education. Five points were accepted, but it is possible that the programme may be rejected en bloc next Sunday. Some of the most influential members are opposed to any programme, a few because of their revolutionary sympathies. I think that without some sound, practical programme the Party can have no success. It must take up some attitude towards questions of the day. Then the policy of trying to embrace Irish Socialists of all shades is, I think, an impossible one. It would do very well for an academic society, but for a political party it would simply mean futility. It is folly to preach socialism without having some means for bringing it about, and it is precisely as to the means that Socialists differ. But as far as I can see, there is no one connected with the Party who has anything like sufficient insight into politics. Mr Sheehy-Skeffington is a visionary. Mr F. Ryan has ideas, but lacks force to make them effective.

A few days ago I got a small book called *The New Ireland* by Sydney Brooks (6d).[53] In a chapter on 'The Church' he gives an account of the early history of the *Peasant* which reads like a resumé of *The Plough and the Cross*. The Mr Milligan, stock-broker, with his farming schemes in Meath, whom you will recall, turns out to be a Mr McCann, ditto, ditto, who founded *The Irish Peasant*.[54]

29 John (Cork) to Michael (Dublin), 2 July 1909

I suppose you have seen the splendid leading article in the *Nation* on the Maynooth fiasco.[55] It appears that the bishops have not yet deprived O'Hickey of his professorship. I am rather sorry that they have been so timid. It might mean an addition to the ranks of avowed modernists.

I need hardly say I wish the new Irish Socialist Party every success. Have the bishops yet published its existence from altar or pulpit?

If you wish to read Meredith's *Richard Feverel* I will send it next week.[56] I got it about a fortnight ago and am at present reading it for the 2nd time. It is as Tonson says full of defects, yet it is a fine novel. It belongs rather to the romantic rather than to the realistic school. Some of the most beautiful passages remind me of the best parts of *The Plough and the Cross*.

30 Michael (Dublin) to John (Cork), 5 July 1909

Last week's article in the *Nation*, to which you refer, is achieving celebrity in the *Independent*. That paper, true to its name, gave a summary of the article last Friday. It appears there was some unintentional misquotation, to which Dr O'Hickey took exception in Saturday's issue. At all events there is a letter in the *I.I.* to-day from W.P. O'Ryan about the article.

The Socialist meeting was resumed yesterday, and the society at last definitely formed names being received. The remaining points in the programme, to which I referred last week, were adopted. Strange to say no one took exception to the secular education 'plank'. I imagine this would not have been the case if it had been discussed. As a matter of fact, it was merely proposed, seconded, and passed without discussion. The only point in the programme to which I could take any exception is woman's suffrage. But, of course, it is inevitable in any socialist organisation. A beginning, then, has been made, but it remains to be seen what use the Party will make of its opportunities. It has much more to fear from itself, in my opinion, than from any bishops.

You need not send *Richard Feverel*, as I would not have the time to read it at present. From what you say, it seems to be a bit too idealist for my taste. Would you like to read Sydney Brooks' *New Ireland*? It is short, too short, but exceeedingly well and sympathetically written. The writer, who is an Englishman, takes practically the *Irish Nation* view of questions. He brings, among other things, the Irish Party and the Church into proper focus, and one can agree with nearly everything he says. I will send it immediately if you care to read it…

31 John (Cork) to Michael (Dublin), 6 July 1909

I can't see why you object to woman's suffrage being included in the programme of the Soc. organisation. I regard woman's suffrage as inevitable and desirable. I seem to have given you a false impression of *Richard Feverel*. The fact is that realism, as it is called, is blended with idealism in the book. Meredith idealises prosaic love, then he 'realises' it. In the commencement of the novel idealism predominates towards the end realism. I will send it when you wish. I would like to read *New Ireland*.

32 Michael (Dublin) to John (Cork), 6 July 1909

I quite agree with you that woman's suffrage is inevitable. Indeed, I believe nothing but a social convulsion could prevent it. To say that it is desirable is, however, a very different matter. When I look ahead at its almost certain consequences I think that few things could be more disastrous to the existence of a modern community than female enfranchisement. I may add that I recognise as fully as anyone can do the justice of the claim, and the unanswerable character of the arguments adduced to support it. There are, nevertheless, arguments on the other side which have nothing to do with 'justice', but are none the less weighty, if not conclusive. You must not imagine, however, that I have any sympathy with those who are actively opposing woman's suffrage. In the first place, their motives are mostly discreditable, and in the second place the foregone conclusion of their defeat makes them ridiculous. Perhaps it might be as well to add further that I think woman's suffrage would be much less dangerous in Ireland at present than in more advanced communities such as England. At any rate, when it comes, we shall see what we shall see.

How are you getting on with your labour troubles in Cork at present? The papers tell us that Cork's trade is crippled. What are your ideas on the matter? Do you think that serious injury has been inflicted on the business of the city?

I shall send *The New Age* to-morrow.

33 John (Cork) to Michael (Dublin), postmarked 7 July 1909

...I think that arguments against woman's suffrage resemble arguments against Socialism. Every man in his heart of hearts realises the justice of women's claim to the suffrage, just as every rich man realises the justice of his neighbour's claim to an equal share of the goods of this world. In each the arguments against justice are the 'good of society' and the 'security of the state'. In the one case, 'society' is a sex; in the other, it is a class.

The strikers and other unemployed here can hardly be said to hamper trade at all. If the trade of the city has been seriously injured which I doubt, it seems to me to be due to the cowardliness or callousness of a few employers. The unemployed, far from being made desperate by starvation, are almost totally inactive. Picketting has practically ceased...

34 John (Cork) to Michael (Dublin), 8 July 1909

Greeting and congratulation and the blessing of Allah and the prophet. Mother tells me you have passed the First Arts exam with honour and glory. May I hope for information at first hand?

Thanks very much for sending *New Ireland* which is exceedingly interesting. I have already read the chapters on Sinn Féin and the Gaelic League and the Church.

This week's *Nation* is very interesting. The editorial as usual is brilliant. I only hope Ryan won't get himself into trouble. He must not forget that the bishops and priests are still a great power in Ireland. They may not be able to alienate the present readership of the *Nation*, but it is in their power to prevent a rapid increase in circulation. You know well that the clergy would prefer the people to confine themselves in the matter of literature to the penny inanities of the Catholic 'Truth' Society or the penny horribles of England rather than read a paper which might elevate their moral character. It is easy to believe, then, that on the slightest pretext they will condemn the *Nation* from pulpit and altar and confessional. What an effect might thus be produced on those whose characters are not yet wholly redeemed from the influence of clericalism! . . .

35 *Extract from the Kerry Sentinel, 4 August 1909*

Once again we have to congratulate two talented young Tralee men, Master Michael Moynihan and Master James McElligott, on the signal success that has attended their scholastic course. We learn that in the First Arts Examination at the Royal University, Master Moynihan has won a first class exhibition value £30, and has also received First Class Honours in French and Honours in Latin and Mathematics ... Masters Moynihan and McElligott are a credit to Tralee, and we shall watch their careers with the greatest interest.

CHAPTER TWO

The Civil Service, 1910–11

Thanks very much for *Madame Bovary* and *Sapho*.[1] I have read the former, it is a very powerful book but perhaps a little too 'realistic'.

What appears to be your exultation in the discomfiture of the 'factionists' is premature as the results in South Mayo and South Monaghan will show. I can't see why O'Brien & Healy should not have nine or ten stalwarts to help them throw out the 'robbing' budget in the next parliament. O'Brien as you have seen has been nominated for North-East Cork where he will be elected. He will then resign whichever seat he thinks most secure and put M. Healy in. Gilhooly & Sheehan are safe, Ginnell and Guiney may get in. There will then be:– O'Brien, M. & T.M. Healy, Gilhooly, Sheehan, Ginnell, Guiney, J.O'Donnell, McKean, Shaughnessy (West Limerick unop[posed]. return) and perhaps Neville Stack and T.O'D. [Tom O'Donnell].[2] What price budget now? Do not think I'm deserting the Budget, an assumption such, would be unjust, unfounded and would very much grieve.

The results of an open competitive examination for twenty-five appointments in the Admiralty, Crown Agents for the Colonies, Surveyorship of Taxes, etc., and for which some three hundred competitors entered the lists, have just been issued by the Civil Service Commissioners, and from these we find that our young townsman, Michael J. Moynihan, has secured seventh place in the British Isles, it being the first, and the only Irish place obtained...

We are proud of our young townsman's genius and ability, and we are proud to have in our midst for the benefit of the community such an admirable educational establishment as the Christian Brothers.

Whosoever would send his son away to college, need only look to the excellent and unselfish Institution in Edward Street, and its product, Michael Moynihan.

Needless to say, we heartily congratulate Mr and Mrs Maurice Moynihan on the latest success of their brilliant son, and as he has yet to celebrate his nineteenth birthday, and as he is in the pink of athletic manhood, we are safe in predicting big events in his future career.

38 M.P. Ryan (Christian Brothers, Mount Sion, Waterford) to Michael (Dublin),
13 February 1910

As one of your old masters in Tralee, I hasten to congratulate you on your brilliant success in the Civil Service Exam.

This is a fitting termination to your splendid scholastic career. I can assure you I have followed each step of your onward and upward march with the keenest interest. I cannot forget the generous act of your good mother in leaving you in the Tralee schools notwithstanding the pressure brought to bear on her to have you and John sent elsewhere. Well I am delighted that she has not to regret her act.

From what I know of you I think I am safe in saying that you are in the beginning of a career that will reflect the highest honour on you. I trust you will keep on your studies for some years here.

I have never heard what your companions – John Vale and I. O'Carroll – have gone to. I daresay they also are doing well. During my stay in Dundalk I was often anxious to meet you in Dublin but I had not your address. I came here to Waterford last September,

Your good mother I am sure is indeed proud of your success. Do not forget to give her my best wishes as also to Mr and Mrs Power of Ballyvelly.[3] What is your brother John doing? I hope he is as good and kind as ever.

With best wishes for your continued success...

39 Mary (Tralee) to Michael (Dublin), 13 May 1910

Tell Uncle John how delighted we all were to see in the *Independent* he was to edit the newspaper.[4] Let me know at once when you hear where you will be stationed. I hope you will be left in London. As those W. Africans are going up, you ought sell them.[5] It would enable me to get the operation over that I must get done,– what I had to neglect for want of money.

How good Uncle John & Lizzie are to you. It is consoling to know, we have them to be interested in us. Don't go out unless with Aunt Lizzie or Uncle John, only of course to your business...

We are very lonely after you. Mamma is in an awful state she is sighing, & crying since you went. Write to her next, you can say in her letter anything you want to tell me.[6]

40 Mary (Tralee) to Michael (Dublin), postmarked 19 May 1910

I am surprised you are not writing. Indeed I cannot understand your action at all. You surely must know by this where you will be stationed & you might let me know ... We are all well but *anxiously* waiting for a line from you.

41 P. Williamson (Assistant Secretary, Inland Revenue) to Michael (Dublin), 19 May 1910

I am directed by the Board of Inland Revenue to inform you that they have received from the Civil Service Commissioners your Certificate of Qualification as an Assistant Surveyor of Taxes, and that you have been appointed to the Dublin, 1st District. I am therefore to instruct you to place yourself under the directions of Mr Surveyor Mulhall at Custom House, Dublin, on the earliest possible date and you should report to the Board, through your Surveyor, when you have taken up your duties.

42 Michael (Desmond House, Great Ormond Street, London)[7] to Mary (Tralee), 20 May 1910

Today being the day of the funeral of King Edward, we were up betimes.[8] After a hearty breakfast, Uncle John and I went out at 8 a.m. and took the tube to Knightsbridge, where we entered Hyde Park and walked to its eastern side. At that early hour, the place was already black with people, but we succeeded in getting a good position quite close to the procession route. For about two hours we stood there, in a burning sun, until at length, about 11 o'clock, the head of the procession appeared. First there came numerous detachments from the Army and Navy, accompanied by bands. These were followed by the Generals and the Admirals of the Fleet. We easily recognised Lord Kitchener and Lord Roberts, riding side by side. Later on came the Duke of Norfolk and Lord Rosebery. Then the gun-carriage bearing the coffin passed; and behind it rode nine monarchs. Among these the most prominent were King George V, the Kaiser, King Alfonso, and King Manoel. These were followed by a few dozen princes of all nations. Next passed the carriages, in which we saw, amongst others, Queen Alexandra, the Duke of Cornwall, and Mr Roosevelt, the latter a homely, benevolent, optimistic-looking man. This closed the interesting portion of the cortège, and we came away with the impression of a very memorable ceremony, and feeling sure that the like of it will never be seen again in the world's history. It took us nearly an hour to get out of the park, as the two main exits were closed, and there was a throng of probably a million people in Hyde Park. The weather was of a most summerlike character, and considerable numbers fainted from the heat and the waiting.

In another week now King Edward will be only a distant memory, and perhaps particles of pink and white will begin to mingle with the colours of mourning in the streets.

I have got no further communication since from the Board of Inland Revenue. I expect to know everything by next week, at all events...

43 John (Tralee) to Michael (Dublin), 12 August 1910

Have I offended against you, in any way? Or, am I to consider your flighty Douglas postcard as a reply to my last letter? Why did you not remain a month in the Isle of Man as you said? Did you tire of Kelly's company?

I notice that *The Plough and the Cross* has appeared in book form. I hope it will be as successful as it deserves.

What do you think of the struggle between Church and State in Spain?[9] It can't be said that the Roman authorities are giving much evidence of that wiliness which you and I were taught to regard as a distinguishing characteristic of Roman ecclesiastics. It was particularly stupid of them at the very moment when they were seeking to obtain a concession to Catholic feeling in England, to kick up a row because a greater degree of freedom and toleration was conceded to the non-Catholics in Spain. I hope Canalezas [*sic*] will stick to his guns, anyway. I don't see why he shouldn't. He seems to have a majority in the country, as well as in the Cortès, behind him. If he does hold on he'll teach the Vatican diplomacy which judged by Protestant ideas, would be rather like teaching a fish how to swim.

So you have been playing the ascetic lately, I have been told. Mother tells me that besides prayer and fasting, you have been wearing a hair-shirt; also that it is your custom to inflict on yourself, morning and evening flagellations. Please send particulars of this, your latest phase.

As for me there is, as you know, none of the ascetic about me. I haven't been doing anything in particular lately. I am still in love with Law and the Kennedy spell is not quite broken. I was rather bewitched by an Abbeyfeale girl yesterday but I shall probably recover. I've been looking out for Mrs Cronin and Daisy since the 1st inst. but have not seen them. Did you visit them when in London?

I am just now reading a very quaint book, *Celtic Twilight* by W.B. Yeats. It is a collection of stories of the 'good people'. The author professes to believe in faeries. I don't know whether he is joking or trying to prove himself the possessor of what is called a 'Celtic temperament'.[10]

Please don't try the 'fasting cure' again except under the supervision of a doctor.

44 Michael (Dublin) to John (Tralee), 15 August 1910

Kindly excuse me for not having answered yours of the 25th ult. I am I consider amply punished in having to deal with a double share of controversial material at once. With cannon to right of me and quickfirers to left of me I am bewildered.

To settle no. 1 first of all, I think it is on a par with Mr Chesterton's usual inanity to say that the Labour Party is the most conservative element in the House, and to put the Liberal Party next to them. Of course he only says it in order to be thought original, but, nevertheless, it was a more than ordinately stupid remark.[11]

As to the suffrage bill, I am entirely opposed to women's suffrage in any shape or form.[12] It is all very fine to say that the bill in question would strengthen the Conservative Party, but that would be very poor consolation when it had ruined the country. No one can suppose for a moment that an Empire relying as every empire must on military power could stand for long with women at the head of it.

...I have not followed the Spanish affair very closely, and can hardly express an opinion. The Prime Minister, however, appears to have taken rather high-handed attitudes. He may have been quite right in giving more religious freedom to other bodies but it was scarcely necessary for him to curtail the liberties of the predominant party. As to his having the country with him, he may have a large number of the people deluded in the specious Radical way; but to say that the people rightly understand or approve of his policy would be an exaggeration.

By the way, your remarks on the question seem to come badly from a man who goes to confession twice a week, and spends half an hour in the church every evening. I am unable to reconcile your theories with your practice, and would like some assistance. I cannot believe that all this piety is affected and yet it is so sadly at variance with your privately expressed views.

You ask about your friend, Daisy Cronin. I did not care to break the news to you before, but alas! she has been very seriously ill lately, and I cannot say whether she is yet all right. You are not likely to see her in Ballybunion this year. You must only bear the cross as best you can, my poor friend, and try the efficacy of prayer – and abstinence.

Next week is the week of the year in Dublin, when it will put on its gayest and most cosmopolitan aspect. The list of attractions this year is greater than ever, and with fine weather there ought to be a record crowd in town.[13]

45 Michael (Dublin) to John (Tralee), 5 November 1910[14]

Il faut m'excuser pour ne pas avoir répondu plus tôt à tes lettres.

Je suppose que tu es très diligent dans tes études et ce que tu trouves les livres intéressants?

Les conférences de la C.T.S. m'ont échappé tout à fait. Aussi les procédés de M. F. Ryan et ses camarades. Quant à ses articles dans la *Nation* ce serait une part de temps de les lire. De ma point de vue, le principal, presque le seul mérite du Vatican est sa opposition à la démocratie, et je regarde tous efforts de détruire cette opposition comme criminels et dangéreux.

En cet égard, je ne puis croire dans cette chute du parti conservateur dont tu parles. Ce serait une calamité trop grande à contempler. Toujours l'espérance!

Est-ce que tu as été au Théâtre Royal dernièrement. J'ai lu dans le *News* d'un concert admirable qui y eut recemment qu'on applaudit vivement, mais hélas! l'assistance n'égala pas les expectations.[15]

Je te prie d'excuser les erreurs…

46 Michael (Dublin) to John (Tralee), 19 November 1910[16]

La situation politique est très sérieuse. Le gouvernement radical, avec une indifférence cynique aux interêts commerciaux de la nation, veut précipiter une élection dans l'issu delaquelle dépend tout le futur de l'Empire. L'horizon est assez sombre car, si le parti patriotique perd cette élection, on voit

'Light after light go down
England and the Kingdom,
Britain and the Empire,
The old prides and the old devotions,
Pass, pass'.
Que penses-tu?...

47 John (Tralee) to Michael (Dublin), 6 December 1910

Mother has asked me to answer your letter as she is unable to write herself. For the past ten days or so her sight has been very dim, the doctors, Molyneux and White, say it is due to nervous breakdown. She is getting better now and tonight can see almost as well as ever.

...It will interest you to know that the great Irish novelist and our very distinguished townsman T.B. Cronin is a candidate for South Kerry. The O'Brienites – he is going on the A.F.I.[17] ticket – did not think him worthy to report and embellish their speeches – he has been sacked from the *Cork Free Press*. So they are going to send him to Westminster to make speeches and laws for the people of G[rea]t. Britain and Ireland. He has taken his sister to the South to uphold him in more ways than one, for it is whispered, that but for the stalwart arms of his supporters he would have fallen through a window from which he was speaking recently at Cahirciveen. O'Brien has given him £350!!

The sitting members have been returned unopposed in N. & W. Kerry. In East Kerry a three-cornered contest is expected – an O'Sullivanite, a Murphyite, and an O'Brienite.[18] Where does Redmond come in?

As to the elections generally it looks as if the Liberal majority will be reduced. In that case do you think the king would create the peers necessary to ensure the passage of the Veto bill?[19]

Why is it by the way that they don't form a genuine coalition government, with members of the three progressive parties in the Cabinet?

Very glad to hear you are coming home next week...

P.S. Mother says if you mean to bring a gramaphone [*sic*] to get it on hire for a few weeks? Also to bring your trunk and all your traps with you.

48 Thomas O'Donnell MP to Maurice Moynihan (Tralee), 14 June 1911

Dear Maurice,
    Have just got this. Am seeing him when I go to London next.

49 P. Williamson (Inland Revenue, Somerset House, London W.C.) to Thomas O'Donnell MP, 10 June 1911

With reference to yours of the 27th ultimo addressed to the Rt Hon. C.H. Hobhouse, MP[20] I am directed by the Board of Inland Revenue to aquaint you that they regret that they are unable to comply with your request that Mr M.J. Moynihan, as Assistant Surveyor of Taxes in this Department, should be transferred to the Admiralty Department.

50 Michael (Dublin) to John (Tralee), 24 June 1911

You were right in assuming that I did not receive your previous letter. It is good of you to try and reproduce it, but methinks that in the effort a lot of the fire of the original has been lost.
    Since Whit[sun] I have been leading what I may call a secluded life. I have been in town only two nights since then, the last occasion being Thursday, when I went in to see the illuminations and the crowd 'coro-nating'.[21] I have never before seen a crowd more densely packed, and it was most difficult to move in College Green and thereabouts. I am glad to say that the feeling of the great bulk of the population was in harmony with the occasion and it was quite clear that the few agitators who attempted to get up a disloyal demonstration in Beresford Place were championing a lost cause.
    We are all looking forward to the King's visit now, and it is not thought worth while to remove the flags and decorations put up for the Coronation, so for the next fortnight the streets will look quite gay.
    Tell mother that I was disappointed with the Board's letter to Tom O'Donnell. Evidently the matter was given over to the Board to deal with, and the moral is that there is very little use in letter writing. The only thing

is to see Hobhouse personally, and I am pleased to hear that Tom means to do this. It will, I fear, be very hard to upset the definite decision of the B.I.R. on the matter, but still there is no doubt that the Treasury is all-powerful, and if they can be induced to re-open the matter there is still hope. Have any steps been taken to secure Fr. Brennan's influence with Boland?[22] I am writing to Uncle John letting him know the latest develop-ment, and I am confident that he will do what he can for me.

When writing tell me all about the coronation celebrations in Tralee.

When you see your friend Mr Finnerty again tell him I 'was askin' for him'.

51 Michael (Dublin) to Mary (Tralee), 12 July 1911

So these wonderful days have come to an end at last. Since Friday Dublin has been a sort of fairyland. Perfect weather, beautiful decorations, enthu-siastic crowds, everything has combined to make King George's visit unforgettable.[23] It is a thousand pities you were not able to come up. I have kept as much as possible in the thick of things these past days. On Friday evening I went to Kingstown to see the arrival, and the illuminations of the Fleet which followed. After seeing the procession on Saturday I was, through the kindness of the Board of Works secretary, one of the few who were privileged to see the opening of the College of Science by the King.[24] Yesterday I took a day's leave to see the review in the Park. There was nothing exaggerated in the newspaper accounts of the reception given to Their Majesties. Everywhere they went it was through cheering crowds, composed, of course, of every class of the population. The people of Dublin have given a magnificent display of loyalty.

Now that you have got your money, you should make no delay in invest-ing as much as you can spare.[25] Rhodesian R[ai]l[wa]y 4% have risen somewhat since I first recommended them, but this is probably owing to the maturing of the half-yearly dividend. The earnings of this railway are going up by leaps and bounds, and though in view of the fixed rate of interest you cannot expect a very considerable rise in value, yet, from the point of security I consider it a 'real good thing'. British N[orth] B[orneo]s are at a low level just now and more than ever an attractive purchase. You will, no doubt, leave the money in the Bank until you need it. Fill up enclosed order, putting in name of Bank, for reference, and I will place it with some broker here...

I am feeling absolutely done up after the week-end. The heat has been terrific all along, and the constant running about in the broiling sun is most exhausting. Hoping you are all well at home.

Please overlook my delay in writing. The fact is I have been so busy having experiences that I could not find time to write about them. We narrowly escaped the witness-box last Friday night. We were going home about 11.30 p.m. when on Butt Bridge we met two French sailors, with whom we entered into conversation. After a while a workingman, in a very befuddled state of mind, came up and began abusing *us*, without any very clear motive. When the sailors noticed his attitude, they got excited and went for him, after the fashion of the Midi. Soon we were the centre of a large crowd, which appeared to take up a hostile attitude towards the Frenchmen. Things were getting very warm, and probably in another half-hour a policeman would have dropped upon the scene, but alas! time and the last tram wait for no man, and I at any rate, was not in a mind for walking to Clontarf. So regretfully we left, and until we were out of hearing the shouting and exclamations of the mob made it seem like a storming of the Bastille. I did not see a paper the next day, so cannot tell how it all ended.[26]

I have had a bathe nearly every day since coming back, and last Saturday & Sunday I went to Howth and got a boat, and had quite a decent time. The days are getting too short now for bathing in the evening, and with winter approaching the call of the city is becoming insistent. So I may leave the 'Green Lanes of Clontarf' very soon. Après ça, le déluge.

I would have called at the Clarence to see Uncle Pat last evening, but did not get into town until 10.30 p.m., when I thought it would be too late…[27]

You are no doubt settled down to a leisurely life again now after the strenuous times of 'the shtrike', even if you have not yet got over the bitter memories engendered by that wanton interference with your daily routine.

Have you heard that John Power is going to Rome on Monday? Uncle Pat routed me up at Nassau Street yesterday and gave me this unexpected intelligence. I am going out to Tallaght to-morrow to see John.[28] Tess is up with Uncle Pat, and very huffed because he would not let her go to *A Butterfly on the Wheel* on Thursday night. She threatens however that he must go to *The Girl on the Train* on Monday. I shall let you know if he does![29]

I have been paying my annual visit to the glimpses of Leicester Square. I lost myself first thing in getting from Euston station to G[rea]t. Ormond St[reet]. Knowing little about the new lines I took the tube for Russell Sq[uare]. the nearest station. I got there all right after going up to Piccadilly where I had to change, and then practically going back again over the same ground . . .

I had very little time for adventures. I was constrained to spend the nights in the thrilling pastime of playing '25'. Sunday, of course, is still practically a dies non. I managed to run into the Coliseum matinee on Monday afternoon, and saw Sarah Bernhardt herself, very eloquent and excited in French as Joan of Arc. I met Jim McElligott, who is now in London studying for the Indian Civil, and I must say I should not like to face the year that he has before him. He is paying a guinea a week for very indifferent lodgings, and what with that and overwork and the climate, it will be as much as he can do to come out of it in sound health.[30]

Uncle John, I am sorry to say, has his usual cold, and Aunt Lizzie is as usual engaged in finding new ways of amusing her guests. She invites you over for a week about Christmas, and you should accept. If you come along with me we shall paint the old village scarlet I do *not* think . . .

54 Michael (Dublin) to John (Tralee), 6 November 1911

I have to thank you for the book which you were so good as to send for my guidance.[31] Already I am busy studying 'how to concentrate', but so far neither rubber shares nor Rhodesians have made much response to my efforts. Consols, however, are rising, so there is still hope. I note with pleasure that I am not apt to be governed by the heart, but have *very clear, calm, judgment!* Following instructions, I am on the look out for scarf pin with a 'sapphire opal turquoise or chrysolite' stone and for hosiery of 'pale pink or nile green'. I shall let you know how these purchases will affect my success. General observations as a man about town, or 'one of the bhoys', make me optimistic.

In spite of my alarm at the prospects of Home Rule, I must admit that such a measure would give an opportunity of remaining in this island which, after all, might possibly be not unwelcome. When the bill is produced we shall see what we shall see. At any rate (if you will excuse this temporary ebullition of my long pent-up muse) at present it seems somewhat of a grievance that

> alike for those who for to-day prepare,
> and those who after some to-morrow stare,
> The Telegram may come by night or day,
> 'Sir you will this day travel here, not there'.
> The wire no question makes of yes or no,
> but east or west directs that you shall go;
> 'the people and the girl* (*No, not Delia Rorke) are here',
> you say; I know it's hard old chap, I know, I know;
> Think not that Fate strikes at your heart alone,
> for let Assistant or Surveyor groan,
> the Board for each finds some unwelcome spot,
> he likes as little as you may your own.
> *Chorus.* Ah! fill the cup, yea, fill the cups that clear,
> to-day of past regrets and future fear;
> to-morrow? Why, to-morrow I may be in Llanfairfechan or
>   on Margate Pier!

Again I crave pardon for above, and I hope to explain it all in good time. In the meantime, reserve your judgment.

55 Michael (Dublin) to John (Tralee), 9 November 1911

It is very discouraging to find that for the long hours I spent in creating immortal verse for your delectation and instruction, your only gratitude is to accuse me of wanting to get married, or being in love or something of that sort. To remove this painful misapprehension I would point out that the 'Rubaiyat of an Ass[istan]t. Sur[veyor].' can harp on other notes besides love of Dublin … Spare your further indignation, then, while I bewail the lot of assts & surveyors –

> weak precis of the game of ways & means,
> played by a heartless Board behind the scenes,
> hither and thither moved and spurred and stayed,
> until old age in mercy intervenes.
> Lo, some I loved, the loveliest and the best,

whose lips were warm, whose hands in mine I pressed,
those too in Dublin must I leave behind,
when I, far called, depart to join the rest of them who were
    my predecessors.
Yes, we* (*Editorial or official 'we' + 'us') that now make
    merry in the gloom,
round Grafton St, must see before us loom,
the shadow of that transfer nearing fast –
well can you blame us if at times we're glum?

I really must ask you, in reading the foregoing, to make liberal allowance for poetic licence. Do not draw unwarrantable inferences, and try to check that flow of intemperate language so rampant in your last letter. And if these lines of mine, the blessed lot, and in what all begins and ends in rot, remember tis in Dublin that I dwell! remember that I'm digging with a Scot! (I had to find that rhyme somehow).

What do you think of Mr Balfour's resignation?[32] Personally, while, as a Conservative, I should like to see him conserved, it seems to me that the present state of the party is a sufficient proof of his innate incapacity as a leader. The sentimental twaddle that is now being ground forth about him has little visible justification when you come to review his work during the past six years. The country is now more than ever trodden under the heels of the Radical despotism, and the wrongs done to helpless minorities are unallayed.

Some curse the penny on the beer,
and some say that the future of the trade looks glum,
but bad though Comrade George's budget be,
'tis nothing to the budgets yet to come.

Fearing that your nerves can stand no more, I hasten to bid you good-night.

CHAPTER THREE

Dublin, 1912–13

Fearing that in your present moral state, a moral lecture would be unavailing, I take the opportunity at the opening of a new year, to say a few words, for your guidance, on politics and social policy.

About two years ago, you may remember, you made a sudden and unheralded change in your political opinions or professions. Anticipating, presumably, a time when, as the reward of prudent speculation, you expect to become a millionaire. You deemed it wise to force yourself into political and social opinions compatible with the possession and retention of wealth.

Under the influence of this pressure, your attitude on political matters has so degenerated as to become a mere mockery of public policy.

Let us consider your views on the question of the taxation of wealth. I think you object to the idea of a graduated scale of Income Tax, which is, perhaps, the most unobjectionable of all means of raising revenue, a direct tax on those who can best bear the burden of taxation; on those who have what they boastfully call a 'stake in the country', and who are, therefore, most interested in the maintenance of the public services. A tax, too, graduated in proportion to the capacity of the taxpayers to pay it, and in proportion to their stake in the country.

For my part, I should be in favour of raising the entire revenue of the country by means of a properly graduated tax on all incomes over £70 or £80 per annum, making, of course, some exemptions and reductions in cases of persons with large families and so forth. Financiers might say it was unwise to have the revenue of the country dependent on a single tax; but that would scarcely be an insuperable objection. At any rate there is much to be said for the idea, and it would be carrying into effect the great principle that taxation should be based, and entirely based, on the taxable capacity of the taxpayer, a principle to which too little recognition has been, hitherto, given.

Another article of your political creed, viz: your objection to State interference in private affairs, is easily overthrown. I might accuse you of forgetting that the State is composed of individuals, and that the welfare of those individuals and the welfare of the State are inseparably bound together. The State, as we know it, exists for the benefit, protection and guidance of its subjects. Amongst the great duties of the State are, the duty of protecting itself from its individual units, and the duty of protecting those individuals from each other. There is also the great duty of protecting future generations from the present one. Thus, the duties of the State, not merely justify interference in private actions, but necessitate it. I doubt if you can suggest a single important action, possible to an individual which does not in some way affect the State, for good or ill.

Altogether, your views of individual liberty are hardly compatible with your professions of conservatism. I have always thought that the love of order was one of the very mainsprings of conservatism, but, we live to learn; I suppose even conservatism is subject to the universal law of change. You seem to think that every man has a right to almost absolute freedom in trade and in private life. In the matter of trade freedom your views are those of the Manchester school of radicals; in the matter of freedom in private life the general application of your ideas would produce absolute anarchy. For my part, my motto is 'order', and it is in socialism that I see the best chance of social order. Conservatism, also, is supposed to involve social order; but, I fear, that is only a forced order, and that were the compelling force removed the entire fabric would collapse. What I seek is a free and natural order erected on a basis of justice and contentment and organization. And if ever a day comes when I shall lose my belief that Socialism means order on that day will I abjure Socialism, and not till then.

Sincerely hoping that in this year which lies before us you will examine your social and political conscience, confess your offences and amend your life.

57 Michael (Dublin) to John (Tralee), 18 January 1912

Your lengthy confession has duly come to hand, and in view of your impenitent attitude I am surely at a loss to know what to do for you. I am aware by experience how useless argument is in a case of this kind.

As against your defence of State interference, I might ask you what functions the state has performed in the past, and what historical basis there is for putting it in the position which it would occupy under Socialism. You will have to admit that the state has never except in periods of decadence, usurped the part of foster-nurse over its individual units. To restrain the individual, not to drive him, has been the useful object of which it has fulfilled.

I cannot imagine what compensations socialism could possibly have to offer for the diminution, or rather abolition, of personal liberty. The average man would probably be better off in no respect, and life would be rendered intolerable by the existence of an army of officials of every government, supervising every little act of one's life. Of course you may say that *your* Socialism would leave a certain modicum of personal freedom & responsibility, but I am speaking of the real tendency of Socialistic legislation, so far as it can be gauged (is this correctly spelt) at present. And even if people did settle down under that sort of thing, can you really suggest that it would be good for them, or for 'the race'? Socialism appears to me a sort of second childhood of mankind, from which all courage and buoyancy & virility have departed, leaving a doating, spoonfed peaceloving old man sliding into the grave. I feel sure that you would think so too if you could divest yourself of your obsession with 'social problems' which really only confuse the issue, and do not decide it. For my part I am rooted in the conviction that Socialism would involve the sacrifice of things more important than the interests of any class, however numerous. And I am entirely an individualist. I do not feel the slightest interest in raising the general standard of well-being or anything of that sort. To see individuals rising above the average is to my mind a much more satisfying thing than to see the whole mass rising together.

If I have failed to impress you, I hope at all events that you see the futility of trying to convert me to your political nostrums...

58 John (Tralee) to Michael (Dublin), 7 March 1912

'The old order changeth, yielding place to new'.

In these days of crisis one recalls almost unconsciously the words of King Arthur. Newspaper headings tell a strange and sad tale. At one point one sees the heading 'Coal Strike; Further Developments'; at another, 'Woman's Suffrage; Glass-Smashing Campaign' elsewhere one finds a heading somewhat like this – 'Chinese Republic; Severe Fighting' and this last is not the least ominous.

Here, in Western Europe, we find everywhere the evidence of social disintegration. The fabric of society is crumbling. I am, as you know, a socialist. That is to say, I have an eye to the future; but I have also an eye to the past. The history of former civilizations, though, I regret to say, it is mainly hearsay to me, seems to show that civilization is not an immortal growth, that, like commoner growths, it has its origin, its zenith and its decline. So it has been with past civilizations, and, as I look around I see what I believe to be unmistakable signs that the civilization of which we are so proud or, at least our order of society, which is, I suppose, much the same thing, is doomed. When I say society is doomed, I speak not of the immediate future, but of a date which may be many generations hence. I would say that the decline of a social system which has taken so many centuries to build will extend over another century or more.

In my opinion, modern society resembles a structure erected on pillars - four pillars, religion, property, class distinctions, and lastly though by no means least, masculine supremacy. Beneath this great edifice and enjoying its shelter are four groups, consisting of Freethinkers, Socialists, Democrats and Suffragettes. Each group armed with crowbars and pickaxes and busily engaged in destroying the Pillar of Society to which it objects; each protesting against the wanton excesses of the others. In the centre is a fifth group consisting of priests and rich men, peers and politicians and a few earnest-looking greybeards. The members of this last group are talking and gesticulating excitedly, pointing to the groups at the pillars and then looking up at the roof as if considering the danger which must result to the building from the exertions of the destroyers. Besides these groups, there are a number of spectators who move about from group to group, watching the scene with amused interest. No one, outside the centre group, seems to realise the danger of the situation. Even in that group the majority are preoccupied with personal and sectional interests rather than with the general danger. Now and again, a member of the centre party goes to one of the corner groups and makes a vain endeavour to check the destruction. Now and again, also, the members of the various groups address themselves to the spectators, seeking to make converts. Thus go on, day by day, this endless destruction and this futile effort to conserve what remains of the Pillars of Society.

Every day that passes leaves the pillars weaker; every day brings the edifice nearer to ruin. Will they be all buried beneath its ruins? Who can tell? Assuming they are not – and it is to asssume a great deal – assuming that they bring the structure to the ground but escape themselves, what will follow? A Socialist state perhaps, where all men and women will be equal. There culture will reign and refinement. There will be peace and plenty. And men will believe that this is, indeed, the paradise round which were woven the dreams and hopes of countless generations. Yes, they will believe it, for a while. And then? Then, I suppose, the Chinese – or the overflow of some other teeming Eastern population will come; whether in the guise of warlike invasion or pseudo-peaceful immigration, who shall say. And, truly, they will make nice work of the delicate china of our social fabric. (How do you like this pun?)

Or, before the groups succeed in destroying our social system, the end may come in another way. I refer to internal anarchy – avowed anarchy. The growth of organised criminality and anarchy, and, unhappily, organised anarchy is not the contradiction that it seems, appears to be one of the features of life in our great cities today. Indeed in some places, most notably in France, where social disintegration seems to have proceeded farther than in any other country, this growth appears to be outpacing that of the power of the law. It may be that it will proceed so far that individual citizens will, once more in the world's history, have to arm themselves for the protection of their persons and property. Police will be useless and the dependence on the central authority, which is the mortar of the social structure, a nullity, universal anarchy would come bringing with it a relapse into barbarism.

Don't take me in all this as protesting against Socialism and woman's suffrage. I remain both a socialist and a suffragist. That is to say, in theory I favour both principles. I believe in their justice; but I fear they are sadly at variance with the spirit of our social system. It seems to me that both are inevitable, but I believe that they will bring in their train nothing but weakness to our civilization. I don't think it will be given to us to take either principle to the point of real success. I suppose we have outlived our period of usefulness, of great achievement. I know there is energy left yet in us, but I fear it will prove rather suicidal than life-giving.

I believe the Chinese have a habit of beginning things at what we consider the wrong end. Perhaps they will start their civilization on socialistic and feminist lines.

Europe or, at any rate, Western Europe is coming under a cloud. In another century or so we will have a renewal of the dark ages. Once more the centre of civilization will move to the East; this time farther east. The world will be ruled from Tokio or Peking. Japan will be the England of the new order.

You and I will look serenely down on a reconstructed world from the Abode of Love. And we will think how much less dismal 'Dark Ages' are in reality than they appear in history. J.P.M.

59 John (Tralee) to Michael (Dublin), 10 March 1912

... I enclose a dividend warrant. It will help to take Moss to the theatre or Con to Dundrum.

It is time I should congratulate you on the brilliant feats of your new party leader. Were it possible to stem the flowing tide of conservatism he would surely be the man to do it. His answers to Mr Asquith's assertions during the debate on the address must have amazed even Austen Chamberlain by the presence of mind, resource and decisiveness which they showed.[1] 'Certainly', I hear you say. Yes, certainly and I should say he'll have a busy time undoing the work of his predecessors, when and if he comes to power. So busy indeed will he be that, I fear, he'll have but little time to display any originality and capacity for constructive legislation.

They say Mr Balfour is returning to the front opp[osition]. bench (that is if Mr Law does not throw out the Government in the meantime) to learn the arts of debating and party management from his leader.

Mother says you expect to be left in Dublin for another year so there is no reason why you should not come home at Easter if 'time' (i.e. Moss) permits.

Mother wishes to know if Moss is a good companion. She also supposes that he is responsible for the brevity of your six line letters to her. What shall I say?[2]

60 Michael (Dublin) to John (Tralee), 15 March 1912

By their fruits ye shall know them. So you too have at last opened your eyes to the real significance of socialism, as a symptom of the decadence of civilization and the break-up of the social order. Your disquisition is a powerful indictment of our contemporary dreamers who are undermining the edifice built up by the labour and wisdom of ages, in the senseless hope of replanning things anew according to lecture-room ideas of perfection. In their utter fatuity they think that the world is following them, whereas in truth their altruistic shibboleths are being translated by each class into levers for the promotion of sectional interests. The miners are throttling the community in the name of justice, while your suffragettes are making war on the community under the same pretext. This patent fact should show the most guileless dilettante economic theorist the vanity of his dreams, but in fact its effect is probably the opposite in most cases. What the end is to be, or whether there is any means of averting the imminent ruin, I shall not guess, but it is becoming more obvious every day that we are on the wrong track. At the moment our position is that we must choose between the successive tyrannies of blatant minorities, and the crushing tyranny of the state. Everything like reverence and regard for established order and tradition has vanished, and the only restraining force in existence is that of elementary physical facts. How the principle underlying such a state of things could ever have appealed to you is more than I can fathom. That it should have taken a national catastrophe to shake your faith in them is still harder to understand. But it is a happiness to know that you have now come over to the Reaction. Henceforth I trust you will be a consistent defender of Throne and Altar, recognising that your four pillars of Religion, Property, Class distinctions and Masculine Supremacy are the only ones on which a true order and a *stable state* can be upheld.

... That young fellow, Moss, has got into a scrape lately, for breaking windows or something (sans l'alternatif d'une amende).[3]

61 Michael (Dublin) to John (Tralee), 9 May 1912

Thanks for your little homily, which is interesting for the sidelight it throws on your steady progress to a conservative outlook on life. Before long I expect you to admit that majority rule no longer has your allegiance, and that whatever risk there be in relying on individual wisdom, it is worth taking for the sake of the glorious chances in it. When that day comes, you will find it easy to drop that superstition about 'effete' aristocracy, which does duty nowadays for profound political wisdom. What is better, you will recognise that even if a particular aristocracy is effete, that is no argument against the principle in general. For already, apparently, you understand that all institutions both democratic and oligarchic have the seed of decadence in them. But their value is in no way determined by that fact and you, with your British sense of fair play, will not overwhelm the old order with abuse and contempt because democracy seems at the moment to have it by the throat...

Fired by your example, I went bathing on Sunday; and found the water quite warm. Three other chaps and I purchased a little rowing boat in Kingstown about a week ago and have taken her to Clontarf. We have had great times during the last two weekends, and are looking forward to a glorious summer.

Have yourself and Leo[4] visited the source of the Curraheen river since?

P.S. Will you please get something for mother's birthday with enclosed P.O. I am unfortunately very busy at present, and unable to do shopping...

62 P. Williamson (Assistant Secretary, Inland Revenue) to Michael, 20 September 1912

With reference to the preliminary examination of Assistant Surveyors held in May last, at the termination of the period of your probation I am directed by the Board to acquaint you that you passed the required test satisfactorily, and you have accordingly been confirmed in your appointment as an Assistant Surveyor of Taxes.

63 Michael (Dublin) to John (Tralee), 4 June 1912

I have not heard from Leo Casey. I understand he is going away to Canada. When is his departure taking place? Perhaps you could induce him to pay us a visit up here before he leaves.

Our little craft with its unsinkable bulkheads is still riding the deep. I am thinking of making the trip down on it for the summer holidays...

I got Lord Hugh's book *Conservatism* yesterday.[5] If and when you read it, it will rid your mind of the last remnants of the Socialist superstition. In a glance over it, I cannot say that I have found anything new, to a true blue like me; but to you, who have got into the bad habit of looking at things from a violently democratic and modernist standpoint, it should prove a mental tonic. Here is a truism which you Reds are strangely oblivious to. 'Nothing is more certain than that the mechanism of human society will only express human character, it will not regenerate it ...We may be sure at the outset that no change of social or political machinery will redeem society.'[6]

Your assertion that society exists to combat individualism seems to me the reverse of the truth. Society exists for the mutual well-being of its units, and it is by encouraging individuality not crushing it out or imprisoning it, that society at once fulfils its chief function and finds its surest source of strength. The general realisation of your ideals could only result in reducing mankind at large to a position of slavery, without even the redeeming feature that it had at the top a class possessed of sufficient stamina and ruling capacity to guide it. Nothing is surer than that such a state, if, contrary to all historical precedent, it can come into being, would crumble like a house of sand.

And as to your idea that society must protect itself against strong men, I know of no analogy or example to confirm that. The exertions of strong or exceptional men have, almost invariably and inevitably, been for the good of society, and where they have succeeded in gaining power, they have used it, practically always, to leave their state stronger than they found it, and often, when conditions required it, to save society itself from ruin and demolition.

I beg of you to bear these little facts in mind when you are day-dreaming, and especially when next you are writing to your most obedient...

64 Michael (Dublin) to John (Tralee), 17 June 1912

I gather from your tone that our cousin did not invite *you* to his 'soirée'. However, you can pay him back when giving your first soirée after election as M.I.P.[7]

I was shocked to find you making such unscrupulous use of my innocent quotation from Lord Hugh. Your 'assumption' that I, any more than the noble Lord, have any desire or intention to regenerate human society either by social mechanism or otherwise, is as unfounded as it is reflectful. My intention was to cure you finally of a fad which, however, I now gather, you have already abandoned. To fling Carlyle at me is an outrage, though your extract is interesting as indicating a decided and welcome retrogression in your standpoint. You have now evidently ceased to approve of the sinister assaults on the social order, or what is left of it, which form the basis of modern politics. It says much for the innate good sense with which I always credited you that you have freed yourself from the influence of the cranks who would establish a new heaven and a new earth on the ruins of the world-old institutions in Church and State on which the stability and continuity of society entirely depend. In the fact that you have now definitely cut yourself off from the old associations I find but one cause for regret and that is that a perennial source of argument has ceased.

I shall send you Lord Hugh's book when I have finished it, which will be some time, at the present rate of progress.

65 Maurice (Tralee) to Michael (Dublin), 29 June 1912

Why don't you write to your mother? She feels it bad. You might at least spare a few minutes every week to do so, knowing how anxious she has always been about you, and how she appreciates your writing regularly to her.

She doesn't know I am doing this.
Your affectionate Father.

66 John (Tralee) to Michael (Dublin), no date (c. 19 July 1912)

On looking at your last letter I find with shame that it is dated June 17th.
My excuse – if such it can be called – is the usual one of laziness.

Your letter reminds me of one of the most fruitful sources of appalling
tragedy in human existence viz. the misunderstanding of human motives
&c. You charge me with misunderstanding or, even wilfully misinterpret-
ing your previous letter and at the same time you say that you infer from
my last letter that I have abandoned some fad not mentioned by name.
Now I don't recollect having made any revocation, formal or informal, of
any opinion which I had previously.

You speak of cranks who 'would establish a new heaven and a new
earth on the ruins of the world-old institutions in Church & State on
which the stability and continuity of society entirely depend'. Now I will
make these words the text of a sermon to which I warn you to attend. I
will begin in the world-old manner on which the continued existence of
pulpit oratory entirely depends. Dearly beloved brother, give ear unto my
words. Fear not cranks! If by a crank you mean a faddist an impractical
dreamer one who has departed from facts, who lives with visions, you need
not fear him; he is harmless. *He* will not build a new heaven or a new
earth. *He* will not undermine world-old institutions. Know you not that if
an idea is not *practicable* it cannot be put into *practice*. I should have thought
that at least, a piece of elementary knowledge. It seems to have been lost
sight of today. It is a strange thing to see you with Lord Hugh (the conservative who, true to the traditions of his house, has 'taught us many new
lessons in parliamentary manners') and a host of aristocratic politicians
and journalists in a state of dire alarm over the propagation of what you
have been pleased to call 'lecture room theories of Society'. Now if Lord
Hugh and you regard Socialism as a mere 'lecture room theory' why *fear*
it. Conservative politicians are unanimous in calling Socialism the great
menace of Society: they are equally unanimous in calling it a lecture room
theory. I must regard it as a striking instance of either insincerity or imbe-
cility in conservatives. Now, my dear Michael I appeal to you, as a sincere
friend to turn your back on this sort of nonsense. Call socialism what you
will but don't call it a lecture room theory. On every hand you see socialism being put in practice. Why not then admit that socialism is a reality, a

practicality; far more so than the world-old institutions in church and state which have lost their meaning and their utility and which a world intolerant of toothless Servility in its institutions is growing weary of.

I appeal to you, for Heaven's sake to cast off this foolish cynical regard for a governing class that has long ceased to govern for a church that has all but ceased to preach. I say 'cynical', because I feel convinced that it is based wholly on the very fact that these institutions have ceased to perform their functions. You pose as a friend of society and yet you would allow [it] to entirely depend on rotten props. I claim to be a truer conservative than you are...

I believe but as little as you do in the equality of men. I believe on the contrary that the aristocratic principle has its roots deep down in human nature. That is precisely why I look to the future without dread. Realising as I do that in a living, moving, active Society those who are best fitted for the task will resume the leadership. I am confident that under Socialism the principle will have scope for a more complete development than it has yet attained. How can you doubt it? For where there is need for government, and where is there not? there, also, is the need for a true, working aristocracy.

I no longer say that I am a socialist. Like all forms of society, Socialism may prove more or less ephemeral. I agree with Lord Hugh that the 'mechanism of society is only the expression of human character'. But a new form of society is an indication of continued energy and virility in the human character and as such welcome. It is a reincarnation of the spirit that abides with men...

I hope you have been paying your duties to Mr Asquith these days and that you have joined in the amazing outburst of enthusiastic homage which Dublin has accorded him.[8]

I suppose you are bathing and boating a great deal in this glorious weather.

I intended all this disjointed chatter to be merely a crude first draft but it has wandered to such length that the very thought of re-writing it makes me shudder.

67 Michael (Dublin) to John (Tralee), 21 July 1912

Your claim to be the true conservative is an old Radical device now thoroughly exposed. As Lord Hugh says, 'it may happen that things may be done (in the guise of Conservatism) which if they could be seen in their unveiled reality, would be instantly rejected, and then the Conservative externals become only a trap, a rotten parapet. Conservatives must take care that they are not cheated by appearances into consenting to changes and developments which may sap and undermine much that is both ancient and valuable.' I would ask you in all frankness to state what you wish to conserve. If as you assert in terms, the aristocratic principle is indestructible, then no effort on your or anybody else's part is required to conserve it, and your belief in its immortality does not make you a Conservative in any sense whatever. A Conservative is, at all events, one who wishes to retain things which are liable to be destroyed. Personally I regard aristocracy in its true and historic meaning, as one of those things and I should be strongly averse to confusing it, as you do, with that officialdom and bureaucracy which would be rampant under socialism. To look upon Insurance Commissioners and such parasites as true and worthy successors to fox-hunting squires and old-fashioned Colonial Governors, is utterly repugnant to me. Frankly, to me all this supercivilization is entirely hateful. Any calamity would be preferable to it. What to you seems progress is to me all decadence and fin de siècle. With Edward Ponderevo,[9] I see 'no promise at all in the Empire or in any of the great things of our time'. And your idea that change is a token of continued vitality is singularly shallow. It is just as often a sign of decay and death.

Mr Asquith's visit has drawn forth all the worst elements in the mob.[10] He might not have been so flattered as he looked if he had known the character of his supporters. The most amusing feature in 'Jacobinism's night out' was the imposing squad of beery looking cabbies on their decayed chargers, who formed the van of the procession. Through sheer compassion the Unionist papers refrained from the caustic comments which the exhibition might well call forth. However we can forget all this if the visit does any good to the measure which, please God, will rid the country of Mr Asquith and his party for ever.

What 'approved society' have you joined? Not the Mollies, I hope. Mr Box has joined them, I regret to say.[11]

I go boating & bathing whenever I get the chance. But the weather is terribly fickle. It was beautiful yesterday, but today there is a continuous downpour.

68 John (Fenit)[12] to Michael (Dublin), 24 July 1912

'I love everything that's old: old friends, old times, old manners, old books, old wine.' Thus said Mr Hardcastle, and if he had added old horses, old women and old country gentlemen I have no doubt you would be in enthusiastic agreement with him. Your unreasoning love of antiquity seems the only thing you have in common with Mr Hardcastle, as, though I have not read the play I have some reason to think him a very sensible old gentleman.[13] Your sentiments have the flavour of the Christmas numbers of magazines and are equally unfit for everyday use.

Your last essay in 'old political commonsense' suggests to me that we open up the whole question of your political position once more. For the purpose of our enquiry we will assume that you really are a sincere conservative. Then, I take it, you must regard conservatism as true political wisdom. The only form of conservatism which anyone, not wholly blind, could mistake for political wisdom is that which would insist on the retention of every old custom, institution or law until he had been clearly proved to be a source of weakness or danger but only until then. Political wisdom will always look first to the essential goodness or badness of a law or institution and only secondarily at its antiquity or novelty. Time may 'make old bareness picturesque' but a wise man is not deceived by the glamour of the ivy, he looks beneath it and sees the ruined wall.

In the current quotation from Hugh Cecil (I suppose he won't insist on the title amongst friends) he makes a remark about danger to institutions which are 'both ancient and valuable' which seems to show that even he doesn't think antiquity all-sufficing. So, you seem isolated in your exaggerated respect for ancient forms. Altogether your position is untenable and I fear that if conservatism generally defends itself so poorly Mr Bonar Law may as well hoist the white flag. Lord Halsbury and you can die in the last ditch.[14]

I really don't remember saying that change, any change, is a sign of vitality. But I do hold that the nation which grapples with its own problems, which lays its own spectres (the spectres of its dead past) is the nation which retains most vital energy. Can you deny that England, striving heroically to solve the problems which beset her, has more energy than poor Spain, encumbered with the unburied corpses of her ancient (and malodorous) institutions?

My dear Michael, I must exhort you once more to cease worshipping the vain 'shows of things'. Come back to reality, back to truth. I remember a time when you claimed and, I believe, truly that you always sought after truth to the end, wherever it might lead you, and, that you always accepted the conclusions of reason even if your most cherished illusions were thereby shattered. Be of that mind once more, seek out the truth and cherish it. Live your own life in your own age, an age that has never been

lived before. Recall yourself to the present time. Don't pin your faith to
dead customs; rather strive to mould those of the present and of the
future. I don't ask you to be a socialist, all I ask is not to be an impossi-
bilist. Don't think you can breathe life into corpses, it is impossible and, in
this case, at any rate, undesirable.

Don't worry too much about mere forms of society, they do not matter
much. The things that do matter, the aristocratic principle and such like
are as the spirit that animates all really living forms of society. These
things are indestructible. In every form of society which has real vitality
you will find them. They leave the earth only for a time when the body in
which they dwelt becomes diseased and begins to decay. They do not stay
long away for you will find them incarnate in the first healthy body that
comes to take the place of the old disused one.

Believe me, all those things which we value most in life are spiritual
things which never die. Have no fear for them; they may disappear for a
time, but, you may always look forward to their re-birth with hope and
hail it with joy.

As for the present time, when I see men getting rid of the old dead
forms which have encumbered the earth and polluted the air so long, my
heart is filled with hope for I know that the hour of deliverance is at hand.

I am glad to hear you were in the Asquith procession. Apparently you
were in the rear directing the gay caballeros. You don't mention that you
attended the Theatre Royal meeting but mother detected your forehead
and hair in a photograph of the platform party which appeared in
Monday's Daily Sketch. In the same paper in another photo you will see an
old familiar face with an old familiar smile of smug self-satisfaction; I
wonder did he warn the Premier against the evils of 'company-keeping'.[15]

The weather has broken here too but last week was very fine and I had
three bathes on Saturday, making nine, up to the present, for the year.

I suppose you heard of the fire here, Galvin's two shops were burned
down and Quinlan's and O'Donnell's, which were rather badly damaged,
escaped total destruction only as a result of the exceptional pressure of
water and the heroic exertions of the military and urban firemen.

69 Michael (Dublin) to John (Tralee), 7 August 1912

In returning thanks for your quotation from Mr Hardcastle (I really forget
who that dear old gentleman was), I would suggest, as a suitable motto for
you, the words of the Latin poet (of the Decadence, mark you). 'Non vetera

amo, nam nova multo meliora.' 'I do not love the old things, for the new are
far better.'[16] It is quite clear that, freed from all the ambiguity and confusion,
your attitude is simply the Modernist one of approval to all current and shifting phases of popular opinion, regardless of their absolute rightness or
wrongness. According to the Modernist philosophy indeed, the ideas of
absolute truth or error are purely illusory. Whatever belief commends itself
to the people in general at any given time is to receive the imprimatur of
'truth' in the newest and most puzzling interpretation of that word. The
criterion of 'truth' with reference to any doctrine is apparently whether or no
that doctrine fits in and harmonises with prevalent attitudes and sentiments.
On this theory a religious belief which has 'lost its significance' today may
have been 'true' one thousand or two thousand years ago. That such a logical mind as yours should have been deluded by a philosophy as steeped in
self-deception and abuse of the elementary meanings of words is altogether
astonishing and inexplicable. The frank partisan, the socialist who imagines
that he has the panacea for all human ills, I can understand. But the intellectual opportunism which is willing to lend its blessing to whatever political or
other movement may command popular approval at the moment, is something new and disquieting. You and your Modernist friends are like men in a
little boat, with no oars to guide it, which drift[s] about at the mercy of the
drifting tides. It were a far far better thing for you to have an anchor of sound
and well-tested opinion which would enable you to survey calmly the various
influences at work around you. Such an anchor is to be found nowhere but
in Conservatism, which builds its political creed on principles which have
stood the test of ages, and are not one whit less valuable to us and to posterity than they have been to our ancestors. Take your stand thus, and you will
perceive that our surest source of strength and our greatest hope for the
future lie in a policy which, while mindful of the just claims of the community, is jealous of the smallest encroachment on individual rights and liberties
and which though, as always, consistent in its defence of law and order, yet
relies mainly on individual virtue and public spirit and initiative, instead of
on the deadening force of compulsion to further the common good. True
reform will consist in making that policy prevail.

70 John (Listowel) to Mary (Fenit), 10 September 1912

I am very lonely after Michael, I don't think I'd feel it so much if I were
at home. I suppose he had Uncle Mick up as far as Mallow with him.[17] Try
to meet me on Thursday and don't forget the key of the house.

Tell father it is time to ask Daly's to send the samples to D. O'Sullivan, Ballylongford. 2s/. nett. is the price.[18]

71 Mary (Fenit) to Michael (Dublin), 11 September 1912

I hope you got to Dublin all right. We are all done up after you. I was never so lonely. The day is lovely & that makes it worse. Enclosed is a letter from John ... It was awful going down to the house alone yesterday after you leaving. John may go the week after we go home from here. Write home & say how you are.

72 Mary (Fenit) to Michael (Dublin), 16 September 1912

I was delighted to get your letter. We are still very lonely after you. The weather is perfect. The corn boat is expected today. They must be pretty sure of its coming as some of the Tralee merchants are out...

There was a shark around the Pier on Saturday. The local sergeant of Police tried to shoot him without success. It was rumoured there was some risk in bathing on account of the Sea monster. We however accepted the risk & had a dip without any serious results...

It is grand that you are not being removed from Dublin.

73 Leo Casey (Tralee) to Michael (Dublin), 16 September 1912

Your welcome letter of this morning to hand. I was most anxious to hear from you.

I was unfortunately unable to keep my appointment on Sunday week last. The pony and trap had to be taken to a funeral...

You will be pleased to know that I have come to a decision with regard to my future career.

The Engineering School in Dublin (N.U.I.) is only in its embryo stage as yet. Consequently I don't think it would pay to take out my lectures in that establishment. So I am going to Cork instead.

I am writing to Cork, by this mail, to find out if there are any rooms to be had in St Anthony's Hall. This St Anthony's Hall is a house of residence attached to the University & as far as I can understand is O.K.

My people do not wish that I go to Dublin so I think it is just as well to fall in with their wishes.

I shall be pleased to hear from you again. Hope you can read my writing. My hand is a bit unsteady this morning ... remember me as ever ...

Leo J. Casey

74 Postcard from Mary (Fenit) to Michael (Dublin), 23 September 1912

Why are you not writing? I hope you are well. The corn boat came on last Thursday.

75 Michael (Dublin) to John (Tralee), 9 October 1912

Thanks for your account of the last days at Fenit. Did you get any information about the old castle and its history?

I suppose you have got into winter clothes and winter habits by this time. I have had some good weekends since coming back, boating and mountaineering. I hope to go in more for the latter in future. I did about eighteen miles up in the hills last Sunday.

It is all nonsense about your not coming up until next year. You must come at the beginning of November without fail. For the remainder of this month, I may say, owing to my insurance folly,[19] I will have to trim my sails pretty close.

I am glad you have found such a trusty counsellor in Montaigne[20]... That you should begin to appreciate this point of view is a triumph of your innate good sense...

76 John (Tralee) to Michael (Dublin), 3 November 1912

I must plead an unsettled state of mind, as my excuse for not writing sooner. When reading Emerson I got into a very pleasant, transcendental frame of mind; I can say I have never been nearer happiness than he has brought me. But Montaigne has destroyed all that. When writing to you last I had not quite realised his pernicious influence. Though I resist his views, his materialism has had a disturbing effect on my mind. Still, I try to forgive him, for, for all his faults he is a delightful, old world fellow.

I quite admit that I have become more conservative but, for practical party politics I have a rooted and growing dislike.

I half hoped that in the shuffling about the Irish Senate someone would propose a second chamber consisting of the present Irish peerage and having an absolute veto.[21] I think such a chamber would be at once the most effective safeguard for the minority and the best guarantee of good government for the whole country. Of course, I know that a proposal like this could not be expected from the ministry which has emasculated the English House of Lords; and in any case that Mr Redmond would not accept it.

So, there is another chance of settling the Balkan question, if only the Great Powers will have the good sense not to interfere. No settlement which would leave even a square mile of European territory to the Turks could be final. I can't see why Europe should bolster up a state which is too weak to maintain itself, and which hasn't even the sense to know its weakness. I don't see why the energetic states of Eastern Europe should not be allowed [to] work out their own destiny. I should like to see Ferdinand crowned at Constantinople as monarch of a federated Eastern empire.[22]

You will please reassure me as to your views on this matter; I trust you to be on the right side in these great questions.

Leo Casey went to Cork on the 10th ult. I have heard nothing of him since.

77 Michael (Dublin) to John (Tralee), 9 November 1912

... The upsetting events of this last fateful month cannot fail to arouse a deep sympathy with the fallen in the hearts of all who value a glorious past. Needless to say, I cannot share in the smallest degree your views on the Balkan question – or as we should now say – the Balkan answer. I am wholly on the side of the historic Ottoman race, of splendid memories, which withstood the armed might of successive Norman Crusades in our own loved Middle Ages and conquered half Europe at a later time, in the heyday of its pride. For the descendants, degenerate though they be, of a long line of ever victorious armies, I have the same essential veneration that I have for our British aristocracy which is open to the same reproach. The crushing blows, the irreparable disasters of these days have filled me with dismay. Words cannot express the bitterness of my feeling towards the triumphant Bulgars. No ethical justice in their cause, no heroism in

arms, no clemency in victory, can atone for their desecration of the sanc-
tified soil. It is a strange nemesis that the great people which once held
sway over all the land and sea from Athens to Moscow, from the Nile to
the Danube, up to the very walls of Vienna, should now be driven back to
make a last and losing stand before Constantine's city, for the only inch of
ground left them out of all that vast territory...

Ah well! whatever we may think of it, Nazim Pasha[23] is going down in
the betting, and we must leave it at that.

With regard to Home Affairs, I agree with you that the ideal solution of
a restoration of the Irish House of Lords could not be expected either
from our doctrinaire Radical rulers or from a party so essentially out of
touch with the best traditions of our country as the Irish Nationalist party.
The whole scheme of the present bill is calculated to push the power into
the hands of the most dangerous and inefficient class in the country. All
the indicators are that the Irish Parliament will be similar in character to
the present Dublin Corporation, which is shunned by all decent men, and
instead of being an object of pride is an object of contempt to the citizens. At first I was eager to see the bill passing, thinking it would in time
prove a National settlement, but in view of the acceptance of the Trinity
amendment (which reflects even less credit on the Government and the
Irish party than on its proposers)[24] and other equally significant incidents,
I feel assured now that the early fall of the Ministry would be as great a
blessing for Ireland as it would unquestionably be for England.

78 Extract from the Kerry Sentinel, 27 November 1912

Manchester Martyrs Commemoration: Speech by Maurice Moynihan

As long as we take pride in the heroes and martyrs of the past and
continue to revere their memory, so long will the unholy spirit of
Anglicisation be kept at bay ... We have nothing to gain by copying
Englishmen or English customs. The English accent does not fit us, and
English-made or English-inspired institutions are not congenial to the
Irish soil ... That Irishman is not to be envied whose pulse is not quickened when he reads [of] the perseverance of Wolfe Tone, of the heroism
of Lord Edward, and of the devotion of Robert Emmet (cheers), his heart
is not in the right place if it does not throb with patriotic fervour when he
reads the glowing sentiments of the men of '48 (hear, hear). And he must
be cold indeed if he can read without emotion the daring and heroic
exploits of the men of '67 (loud cheers)...[25]

79 Mary (Tralee) to Michael (Dublin), postmarked 12 December 1912

I am still confined to bed, but I think & hope I am on the mend. I was very bad on Saturday & Dr White called in Dr Hayes. I have not been so bad since. I am retaining milk & other liquids. I am not allowed sit up in the bed but he is promising if I continue to improve to let me get up for a short time on Saturday. I am sure I will be better when you come home please God.[26] I believe Jo Power came home last week but she did not call here.[27] Han is still in Cork. John will go tomorrow and bring her home. Write & say definitely when we may expect you.

80 Michael (Dublin) to John (Tralee), 9 April 1913

No doubt you feel that it is my turn to write to you.

How are all our friends ever since? Have you fixed it up with Maisie, or do you think her talk about houses was all swank? I am wondering if Eily has given any explanation of her devastating frostinesss on Saturday week. She has not done so in any of her letters, at all events![28]

No bathing since, I suppose. I don't know when I shall have another. People here look with disfavour on so novel a practice as bathing in spring.

Are you praying hard that Montenegro may abandon her fire-eating attitude, and prevent the catastrophe of a general war.[29] The position of England is comical in the extreme at this juncture, but the Nestor of states will deserve well of the business world if she (or should I have said he) ensures peace at the trifling expense of mere personal dignity.

You have doubtless finished the *New Machiavelli* ere this, or did you give up in despair at the later chapters?[30] Anyone can see that H.G.'s essential defect is his absolute divorce from tradition, both literary and otherwise. That he should have ever read so antique a book as *The Prince* is in itself surprising. Reading Wells one might think that the human race came into existence about 1837 and that all 'problems' of life and politics had to be thought out now from the beginning, with no past teaching or experience to guide us. By means of this attitude, he attains a quality of originality which however has no reality beyond his literary style & way of thinking. When he attempts to give definitions to his thoughts, they prove to be the same foolish imaginings, so much better expressed by Plato, More and all that crowd.

Give me Burke, anyway. I am ambling along at leisure with that delightful old anti-Jacobin, glimpsing in their best attire those principles which we now would call High Toryism, but which then were the common basis of all British politics. Burke's weakness, if it is one, is that he really had nothing to argue against. The opera-buffe themes of the Revolutionists were not matter for serious argument, but rather furnished scope for declamatory eloquence. Burke takes his stand on tradition above all things, and if he makes what is vulgarly called prejudice the basis of conservatism he at the same time compels one to see that practically all high feelings & honourable devotions are in the strictest sense prejudices, but not less admirable and right on that account.

81 *John (Tralee) to Michael (Dublin), 14 April 1913*

I don't think you need worry about Eily's assumption of coolness. It was the outcome of constraint, due to the impossibility of expressing her feelings at parting with you, in the presence of so many critical non-lovers.

I haven't been bathing since, though I've been on the mountains 3 times.

I fear that general war won't turn up this time, sorry.

I finished the *New Machiavelli* the day you left. I agree that a divorce from tradition is a decided defect in a writer; and I think the charge may be brought against Wells with good cause. A divorce from the past is of course entirely unnatural and Wells seems to lose sight of the fact that all development must be progressive. I admire Wells' courage though most of his ideas are repugnant to me. I think, too, that he is, at bottom, sincere though it seems to me that he sets down many of these fine things simply because of their eccentricity.

Since finishing Wells I have turned once more to Emerson. I don't know whether there is anything like a precedent for Emerson in the world's literature. Of course he needs none. At any rate, I know no writer who stands on the same plane with him. He gives life a dignity which these others are incapable of expressing. Other men believe in the soul; Emerson is all soul. He is above the circumstances the joys and sorrows of life. He always stands for the highest ideals. He is really in direct communion with the Spirit of the Universe. He is himself the best proof of this doctrine. When I weary of men whose minds are bent on petty circumstances, who are but circumstances, who fight for or against petty reforms, who do and rule and think and judge by rule of thumb, I can always turn to Emerson and find him serene, inspired. True, when I think of him thus I am apt to idealise him. In practice I often find even him limited; but it is he who has given me this very standard by which I judge him; and, if he fails of it, it is because his highest inspirations are inexpressible.

At any rate every time I turn to him he makes me yearn to be rid of all these insincerities and subserviences of my life. He makes me wish to stand forth as a man and to have done with cowardly deference to the opinions and traditions and institutions of other men. Of course, I always find my cowardice too much for me. At least, he gives me an ideal and that is something.

I have also started Kant and have got through 70 pages with very limited comprehension. As a lesson in metaphysics the experiment is destined to futility; but the habit of trying to concentrate my thoughts may give me some of the much-needed quality of concentration. It may interest to you to know that 'who were you with last night?' has been singing in the theatre here. We are progressing!

82 Michael (Dublin) to John (Tralee), 22 April 1913

What between the Tralee Mountains and Kant & Emerson, you must be subsisting on very rarefied air at present.

As far as Kant is concerned, although personally I have practically given up all such reading, and truly believe that it leads nowhere, I would venture to say that for anyone to begin his acquaintance with metaphysics by reading Kant is much like starting Greek by taking up Homer. The chances of comprehension are equally limited. You would need first of all to get a general grasp of the subject from an elementary handbook. However, I shall be interested to hear how you persevere. Kant's great service was his powerful demonstration of the inconclusiveness of all argument about infinities, and, consequently, of the futility of reason as a guide to conduct. I would not dare to speak with disrespect of the Schoolmen, and the traditional desire to find a metaphysical basis for faith and moral sentiments. Deeper reading of experience, however, as it seems to me, has shown that any attempt to reconcile, or at all events, found religion on logic, is in the end as unsatisfactory, although less repugnant, than the rationalist attempt to found morality on utility, or enlightened self-interest, as the old phrase goes. The emotional or religious principle, and the rational principle are not only distinct, but often conflicting. Doubtless, this doctrine is the essential heresy of modernism, and one can understand the church's condemnation of it when one considers the element of uncertainty it introduces. The Encyclical

Pascendi is illuminating and logical enough on this point. Yet I cannot help believing – and my belief is founded on the whole history of Christianity – that at bottom the true spirit of the Church is at one with the so-called Modernists on that vital subject. When you consider that Christianity rests entirely on a Revelation, and that *faith* has always been the description of the Christian attitude, you will, I think, see the truth of my contention. The very claim of inspiration & Infallibility made by the Pontiff is in itself a recognition of the fundamental verity that religious & moral truths are ultimately to be found by the heart, not by the head.

Eliminate then from Kant a superficial scepticism (corrected I believe in the *Critique of Practical Reason*),[31] from the Modernists a certain crudeness & lack of respect for authority, and from the Church a quite praiseworthy loyalty to the great thinkers of the Middle Ages, and you will find that all three are really on the same side.

The whole subject, of course, would stand a good deal of elaboration, and will indeed be treated fully in vol. 1 of the philosophy of life, politics &c &c shortly to appear from the pen of

MJM

83 Mary (Tralee) to Michael (Dublin), postmarked 25 April 1913

The enclosed appeared in the *Kerry [Evening] Star* this evening.[32] Will you write a few lines saying you have no intention of resigning your present position. That will be quite sufficient. You can send letters to both *News* Office, & *Star* to appear in Monday's issues. I hope you will send wire as I told you in my letter of this morning. I do not wish your name to go before the public for failure. We may as well use a bit of energy & say we would not accept such a *humble position* . . .

Say something to the effect that you were surprised to see your name mentioned as a possible candidate for Co[unty] Sec[retary], as you had *no* intention of resigning the position you hold.

84 John (Tralee) to Michael (Dublin), 17 May 1913

The retirement of a public official after thirty years service of his native county must at all times touch a feeling heart. When the official is P.M. Quinlan, King of Men, and the occasion of retirement is ill-health, consequent on over-work in the interests of the ratepayers, then indeed must the soul of every right-thinking man be stirred to its depths. Now I know that you are a right-thinking man hence, I know your grief on this occasion must be nigh unbearable; but I appeal to you, both as a right-thinking man and as a staunch upholder of the hereditary principle if you find no consolation in the knowledge that the great man is to be succeeded by his distinguished son.[33] It is true, unhappily, that the equally important principle of primogeniture is being disregarded. Still it is a great thing in these degenerate days to find a great public body like the Kerry County Council determined to uphold against all comers a great and time-honoured principle which has fallen on evil days. As you might expect, People's Friend Quinnell is denouncing in unmeasured terms the arrangement of His Majesty and his Privy Council. Of course, King's friend Ryle is relentlessly showing up the demagogue.[34]

You have quite frightened me off Kant, I regret to say. I have turned from him to Marcus Aurelius, to Aeschylus ... Within the past week I have got a book of Churchill's *Richard Carvel* which has been recently published in Macmillan's 7d series. It is an excellent book as novels in general go, but it is distinctly inferior to Churchill's recent books. I will send you this book if you promise to read it but I would rather you'd make Churchill's acquaintance through *Coniston*.[35]

I have also got the *Iliad*, Chapman's translation (Morley's Univ[ersity]. Lib[rary]). I have read little of it yet but enough to make me regret not waiting until I could afford Lang's splendid prose translation...[36]

85 Michael (Dublin) to John (Tralee), 20 May 1913

As you surmised, it is a matter of great consolation to me that down in Kerry they still stand upon the ancient ways. Especially was I gratified by the resolution proposed (and passed by 40 to 15) in the Tralee Board of Guardians, by Mr Michael Aherne, that Pillar of the Old Tory, in which after a crescendo of praise he winds up with the chivalrous opinion that 'after all, there is nothing like breeding & training'. Then, too, Patrick's own invocation of his ancestors adds a greater emphasis to the significance of the occasion.[37] This followed so quickly by the Newmarket election, has made this glorious May a one to be remembered. This day three years ago by the way we had a similar reminder that though kings may die, or as in the present case, abdicate, kingship and hereditary right live for ever. (You will understand that I allude to the public funeral of His late glorious Majesty, of blessed memory, on May 20th 1910.)

I am afraid Jack Quinnell is a newspaper proprietor of the Lord Northcliff type, only much more unprincipled. Loyalty to Church & King, loyalty to the old social order, and to the great principles on which these things rest, are as nothing to him when there is question of making a few miserable halfpennies by flattering Demos. I suspect the Quinnells must be of Cromwellian origin. On the other hand, his Norman ancestry shines out in the conduct of Mr Geo. Raymond 'honourable man that he is' (I quote from the Master).[38]

I trust you found Marcus Aurelius rather dry reading. It is excellent though in parts, but this rigid stoicism forms no sort of philosophy for practical men. To avoid pleasure and ignore pain is an ideal of conduct as illiberal as it is impossible.

Before sending *Richard Carvel* I should like you to tell me its subject & period.[39] At present I am reading Montesquieu at such odd moments as I can spare. His easy scepticism & not ill-natured satires are amusing, if not convincing to a hardened optimist like me. M. is one of those whose *forte* is to abuse & belittle the prevailing fashion & institutions of their age. His lightness & grace of touch make him tolerable, but every now & then one gets the uneasy feeling that he is a 'damned Radical' at bottom. I can stand satirical writing, provided it is not too serious or embittered, but the mere implicit suggestion of reform makes me feel as if I were on the roof of a tottering building. When I say reform, of course, I speak not of reform in conduct, but the undermining of beliefs & the destruction of institutions which are far more expressions of good, rather than the bad, side of human nature.

86 Michael (Dublin) to John (Tralee), 3 June 1913

You must have been very agreeably surprised by the account of the attack on the Provincial Bank manager.[40] It really looks as if the Golden Age were coming again in Kerry, does it not. This is only the latest in a series of portents which all point to the same explanation. Mr Michael Aherne, by whom I am profoundly impressed, appears to be the prophet and prose-poet of the New Jerusalem. His latest declaration, that 'we are not democrats, we are nationalists ... and support the man who fires the shot', affirms, in inspired language, the essential unity of all the old prides and the old devotions. You in Kerry must, indeed, have thanked Heaven for such a man, during this last critical time.

You can send *Richard Carvel* just to break me in to Churchill. I am sorry to hear, however, that the hero consorted with Fox.

I fear that Emerson & Aurelius, however good in some respects, are developing in you a most regrettable lack of reverence for things as they are, and for outward forms. As you must well know, religion, monarchy, and the whole social order, or what is left of it and them, owe very much indeed to this feeling of respect for pomp and ceremonial and state; and respect for men's office and rank apart from their individual characters. To your Emerson a bad Pope is but a bad man, and only to be regarded as such. To me, and surely to you also, veneration for his position would outweigh all his vices, if his claim to loyalty were in question. And as for hypocrisy, which your friends are so fond of denouncing, I need say nothing beyond quoting its old definition as 'the tribute vice pays to virtue'. Repent in time, then, or before you know where you are you will have relapsed into the errors of Philosophical Radicalism.

87 Michael (Dublin) to John (Tralee), 18 June 1913

Thanks for *Richard Carvel*. I am reading it steadily, in such time as I can give. I can only say yet that the character and ideals of 'Mr Carvel' appeal to me strongly.

I went into a bookshop yesterday, and lost my head so far as to buy two volumes of your Emerson, in the new Bohn series. Nothing could have been farther from my mind when going in, which I did with the object of examining Coleridge's *Aids to Reflection*,[41] a book recommended by My Lord Hugh Cecil. However, as I saw nothing about Conservatism, & much theology and pious meditation, I did not purchase, but gambled on Emerson instead. I hardly expect to spend much time over him, though I find the *English Traits* rather interesting.[42]

The event of last week was, of course, Larry's visit to Dublin.[43] True to his traditions, champagne corks were flying in all directions down at the Manchester & Provincial last Tuesday week, and doubtless on the other days as well. What between Larry, the gay proprietress Mrs McArthur, and the pretty barmaid with a delightful Ulster accent, it was a pleasant day for me. There is no mistake but L. knows how to go the pace, and the presence of his daughters had not much of a restraining effect. Generous to a fault this man, but a terrible old rake at bottom.

88 Mary (Tralee) to Michael (Dublin), postmarked 28 June 1913

Thomas Anthony is very big & strong, & I hope will sometime relieve you
& John of many responsibilities.[44] You must have been surprised to hear
you had a new brother. Father was thinking of going up to Dublin tomorrow & I am trying to persuade him not to. I am up today for the first time.
We are taking a lodge in B[ally].Bunion from August 1st. Will you arrange
to come then. You had better go to Kingsbridge tomorrow in case Father
may go. Stay with him until he is coming home & get him to eat something.[45]

89 J.E. Chapman (Inland Revenue) to Michael (Dublin), 16 August 1913

I am directed by the Board to inform you that they have ordered that you
be transferred to the Croydon 2nd District...

CHAPTER FOUR

Home Rule and the Approach of War, 1913–14

We are all very lonely after you ... How is Aunt Lizzie I hope she is better. If she wishes I could let Han go to her for a month & she would see after things & give her a rest...

There is no life here since you left. We go to bed at half eight. The show is going tomorrow. They had no business after you leaving. Ivy has not been seen since but she sent a message regretting my coolness towards her. I am so sorry but even you (infatuated & all as you were) must admit she carried things a bit far.[1] Will you write a long letter to say how you are situated & if you like the place etc. I am glad to be going home it is unbearable since you left us...

91 Michael (Croydon) to John (Tralee), 8 September 1913

Here I am at last trying to settle down after an over-strenuous week. I have just returned from a walk among the quiet Surrey lanes, the first glimpse of the countryside I have had since leaving Fenit. Piccadilly Circus is all very well in its way, but I am thoroughly sick for the time being of ragtime venues and tramping through the flaming streets, and perpetual gabble in painful French. For what between a young French boy who was staying at G[rea]t. Ormond Street,[2] and les belles Françaises of the Square, I had almost ceased to speak English. Happily I am now granted a brief respite, during which time I can garner experience of other aspects of the old English social order.

I think I can say that once I had to come to England at all, I could not have lighted on a more delectable place than Croydon (if one overlooks the want of the sea, that greatest of all joys). It is full of beautiful scenery, and rich in historical and antiquarian interest. March of mind and wisdom of our ancestors jostle each other here at every turn. The relentless encroachment of urban civilisation, so well depicted by Wells, goes on increasingly, turning pretty byways into streets of elegant villas, and quaint old commons into parks, leaving here and there an ancient church, an ancient inn, to look bewildered and out of place, amid strange new surroundings. 'Blow, bugle, blow.'

I little thought when leaving Dublin, that it would stand so prominently before my eyes for a week after. I saw nothing of Larkin's business, for on that Saturday night Box and Vale[3] and I were entertaining the Winter Gardens in the Theatre Royal with patriotic and sentimental songs and did not approach at all to the quarter of the town where the trouble was. But ever since it has been nothing but Dublin, until yesterday when wandering into Trafalgar Square I found a large socialist meeting of sympathy with the strikers. Familiar touches made one fancy oneself back, such as the *Daily Citizen* placard 'We stand for free speech and Damn Murphy'. I had a fierce argument with Uncle John yesterday at dinner, but I slid away as he was getting far too hot for my taste . . .[4]

I expect to go to town every weekend, and perhaps will run down to Brighton some Sunday this month. We are on the main road to the famous old watering-place here.

How is poor old Fenit getting on? Now that its shining star has left,[5] how forlorn must be the beach by day and the village green at night! Sunt lacrimae rerum, but with time, alas! all tears are dried and what is old can never last.

92 Michael (Croydon) to John (Tralee), 23 September 1913

I should be more grateful to you if instead of prescribing cures for Conservatism you could give me an antidote against the virus of radicalism. Wherever I go I am exposed to this dangerous infection. The landlady's married sister who is on a visit to the household is an ardent champion of 'justice', votes for women, strikes and strikers. Uncle John, who on all subjects is a heated debater, is a declared enemy of social order. At both houses the *Daily Chronicle* is served up for breakfast. My only tonics are antiquarian guidebooks, National Portrait Galleries, my Lord Chesterfield's Letters, and *The Observer* on Sundays. It is consoling too that Croydon and all Surrey is represented exclusively by Tories in

Parliament, so you see we are well able to keep the flag flying here.

I am interested to hear that Ivy has returned to her country seat. She is due in London in a few days time to get married, but perhaps she has charitably postponed that *miserabilis dies* and will remain to grace another summertide at Fenit.

To keep up the connection, so to speak, I have got a book of short stories by Morley Roberts, entitled *Salt of the Sea* dealing with life on board tramp steamers (like the *Marguerita* for instance). It is not up to expectations, being rather vulgar, semi-serious, and inclined to run to cheap sentiment. However, I shall send it to you, when I finish it (if I ever do so) and you too can use it to bring back the smell of the green waters when October days have come.[6]

When writing next you might send me on those German textbooks (3 or 4 in all) of Hugo's, if you can find them. I have been struck with the rather silly idea of resuming my German studies and the temptation to do so will be greatly diminished, if not destroyed, by having the books close at hand.

93 Mary (Tralee) to Michael (Croydon), 1 October 1913

I was delighted to get your letter yesterday. It was surely a strange coincidence that you & Ivy met so soon after her arrival in London. It is certainly a relief to have her married and done for. She was the cause of a lot of trouble since her maturity.

I paid a visit to a Palmist on last Monday & one of the many yarns she told me was this. She said a great friend of mine a young dark man would be married in the near future to a very fair woman, & this would be a source of much trouble to me, but I would get reconciled after a while.

You can imagine my feelings when I knew Ivy had gone on. John would have it that it was you & Ivy. It kept me awake for a few nights. You must think me very good to let you know her whereabouts. She has not yet written or wired to say the knot was tied. May God grant it is & that she will not give any more trouble except of course to Poor Thing...[7]

I showed your letter to Han. She is inclined to think about going away to school. She prefers a domesticated life to any & does not see the need for any more study. Needless to say I do not intend giving in to her...[8]

94 John (Tralee) to Michael (Croydon), 9 November 1913

It is time to assure you that I still eke out a not wholly miserable existence. At this moment, the house shelters that once dainty plant, the Ivy Greene, now, alas, in this drear winter time, deprived of all its freshness, all its greenness (verdancy), reduced, in fact, to the merest leafless Twigg.[9] Still even in this state it serves to remind one of summer and Fenit and of your youthful follies. It even gives one hope that spring will come again with all its verdant freshness; summer with its fullness, its repletion. Not, indeed, for this plant, for this Twigg, at least will never be Greene again, but then for others.

Leo Casey is home for some time. I have not met him, but it is said that he failed in his exam. I don't know whether he intends returning to Cork, like enough he is in the throes of indecision, as usual.[10]

Doubtless the reduction of the Liberal majority in Linlithgow, and the defeat of the Liberals at Reading (for I suppose that is certain) have filled you with delight.[11] For my part, I know not how to take these blows – I am sorry lest they may injure the prospects of the Home Rule bill; I am glad because they may make the Government hesitate before they coerce Ulster, and again, I am sorry lest they result in partition as a 'settlement'. It is but part of that scepticism which has become, which every day becomes, more and more a ruling principle of my life and which goes down even to the fundamental things of life.

This scepticism, it is the only thing of note in my religion these days. I call it scepticism but it is rather an affinity to that which is true, or good, or wise (using these expressions subjectively), and making no claim to any recipe for the discovery of objective truth in all the isms. Needless to say I find in every creed and every system much that repels me as well as much that attracts. It seems as if there were no place for me in the order of things; and yet, I do not believe that this is so, for that were blasphemy – almost the only form of blasphemy I recognise in these days.

95 Michael (Croydon) to John (Tralee), 17 November 1913

It may interest all of you to know that the S/S *Margarita*, from Rosario, arrived at St Vincent on the 13th inst, and left on the 14th, bound for Waterford where she will doubtless arrive about the beginning of December. She will probably have left before I pass through that city, as I hope to do about the 20th Dec.[12]

You know of course that one of our Kerry peers, Lord Headley, has turned Mahommedan [*sic*]. I see it mentioned that before he succeeded he was an architect, so I was right in my conjecture that it was he who called into the office in Dublin about two years ago.[13]

Larkin is the man of the hour in England just now. *The Times* devotes a couple of columns to his speech this morning, more than it would give to most Cabinet Ministers. (I may mention that we get *The Times* every day at Lansdowne Road.)

If your difficulty is how to choose between the principles of different parties, mine is to find a shred of principle left in any. There is, for me, nothing to choose between the profligacy of Liberal ministers who release Larkin, almost openly because he cost them votes, and that of Tory newspapers which in a gingerly fashion try to use the Dublin labour movement as a stalking horse against Nationalism. Add to this the criminal hypocrisy of both parties (of all indeed) towards the 'Ulster question' and one gets a vision of political depravity far lower than any that existed in the days of open bribery. My indignation is not diminished by the fact (whisper it not in faith) that I wrote a letter to *The Times* advocating the 'Irish House of Lords solution', and the rascally editor neither printed, acknowledged nor returned it!

As for Ulster, I do not share your anxiety lest they may be coerced. My fear is that they won't be. I admire their *apparent* readiness to fight for their principles, which, contrasted with the spiritless apathy of their opponents, makes one feel ashamed of the latter. But the extreme insolence of their attitude, especially the suggestion that it is for the Government, forsooth, to begin overtures to their lordships, has really made them undeserving of consideration. Although they are alien in race, religion and sentiment, and not at all a necessary element in the life of the country, still, as, unfortunately, they cannot be transported, and have to be put up with, no one would mind meeting them half way if they showed a national spirit. The one concession which would be consistent with the honour of the country, would to me, of course, not be a concession at all, but a guarantee of stable government in Ireland, Ulster or no Ulster. I refer to the establishment of a more conservative constitution. No public man, no newspaper has dared to suggest this, but they still keep harping at 'exclusion', which nobody, not *The Times*, not Ulster pretends to want. Failing a proper settlement, the next best thing is for Redmond to stand firm, and resist any attempt at exclusion, or further restriction. I hope and believe that he will do this, and if the Bill goes through as it stands, and the Orange crowd try their little game on, one must rely on the Irish soldiers in the British army, at any rate, to obey the order to shoot. Our Ulster Scots might then have a new anniversary to replace the 12th July, and to be celebrated with their drums neatly muffled in black.

I shall not annoy you with the reams I *could* write on the subject, but await your views, which are rather implied than expressed in your last.

96 Michael (Croydon) to John (Tralee), 6 December 1913

You need not confound my attitude towards the existing Unionist Party with that of one who is 'shedding his Toryism'. It is rather that of one who, regretfully, sees them abandon all the historic position of Toryism, ostensibly in the interest of an unruly gang in the North of Ireland. To read 'Tory' speeches and articles attacking the now defunct Lord North, and anxiously quoting precedents to justify revolution, is much more than I can stomach. The politicians of an earlier day at least professed principles (whether they believed in them or not) and did not change from Jacobites to Jacobins and vice versa to catch a few votes. I grant you that that was in the days when vote-catching did not matter, before democratic despotism had made honest or consistent government impossible.

I notice that all Sir Edward Carson wants now is that Ulster shall have the spending of taxes raised there. Rather a sorry ending to all the deep emotion, is it not?

It is strange to find you so far taken in by it all that you think the fear of intolerance is genuine. Every living man in Ulster and in England knows that the Irish Catholics are the most tolerant people on the earth, even when compared with peoples whose tolerance has the broad basis of indifferentism. What they do fear and hate is the idea that the Catholic Church should take its rightful place in Ireland, or that the Catholic point of view should have its proper influence. 'Loyalty' to the Empire has nothing to do with it, except that it happens to be a convenient whip with which to flog the Nationalists. It is laughable to think of these rapscallions burning with love for an Empire which exists only in name, and the component parts of which are under no sentimental illusions as to their relationships.

Personally, failing a settlement on 'my lines', I see nothing for it but to press the present bill. It is difficult to imagine what further 'safeguards' they can put into it, and any concessions can only be on the lines of giving more or less autonomy to Ulster, which will scarcely be agreed to by the

Irish people. You have heard indeed of the new Oliver who has come to bring peace, not now, like his prototype, with the Bible in one, and the sword in the other hand, but with a General Election in one hand, and a yardwand in the other. (The author of *The Alternatives to Civil War* is a draper in Oxford St.)[14] He is very fairminded, it is true, but goes far away from realities when he suggests that any adverse British election could influence or abate the Irish demand in the slightest. The voting of that hundred-headed hydra, the British Public, cannot settle the question now any more than in 1886 or 1895 [*sic*]. The matter is, in effect, outside the jurisdiction. When the 'oppression' does come, they will, I daresay, make themselves heard, much more loudly than they do in South Africa today, where they cannot assert the 'privileges' of British subjects against the real oppression of their own erstwhile enemies.

97 Michael (Croydon) to John (Tralee), 10 January 1914

As I understand you became reconciled to *Saraconisca* [*sic*] after all. I am venturing to send you the remaining books of the series. The sequel to *Saraconisca* is *Sant 'Ilario*, then comes *Don Orsino*, with *Corleone*, I hope, a good fourth. Of course, you have *Don Orsino*, which I left behind me.[15]

I do not know whether *The Path to Rome* will justify its reputation.[16] Persevere, anyhow, & tell me what kind it is. In glancing over it I notice he brings in the inevitable story of the Man born in Croydon. It is remarkable what a number of modern writers have heard of this place.

In an endeavour to ascertain your mental diet at the moment, I asked, in vain for *Public Opinion* at Charing X [Cross] book-stall last night. I got *The New Age* instead, and will send it on to you in a day or so. You will notice three things about it. First that the price has been raised to sixpence, second, it is not so good as when it was a penny and most remarkable of all phenomena in modern journalism, that it has no advertisements. This is evidently in pursuance of a settled policy, the result of which it is not difficult to forecast. Of course it has not always seemed to me illogical for a socialist paper to accept 'capitalist' advertisements or identify itself in any way with the 'Profiteers' (the very latest term of abuse). But this admirable consistency will probably prove the death of *The New Age*.

Laziness has prevented me from writing to Duckworth's about the Lives of the Saints series, but I hope to do so before long, and shall feel very happy to introduce you to St Francis of Assisi, Ambrose, or whatever one you are most interested in.[17]

Your researches may be helped by knowing the latest theory about ghosts, put forward by *Times* correspondents recently. They are, we are informed, the outcome of impressions on matter, that is, on the rooms, furniture &c where the deeds that become visualised were originally perpetrated. These deeds, & the forms of the actors, are recorded on the surrounding objects, just as the voice on a gramophone record, and afterwards are reproduced before those sensitive to the vibrations. I shall not presume to comment on these subtle speculations, but leave you to form your own opinion.

Wishing you a very happy birthday.

98 Michael (Croydon) to Mary (Tralee), 31 January 1914

I am very glad to hear Denis is getting on so well at school, and setting a good example to Han & Maurice.

The news of Nellie Brosnan's engagement has come with dramatic suddenness. So far as John is concerned, after the first pang is over, it will probably rouse him from his lethargy, and act as a warning to make sure of Maisie before it is too late... [18]

99 Mary (Tralee) to Michael (Croydon), 8 March 1914

I was expecting a letter from you for the past week. I hope there is nothing the matter with you. Your father is just the same. He cannot walk at all except up & down & his own room, & the Doctor would not let him try. He says the only way he can get about again will be driving. He is very wasted. Uncle Denis is dying. [19] He is half unconscious for the past week. Bad as he was it is hard to see all one's family going. It is very fine weather here now. I was looking forward to seeing you in April & have not given up all hope yet. If Father improves anything I may go for a few days or could send Han...

I suppose I must try & get a pony & trap to take your Father out or else take a place in Fenit for a prolonged period...

100 M.W. Cullington (53 Oakhill Road, Putney) to Michael (Croydon), 13 March 1914 [20]

I saw Capt. Bell on Wednesday night, & he told me you had written him about attending camp at Easter without a uniform. Pray be not perturbed about that. If you have yet been measured for your uniform probably it will be ready in time. If it is not, they may be able to fit you up with a scratch uniform. If they can't do that, you can go in the oldest & holiest suit of civvies you can raise.

Of course you can do drills without a uniform. I am really not sure whether you need have a gun & bayonet. If you have not got one they would probably lend you one if you turned up for a drill.

I am very glad to hear you think of going with the reg[imen]t. at Easter. You will find the ten drills a great lift. I am undecided about Easter myself. Hope to see you at the smoker at head Quarters on Tuesday at 7.45.

101 Mary (Tralee) to Michael (Croydon), 15 March 1914

How is it you have not replied to my letters or more. You know the state I am in about you & it is cruel not to write. I am imagining all sorts of things happening to you. If you are well get someone to write & if you are in any trouble write & tell me & you know surely I would go to the ends of the earth to get you out of it ... Father is much improved but is confined to his room still.

102 Michael (Croydon) to John (Tralee), 17 March 1914

Churchill's splendid speech on Saturday, and the Prime Minister's firm attitude last night, seem to have made a magical change in the situation.[21] The Unionists were, as one of their organs, the *Daily Mirror*, put it, completely nonplussed, and this morning's press was a revelation. Instead of the indignant shrieks and desperate threats of war which one might have expected, every Unionist leading article is couched in terms of mild though petulant protest. Scarcely a word now about civil war, the bubble is burst at last. Not only that, but the whole business is thrust away in some back page, quite overshadowed by the 'Naval Scandal in Japan'. Of course we are not out of the wood yet. There is still a danger that the Unionists will accept the concessions proffered. They will have to eat humble pie in any case, and this is their last chance of getting a little flavouring with it. But it would be disastrous for Toryism as well as for Ireland if they were to get their reward for their liaison with Jacobinism.

As to the future, any coercion that the Ulsterites have to suffer will be good for them. All people, I think, can either be lead [*sic*] or driven, and as these people plainly are not amenable to any kind of persuasion, driving is the only means left. If unfortunately, they cannot, in this enlightened day, be forced to become good Catholics, there are still means for forcing them to become good taxpayers, and their unwillingness at first to submit to this is likely to be our only diversion in the way of civil war. They can easily explain to the disappointed ex-colonels that they meant their civil war to be other than perfectly civil.

I have read *The Path to Rome* with great interest. It is a many-sided book, but what chiefly struck me in going through it, was the additional evidence it afforded of the reality of that curious psychological phenomenon, the constant union of conservatism, religious orthodoxy, militarism, and 'conviviality' in individuals, and in communities of individuals. There appears to be some spiritual bond uniting these four impulses. That Auctor is a case in point you will readily agree. The whole history of the Irish people bears out my thesis. So does that of Toryism in this country, it being always identified, in its principles with the church, the ancient institutions, and a spirited foreign policy; and in its adherents, the jolly Cavalier, the *fox-hunting squires* and the Regency bucks, with the worship of Bacchus.

The Catholic Church has never discountenanced war, as some heretical sects have done, and without irrelevance I may refer to the first miracle recorded in the gospel, at the marriage-feast of Cana, and to the essential part that *vinum* must for ever play in Catholic dogma and ritual.

Lastly, I will mention the devoutness and dissipatedness of soldiers generally.

Unless you are prepared to maintain that my idea is illusory, I should like to know what is your explanation of the matter. You need not spare paper in replying, as a lot can be said on the subject.

103 Charles Clarke (C/Sgt. B Company, Civil Service Rifles), to Michael (Croydon)
17 March 1914

Re Easter Training: Draw your Equipment in the ordinary way from the Stores. As to clothing, arrangements will probably be made to fit you out for Easter but I will let you know details later when I know how many recruits of the Company are in the same boat. If all fails come in plain clothes. Trusting you will enjoy your stay with us.

104 John (Tralee) to Michael (Croydon), 22 March 1914

I must disagree entirely with your view of the political situation. Perhaps, as you say, the English unionists would be glad to withdraw their support from Ulster now that danger is nigh. But, after all, the real danger, if it is real, comes from Ulster herself and I cannot believe that fifty or sixty thousand men are engaged in a conspiracy which has no more serious object than that of bluffing the Government nor, granting their sincerity, can I believe that a change of attitude on the part of the English Tory party would deter them from fighting. There is so much scepticism in our times that no one will credit that there is still a people ready to risk life and property for a cause.

To turn from the Ulster Volunteers to their leader, do you think Carson is a coward to draw back before bloodshed? Do you think that, after leading them on for two or three years, he will desert them now, even if he does not really believe in their cause. I don't, I think of him as a man of grim, satanic determination, a desperate gambler, too, who would readily stake his own life and the lives of a whole people on the throw of a dice. I must recommend you to an article (which I enclose) by Ja[me]s. Douglas on 'King Edward VIII'.[22] Except on reading Aeschylus I have never had such an intimate feeling of being up against great elemental forces which it were folly to resist.

I have given you my inferences from the apparently admitted fact that there are fifty or sixty thousand men (at least) in Ulster who have drilled ostensibly for the purpose of resisting Home Rule. The press here or, apparently in England, makes no sincere effort to help us estimate the importance of this fact. The papers are full of Ulster, we hear of Volunteers drilling, of convoys of arms and ammunition, of watchmen in every church tower in Ulster waiting for the signal to sound the tocsin which shall be the death-knell of all our hopes of a united Ireland; and, editorially, we are told, on one hand, of a terrible civil war which shall deluge Ireland or even the Empire in blood, on the other hand, we read of a campaign of bluff organised for the purpose of destroying the Parliament Act and restoring the supremacy of Lansdowne House. We are assured also, with that inconsequence which is characteristic of party journalism, that the Tory plan of a Referendum on Home Rule is part of a gigantic conspiracy to destroy democratic government by making the democracy supreme.

Midst all this babel of opinions comes the news that troops are being concentrated in Ulster, that hundreds of officers are resigning and that guards have been doubled in all the barracks in Ireland where ammunition is stored, not excepting Tralee. Following this comes a rumour here, unconfirmed however in the Sat[urday]. *Herald* that rioting took place in Belfast yesterday.

I have come across a little book on the Red Branch knights which gives an account of a siege of the fortress on Cahir Conree just about 1900 years ago.[23] Cuchulainn the great Ulster hero was the commander of the besieging Red Branch. Then as now Ulster was ranged against the rest of Ireland. The book is full of the heroic traditions of our race and should bring delight to such an ardent militarist as you. I shall send it to you if you wish to read it.

With reference to your incursion into the domain of psychology. Your observations are probably correct but the causes of the phenomenon are difficult to ascertain. All Christian orthodoxy has its centre and origin in sunny climates. The people of such countries are always lovers of beauty in art, music and ceremonial and their Church inevitably develops an elaborate and gorgeous ritual, this reacts still further on the temperament of the people and even changes the character of adherents of the Church in northern countries. This would perhaps account for the gaiety and conviviality of the orthodox. Their respect for religious authority may also have its source in their happy-go-lucky temperament, which has resulted in the devolution of all the worries of theological speculation on a gradually centralising authority. This in turn by ridding them of a load of care would result in the enhancement of the characteristic from which it originated.

The conservatism of the orthodox may result from the changed traditions of the Church and its long association with ancient political institutions. Their militarism is a remnant of the days when the Church was established in every state in Europe, when Te Deums were sung and trophies hung in the churches after victory; when the bishops and primates blessed the colours of regiments and when Popes formed 'Holy' Alliances amongst the states of Europe.

Your reference to the 'devoutness and dissipatedness' of soldiers raises the whole question of the Church's attitude towards morality. The fact is that with the Church morality is secondary and consequential, religion primary and causal. Of course, this is what one would expect from a religious body, but it was probably the cause of all the moral corruption which had ever existed in the Church and, therefore, of the Reformation. The reformers thought religion existed for morality, and, as you know, their opinion has had a great influence on Irish Catholicism and even, in a lesser degree, on Continental Catholicism.

I need not say that the Church is in absolute harmony with the teaching of her founder in this matter; and indeed Protestantism at its worst is a recrudescence of the harsh spirit of Judaism in this respect. You will find an exposition of this essential difference of attitude between the Church and Protestantism in Tyrrell's *Christianity at the Crossroads*.[24] Should you come across a book named *Marie Claire* don't pass it by. The writer is Marguerite Audoux, a Parisian sempstress. It is quite unique in my experience, a simple record in beautiful 'childlike' language of unimportant happenings in a French orphanage and on a farm where Marie Claire worked first as a shepherdess, then as a sempstress.[25] It is withal a marvellous study in psychology (evidently an obsession with you at present)...

105 Michael (Croydon) to John (Tralee), 23 March 1914

Before you get this you will have learnt that Brigade-General de la Poer Gough has had matters satisfactorily explained to him, and will resume his command.[26]

Writing this midnight, it seems to me there are three possible things which can happen now. (1) The Government will give in to military despotism, and democracy will have got a stab which will cripple it for a generation. This to me would in some measure atone for the bitter disappointment of Irish hopes. (2) The Government and opposition will stand firm and there will indeed be bloody rebellion, and Ulster will get her reward. This is the outcome which I earnestly pray for.

(3) The opposition will accept the Government's proposals and peace will be secured at Ireland's expense. This, the worst tragedy of all, appears happily, to be unlikely, in view of the bitter words of the past week and Law's speech today. I will not waste time giving reasons why I think the Government must and will stand firm. They are obvious. No Government that ever existed, autocratic or republican, could surrender under such circumstances without shattering the foundations of civil order.

As you know I have held varying views about the question, its nature and its rights. Today I feel that it is not, as I once thought, a merely religious question. Nor is it economic. That Ulster is not concerned about her material prosperity I am at last persuaded. No. These Ulster Protestants are aliens and bitter enemies of Ireland. Unrelenting hatred is their attitude towards the Irish, and unending hatred they deserve in return. Would that there were an Irish Carson to kindle and fan it. But now we are all opportunists. Dearest principles, honour, truth, everything that can make a man love and trust his countrymen, have been sacrificed on the altar of a Peace that heareth not.

Peace sitting under the olives and slurring the days gone by. Patriot Derry arouses even English Unionist admiration by sacrificing her route march. What else has Patriot Derry or Ireland got by it. Sneering Orange scum will answer.

If all lessons given to Ireland were not thrown away, one might say that the lesson of Carsonism is that no peace hero will do. Carson is right in thinking that the Commons House [*sic*] is no place to decide this matter. It is not a political problem at all, in the sense of a divergence of opinion amongst the citizens of a state. It is a conflict of races, of traditions, of everything in fine that separates one state from another, excepting, unhappily, a separate organisation, which is of course, the rub.

I am far too much of a pessimist to hope for the felicity of war against Ulster. Perhaps it is my disbelief in the possibility of any extensive operations at any rate that has induced me to take up the latest pastime. Know, therefore, I have joined the Civil Service Rifles and that if you had been passing Somerset House this evening at 6.30 p.m. you might have heard the 'tramp of armed men' and the swift word of command, and looking in, observed yours truly, with rifle in hand, trying to learn the rudiments of military discipline, in a word, drilling – a word of awful import nowadays.

We shall D.V. do a few days training at Easter, and a fortnight's camp in August, unless events move very rapidly beforehand. Being only liable for service in the United Kingdom, a German invasion or Ulster rebellion are the only eventualities which will see us take the field.[27]

I like your ingenuous explanation of the cor[r]elation of Catholicism, militarism &c. My own is, I suppose, substantially the same, namely that it represents the triumph of the emotional instincts over the rational. That this is so reflection will bear out. You will remark that in the last resort, the apologists for religion, for conservatism, for war, for art (as you had properly mentioned that), for Bacchus, rely on appeals to to the emotions, regardless of utilitarian or practical considerations, which these latter predominate in the unholy host of Protestants, atheists, pacifists, Philistines, eugenists, temperance fanatics, and socialists. Even where one may agree with any of the latter, they leave one cold. It is a case of 'my head is with you, but my heart is against you'. I think that we have here something more than a fortuitous historical association between the papacy & war &c. It is because these things are products of the same type of mind that they are so constantly found together. I think that *The Law of*

Civilisation and Decay throws some valuable light on the subject, although the author's dissecting-room methods are very disgusting.[28]

You need not send me any more books at present. I have all the Crawford series to go through yet, and no prospect of doing it.[29]

106 John (Tralee) to Michael (Croydon), 30 March 1914

I regret that you should take up such a partisan attitude on the Home Rule question. I don't know that I love the Northerners any more than you do; at bottom I think you have far more in common with their covenanting temperament than I. But to me, the good of the country is far more important than any question of party or racial strife.

The Protestants of Ulster are there – very much there – and there they will remain. (I should like to know how you propose to exterminate them.) If I were to admit that their presence is an evil, which I don't, then I think it is to make the best of it. You know that our great weakness through all our history has been disunion. It is so today; rarely have the lines of cleavage between our factions been more marked, rarely has our need of unity been greater. If our future history is not to be, like our past, a record of failure and disillusion and bloodshed, we must change all that. We must draw all our parties and factions together and make them ready to sink their differences in face of the common enemy, instead of the exclusion of Ulster, as Sir R. Casement says, we want the exclusion of England.[30] The Home Rule bill is certainly not the way to do all that. It arouses fierce antagonism in Ulster, and to us it is wholly unsatisfactory with all its reservations and limitations. It is my opinion that a bill like the Irish Councils bill would be acceptable to Ulster and would offer a basis for the re-union of the country so that in ten years time we might have all Ireland united in demanding a full settlement of the Home Rule question.[31]

You speak of the conflict of races, traditions &c. I grant it, but you must remember how that conflict had been kept alive. You might remember too that the fact that the divergence between us is so wide is all the more reason we should strain every nerve in the effort to bring about unity which is essential to our National existence. For my part, I do not yet despair, I recall that the Protestant Volunteers meeting in Dungannon in 1782 recorded their joy 'as Irishmen, as Christians and as Protestants in the relaxation of the Penal laws'.

107 Michael (Croydon) to John (Tralee), 5 April 1914

Many thanks for sending me copies of *Public Opinion*. As you surmise, I can see the point of view of the Ulster Protestants as well as anyone. I can understand their contempt for their Catholic neighbours, and their dislike of being governed by people whom they have always despised. I know too that they are, if possible, more remote in character from Englishmen than from the Celtic Irish, and that their love for England is the shallowest pretence. *But* - the greatest evidence, in my opinion, of their superiority to the mere Irish is in that quality which you, and O'Brien,[32] and Uncle John, and all the English, reprobate so much in the Irish, while *openly admiring it* in the Ulstermen. I mean their vigorous self-assertion, rejection of all compromise, and determination to submit to no majorities and no power except their own. I too admire their spirit, but where I differ from you, O'Brien, &c &c, is that I should admire it still more in the Catholics, if it existed. Your idea of peace and compromise implies that *all* the concessions shall come from the National side. In practical politics you are probably right, because evidently as the armed men of Ulster will not budge one inch, it is up to the Irish majority, and the Parliamentary majority, to sue for peace on the best terms they can get. But can you seriously mean that in the event of such a surrender you would feel admiration, or indeed anything but loathing, for the 'forbearance' and 'moderation' of the Nationalist element? The ultimate test of any idea is the willingness of its followers to fight for it, and there is no place in the sun or under the moon for the Irish National idea if its adherents stampede at a critical time. And I may confidentially say, a surrender would mean an abandonment of the Bill, or any substitute for it, altogether. You think an Irish Councils Bill would be acceptable to the Protestants. But might I ask you to consider the position. The death of the present Bill would mean the death of the Government, and even if they managed to come back by the aid of a lying campaign against the Army, which is very doubtful, they would be faced with an Ulster, flushed with its own victory, which no election could affect. An Ulster very little inclined to compromise of any kind, and which would treat the introduction of an Irish Councils Bill as a confession of defeat and an incentive to stand firm. It is perfectly certain that they would not accept it, and then the Government would have to face the same situation as at present, that is, they would either have to coerce Ulster or drop the measure. And do you consider that while the present fairly generous Bill does not justify coercion, the other wretched proposal would?

Be assured then, that every concession to Ulster feeling, every effort at conciliation, is at present openly regarded by the English Unionists, and still more by the Irish Unionists, as a sign of weakness on the part of the Government, and as an encouragement to the belief that the Bill will never go through in any form. And are they not justified? When one party to a dispute wants compromise, and the other will have none of it, is there any doubt which is the beaten side?

The Army crisis gave both English parties a deuce of a fright last week. They were perilously near to opening up the fountains of the deep, and swamping the whole social fabric. They were recalled to their senses by the speeches of the Labour members. The dangerous consequences of the doctrine of optional obedience were brought home to the Tories. Not that the silly threats to arm the Railway strikers were taken seriously. As Hubert in the *Sunday Chronicle* well said, 'When Mr Thomas talks of arming his followers he does but vapour; he knows well enough that his followers like not arms nor the bearing of arms.'[33] This salient fact, combined with the fact that many responsible Liberals would resolutely oppose any electoral campaign directed against the Army, minimises the gravity of the precedent created by the Curragh outbreak. But the incident is a clear proof of the pitfalls of action based on an immediate expediency, and of the necessity, in the best interests of the country, of rigid adherence to Tory principles, on the part of the Tory party.

108 Michael (Croydon) to John (Tralee), 13 April 1914

I am sending *Times* supplements. I do not care for H. James's articles. He seems to write a great deal without conveying anything concrete.[34] I am glad *The Times* has an increasing circulation in Tralee. Notwithstanding certain defects it is in my belief the best newspaper the world has produced and it is not likely to be ever improved upon now.

Our battalion paraded in marching order at Somerset House on Thursday evening and entrained at Charing Cross for Caterham. Arrived there we had a foretaste of the hard work before us, in a stiff march up a hill to the Guards' Depot. Perhaps a short description of our life in barracks there may interest you.

Lights out at ten o'clock, and one has to be sharp about it. One need not be in bed or even indoors at that hour however, and a would-be sleeper is kept awake until at least twelve by a noisy crew of latecomers. At 6 in the morning the bugle sounds for reveille and at seven we parade & drill in the square for one hour before breakfast. After breakfast a long march or manoeuvres on the downs, including a sham fight on one day. I can tell you it was the deuce to keep running up hill, against wind and rain, with heavy rifles, stopping at intervals to fire imaginary shots at the retreating enemy. In the afternoon there was another drill. On Sunday the sheep were separated from the goats and all 'R.C.s' (there were only about a dozen of us) went off to 9 o'clock Mass, the fairly large church being crowded also with Irish Guards. The heretics had their church parade at 11, and were marched off, dissenters and all, to the Anglican Church.

The chief drawbacks were the incredibly hard beds and pillows, which did not however prevent sound sleeping; and also the food which though wholesome was not always appetising. Among other things one learned to put up with any sort of eating arrangements, but to be intolerant of a dirty bayonet or a man out of step.

It was glorious while it lasted but the days went too soon.

It has whetted my appetite for camp which will be still more spartan in its character.

109 John Power (Desmond House, 2 Great Ormond Street, London W.C.) to Michael (Croydon), 26 April 1914

I was disappointed you did not call this evening. I had intended to ask you to resign your membership of what you call the 'Civil Service Rifles' & I now ask you to do so.

I sincerely hope you will have acted on my advice before next Sunday, when I hope to see you again.

Your affectionate uncle, John Power.

110 Draft reply by Michael to John Power, no date (c. 27 April 1914)

When I began to consider joining the Civil Service Rifles, or was, you must not imagine that I was either blind or altogether indifferent to the obvious criticism which such a step would arouse amongst many of my friends, and the misinterpretation, whether honest or wilful, to which it was exposed. Believing however, as I still believe, that my motives were neither unworthy nor inadequate, I made up my mind to face any criticism of that kind.

I yield to none in my love of country, but I am unable to see any hope of serving it in the detailed and uneventful way of life which you apparently think I ought to adopt as an Irishman living in England. On the contrary my idea of patriotism is, perhaps mistakenly & unfortunately, a very old-fashioned one, & has nothing in common with later ideas of ordered progress & industrial development. Therefore to me the only way of serving Ireland is fighting for it, and I should be the first to welcome the opportunity of doing that. Though scarcely daring to hope that it will come, in such times as these, I can at all events be ready for it, and if every Irishman were to follow my example the chance of its coming would not be so remote. To me indeed it is pitiable to find that while Nationalist Ireland has no weapons but empty words and irresolute deeds, the enemies of Ireland can show a strength of purpose and an energy of resource which, if employed on the right side would make Ireland irresistible.

Considerations such as these combined, as I say with a perhaps excessive distaste for peace and for modernity, have brought me to my present position which is far too bound up with my present philosophy of life to be shaken by petty criticism.

I am glad to add that there is no misunderstanding of my motives at home, as enclosed letter from John received, curiously, at the same time as yours yesterday morning will show. Please let me have it back.[35]

Hoping to hear from you soon.[36]

111 P. Williamson (Assistant Secretary, Inland Revenue) to Michael (Croydon), 30 April 1914

At the examination held in February last you displayed sufficient knowledge of the Tax Law and Practice, of the making of Assessments, and of the general conduct of a Surveyor's business to warrant [the Board] in regarding you as qualified to receive a Treasury Commission as a Surveyor of Taxes in due course.

112 Michael (Croydon) to John (Tralee), 10 May 1914

Thanks for the *Irish Volunteer* which I found awaiting me on my return from drill the other night.[37] The formidable force whose doings it chronicles is treated by Tory papers here with great respect, due more, I think, to politeness than to alarm. Doubtless they feel that dummy rifles and 'winged words' will not circumvent Mr Asquith's armed guards with ball cartridges, mounted day and night at all Southern depots. However, this English complacency *may* be mistaken. The deadening influence of the long years of peace and order and comparative prosperity is hard to shake off, but it could perhaps be done in Ireland, if soldier leaders were found. Col. Maurice Moore may be one of the right sort, may in time become Maurice Mór.[38] This name has the real 'Wild Geese' ring about it.

There is an idyllic drama in the words of love with which the *Volunteer* speaks of the brown barrel of the rifle. They have made me very proud of my Lee-Enfield which is always at hand, with bayonet fixed (but sheathed), for we take absolute charge of all our equipment during our term of service. I had my first shoot a few weeks ago and did fairly well at 200 yds. I shall be going out again on Thursday and on Saturday week comes a weekend musketry camp. It's a rum game, taking it all round. It gives you a sort of double life, in one of which you feel as near to the Mexican Rurales as in the other you are to civilised men about you.

I hope you will send some more copies of the paper, and as for *Public Opinion*, if it has ceased to interest you, it repels me by its relentless chronicle of the progress of movements which I hold in abhorrence without exception. I do not care to be reminded of these things too often. Like the proverbial ostrich, I get the spiritual or mental blessings of security, without the reality, by burying my head in the sands. I take *The Universe* every week but I am getting rather disgusted with its weak-kneed and English attitudes, e.g. read the article on the toast of 'The Pope and the King'. That kind of low opportunism never brought, and I hope will never bring, anything but contempt on any cause, and the Catholics who are afraid to put the Head of the church before a wretched doll, even in a toast, are of the same breed as those who in another age put one who, at any rate, *was* a King before the Pope of that day.[39]

113 John (Tralee) to Michael (Croydon), 22 May 1914

Since I wrote you last an important event has occurred in connection with the Irish Volunteer movement.

Mr Devlin's mighty organisation, having looked askance at the movement since the beginning, has now, at last, signified its gracious approval, and has instructed the country branches of the Order to co-operate with Sir Roger Casement and the other 'cranks' who have created the I.V.F. One result of this accession is that the public boards all over the country are at the old game of passing resolutions; another, that new branches are being started all over the country; a third perhaps is yet to follow (D {& J.D.} V) namely – that money will be collected here and in the G[reater]. I[reland]. beyond the seas to equip the force.[40]

I am sending you this week's *Irish Volunteer*.

I must revise my opinion of the *Times Literary Supplement*. I find that I can read, with pleasure, every article in it with the exception of the novel reviews. I wish you would get it . . .

114 Michael (Croydon) to John (Tralee), 2 June 1914

It appears to me that you do M. Barrès an injustice, and if I may say so, put a rather strained interpretation on Christian precept, when you attempt to show that his *Civilisation du Christ* could only mean the quite human, or if you like, inhuman, social fabric of the Middle Ages.[41] The text you quote 'My Kingdom is not of this world' instead of supporting you, is a sure refutation of your argument. If it means anything, it means that Christian 'civilisation' is not a perfect political state; has, indeed, nothing to do with ideals of society, but consists [of] the reign of the Eternal Goodwill in man's hearts, inspired, of course, with faith in the Christian revelation. So far from doubting the possibility of such a 'civilisation', I confidently affirm that it has existed all through the ages, and is as active a force today as ever, nor is it less real because it has not brought about perfection in human relations. It has its life in the soul, and all men are its devotees more or less, however their action may appear to belie that; indeed it has its strongest hold, as often as not, on those whose outward lives appear least meritorius. I am not preaching novelties, but reminding you of well-accepted teachings of the Church. If you will purge your mind of modern materialist ideas of political and social reform, you will be able to see the 'Kingdom of Heaven' readily enough. And before criticising the alleged failure of Christianity, remember again that the greatest 'evils', from a mere social or political point of view, undoubtedly afford the highest opportunities for the development of the Christian idea in the soul, and from a spiritual point of view, the world has everything to lose and nothing to gain by their abolition. It is my deep conviction of these things that makes me look with so much dread upon all projects of reform! And I regard those who think that Christianity requires *wholesale* attempts at ameliorisation [*sic*] (you being I am sorry to say, temporarily among the number) as rank heretics. The other text which you call to your aid does not help you. Quite the reverse. Firstly, the command to sell *all* your goods to feed the poor was addressed to one individual, not to all men. Secondly, when carried out, it leaves the man who has done it in the same condition of penury as those whom he has partially relieved, so that it in no way helps those who want the abolition of poverty.

It is, after all, a pity that the Sermon in the Mount should be so misunderstood. Many good men have been led astray in this way, and I hope I am not too late to save you from their fate. If I have not convinced you, there are many other points that I have not touched on. But if I have not said enough to prove to you that 'there is a soul of good even in things evil', I trust, at all events, to have removed from your mind the notion that Christianity has failed in its mission. It may have failed to bring about a state of things which you still regard as desirable, but that was never its object. It has brought men a mystic religious ideal which permeates them all in some degree but which in its larger acceptations they are free to embrace or reject at their will.

I enclose a cutting from *The Times*, which shows a very fair, if not sympathetic, attitude towards the National Volunteers. It is curious to note the favourable contrast drawn between the latter, and the official Nationalist party which is now attempting to obtain control.

115 John (Tralee) to Michael (Croydon), postmarked 5 June 1914

... You are not satisfied of accusing me of thinking the 'Kingdom of God' to be the realization of a political ideal, you also think it necessary to preach to me of the advantages of social 'evils'. Clearly, you have forgotten last Christmas, and the nights you kept me awake striving to convince me of the reality of evil...

I think you owe me an apology by return of post for a letter which has been 'a tissue of misrepresentations from beginning to end' as our leader Mr William O'Brien would say.

116 Michael (Croydon) to John (Tralee), 7 June 1914

Perhaps I owe you an apology, but you must have the patience to listen to a lengthy one. I see now, or seem to see, that the house of cards which I successfully demolished in my last letter was not your house at all, but one which I built up from my own imagination. The fact, the ridiculous fact, is that I was writing them under Whitmonday influences. I went out that day, and amongst all the things that I saw, found nothing of which I disapproved. I missed the midnight train from Charing X [Cross], got the last tram as far as sunny Streatham, S.W., found even the conductor a good man struggling with sleep, and had to walk five miles to Croydon, where I arrived at 2 am. Shades of Clontarf, how often have I missed *your* last tram, and thought it toil to have to walk two miles to my place of rest, where Brian's Kernes lay sleeping forevermore! But it is a long way down to Croydon, it's a long way to go...

Even that, however, did not disturb my exposure, and I still heard the angels singing when I wrote to you, a couple of days after.

I was awakened from my dream of the fitness and permanence of things by hearing of the invasion of poor old Fenit by British ships,[42] and the burning of the Norman churches by suffragettes. Matters of small account in the inverse, perhaps, but the spectacle of England's hand coming down once more on the cowed form of a once great nation, of modern 'reformers' destroying without pity the reverend walls which early faith had built for God, such things had no place allotted to them in my simple scheme, so I have had to revert to my Christmas attitude regarding the existence of evil. In doing so, I have, I think, attained to a true conception of Christian and Pauline teachings...

In spite of your denial, I am almost tempted to accuse you again of mixing up 'sociology' with religion. If you do not do that, you go very near it, by discussing religion as if it were purely a moral code regulating human relations. It is this line of thinking which has led you astray.

117 Mary (Tralee) to Michael (Croydon), 10 June 1914

What holidays do you mean to take. I expect at least four weeks. You will have no time if you take less & after your long absence it is the very least you may take. Mamma was very ill for a few days last week but is on the mend now Thank God. We are not done with election work yet as the bills have to be put in and paid. I wish it was over...[43]

We are all looking forward longingly to see you. It is all 'when Michael comes home'. John is getting a hard hat for the occasion.

118 Mary (Tralee) to Michael (Croydon), 13 June 1914

...I am out all day today settling bills and trying to keep things going. Denis will make his First Communion on Saturday...

119 Mary (Fenit) to Michael (Croydon), 15 July 1914

I have just arrived here dreadfully lonely. They are all silent & when they do talk it is 'poor Michael' all they can say. I am sending parcel this evening & shall send socks tomorrow. Father went to town again today & must go in tomorrow to finish taxing of accounts. I hope you are not lonely & I may go in September. If I can at all I shall do so. It is raining here all day that is one consolation. If it were fine I would be in an awful state to think you were not here to enjoy it . . .

120 Mary (Fenit) to Michael (Croydon), 20 July 1914

Many thanks for your letter and cheque. You sent too much. We are very lonely after you. It is like a desert since you went. Bridie wrote the latest to you a few days ago . . . [44] We had not one fine day since you left . . .

121 Michael (Croydon) to John (Tralee), 22 July 1914

We are now beginning to take an active interest in the forthcoming camp. We parade on Saturday week at the congenial hour of 12 midnight, march to Paddington through the night, and start from there at 2 am. I don't know why they fixed these unearthly hours, but ours not to reason why! My address will be a rather large if not imposing mouthful Private MJM, B Company, 15th Battalion, County of London Regiment, 4th London Infantry, Brigade Camp, Perham Down, Andover.

What did you think of the article on Emerson in last week's *Literary Supplement*?[45] It is the first time I have seen him so severely criticised, and I think you will admit the force of the observations. He was one of the last of those rusticated philosophers to whom 'life' only means the easy round of a pleasant country house, and the exploration of old books. Since his day the gulf between the world of letters and the world of action has, for good or ill, been bridged over, and the writer of today, whose books are to make any appeal, must mingle much with the fevered life about him, and he a man of the world just like his neighbours the stockbroker or the boxer . . .

122 Mary (Fenit) to Michael (Croydon), 26 July 1914

I got your welcome letter. I would have answered before but am simply dead from being up at night helping to entertain Han's & Bridie's male friends. I am afraid this place has spoiled them. John is getting fearfully dissipated. The weather is terrible. We are not able to go outside the door, wet & wild. John even had to give up bathing...

123 Mary (Fenit) to Michael (Croydon), 28 July 1914

I hope you will not get cold camping out. Be sure & send home socks to be washed. I shall send them back by return of post. The weather is still awful...

We are going home on Friday & we are not sorry...If I got a salmon, shall we send it to your landlady if you are not at home...

124 John (Listowel) to Michael (Croydon), 29 July 1914

I am not in the least appalled by your midnight parades and small hours marches. Have not, I, myself, covered the distance between Fenit 'Island' and the mainland four times between the hours of 12.15 and 1.40 am?...

I have read the article on Emerson and been somewhat surprised at its tone. Of course, there can be no question as to his aloofness and refusal to mingle with the life about him. And yet I doubt if it was what one might call intellectual aloofness...

It were passing strange indeed if I did not refer to the Dublin Murders.[46] I was in a state of fierce indignation all Monday and, indeed, had almost resolved to join the Volunteers at once; but the soothing speech of our trusted leader has calmed my excited nerves.[47] I have no time for comments, it is 9.10 pm and bed-time – I must repair the ravages of my (almost) all-night sittings and prepare for more to come.

I shall probably not write to you at Andover; the address is appalling to one in my state.

125 M.W.Cullington (Inland Revenue Offices, Putney) to Michael, 30 July 1914

I am looking forward to camp when we shall leave a few of our cares behind for a fortnight. I should not be a scrap surprised if we left camp only to go on garrison duty in some damned place. I don't look forward to that with glee I will say. 15 days camp with a few days at Easter is all very well but I am not keen on 6 months or a year. Still it would be a thorough rest for our jaded brains. Whatever happens it is exceedingly unlikely that we shall see any actual scrapping but if we do it will be pretty severe. I don't know that I have many tips that I have picked up in 5 years. The great thing is not to care whatever happens. I forget if it says anything in orders about tea-cloths. You will want 2 (we wash our own plates). I suppose you have noticed with great joy that our grey uniforms will not be required. Indian rubber shoes & a sweater are desirable if you have got them. I don't know whether you have the habit of wearing pants all the year. I find that those khaki breeches cause my legs to get covered with pimples by the end of the first week if I wear no pants. So I wear pants; if you are blessed with a thick hide I don't suppose they will be necessary. I shall take a bathing costume in hopes that I get a chance to use it. We had bathing at Abergavenny.

I expect to be up at Somerset House shortly after 11.0. I shall see you before midnight anyway.

126 Michael (Croydon) to Mary (Fenit), 3 August 1914

Our camp has ended suddenly. We went there on Sat[urday]. night and during Sunday made all the necessary preparations for a full stay. But last night, half an hour after we had gone to bed we were called up and amid much excitement and conjecture brought back to London. We are under orders to assemble to-morrow at eleven am with mobilisation kit, but no Royal Proclamation of mobilisation has at this early hour (I am writing at 7.30 am) been issued. The only certainty about our future movements is therefore that we cannot in any casualty [sic] be sent abroad. We shall probably have a long absence from civil occupation, but our duties will not be of a nature to make us actual combatants. Only in the event of an invasion could we possibly be brought into conflict with German troops, and even then the balance of the Regular Army left in England & the Special Reserve, would be first called upon. But invasion is exceedingly improbable. War has not yet been declared by England but very soon after it is the German Navy will probably be destroyed. I am looking to the future with no feeling of personal inquietude, and you will see that there is no ground for any.

The real trouble for the people of this country whether they be acting the part of soldiers or of civilians will be financial and industrial. In this situation unprecedented in the history of the world which now so suddenly confronts us, it would be foolish to ignore the imminence of a period of grave anxiety and trouble for all of us. But I trust that you will all face the unique situation coolly and with composure. Only by the people going about their ordinary vocations as far as possible and avoiding any panic feeling or action, can the commercial distress be minimised. With God's help, Ireland, with its prosperity rooted in the soil which in such times will increase rather than diminish in value, will come out unscathed from the ordeal.

I do not know what my address will be in the near future but you can meanwhile write here & letters will be forwarded.

I am sending home all my goods & chattels which I do not want at present. It will save paying rent for my lodgings should my absence be prolonged. On mobilisation we get £5 bonus & also I understand civil servants get full civil pay. As our expenses will be small I hope to be able to send you a more substantial sum each month, if the crisis endures so long.

P.S. Are you staying on at Fenit or not?

If prices of butter &c go up much, as they are sure to, Ireland will benefit very considerably, as the chief source of supply for this country. It would be worth John's while, if it could be managed to enter the market as a direct exporter of produce.

127 Mary (Tralee) to Michael (Croydon), 5 August 1914

Your letter I received this morning alarmed me very much. They were all consoling me saying you were in no danger. Fr Duggan also only laughed at my fears.[48] May God grant they are right. Take all the care possible of yourself & I have confidence in God's goodness you will be alright. Will I send your shirts & socks I have them ready for you. I did not get your trunk etc. God help me, it will be awful when I do get it without yourself. We have only to pray & ask God & his Blessed Mother to remove this cross.

We may perhaps be able to laugh together at all our anxiety before many months. Provisions have gone up considerably. Sugar 5s per stone today. We have put in a supply & flour has gone up a lot also.

We had an awful difficulty in getting money today to buy the butter. I had to go out begging & managed to get a loan of £12 & a promise of £70 in the morning. Mr Revington who is a brick always sent it down to the house to us.[49]

Goodbye my love and may God guard you. Send home if possible your soiled clothes. They shall be sent back by return...

We left Fenit on Friday. Fr Duggan sends badge and medal. Wear the enclosed badge & it will keep you from all harm.

128 Mary (Tralee) to Michael (Croydon), 6 August 1914

I got your letter today. It was a relief to me as the suspense is dreadful. I was crying all day yesterday & imagining all sorts of things. Thank God my mind is not so disturbed today. I am sure there is no danger but still I get frightfully nervous from time to time ... There is an awful panic here. All the reservists are going away this evening & the people are very excited.

If you are sent anywhere wire me your address. They say here the war cannot last long that is one consolation & they say it would be impossible that the Germans could get into England. Julia Brick of Caherbreagh is in Belgium & cannot come home. They were fighting on yesterday ¼ of a mile from the coast & of course there is no reliable news today. Her poor mother is distracted. God help Mothers. Goodbye now my own boy until tomorrow when I shall write again to you. May God keep you & save you for me.

129 Michael (B Company, Civil Service Rifles, Somerset House, London) to Mary (Tralee), 8 August 1914

We are now convalescent, if I may describe the fact that we are again allowed out of doors. Owing I suppose to our prominent situation a good deal of interest is taken in our proceedings, & you may have noticed photographs of our sentries in the *Daily Sketch*. Yesterday afternoon as we were going down to have a bathe with towels in our hands, the terrible cinema man mowed us down with his machine. So you may see us on the pictures one of these days.

I do not know yet when we shall be leaving here, nor where we are going to. There is talk of St Alban's in Hertfordshire. We are, I need not say, on for this business as long as the war lasts. It will be a fine rest from Taxes. We shall get full civil less military pay during the whole time, & be reinstated at the end without loss of seniority. So whoever suffers through the war, it will scarcely be us.

I believe the Government means to prosecute this war to the bitter end. They are taking no chances, and it is said that troops are already being poured into France although not a word has appeared about it in the papers. They have asked us for volunteers for foreign service, and a very large number have offered. I should gladly do so if I had your permission. War has pretty well lost all its terrors for us. Simply hard physical work, with a risk of an early demise, that is all.

It is impossible of course to prophecy [*sic*], but the business may be over sooner than expected, as Germany will not easily get over her early reverses. According to all human calculation they have no chance against this country on sea. Personally I should like to see things a bit more evenly distributed, as they deserve some measure of victory for their defiance of the world.

You have the Equitable policy somewhere at home. I never had it in my possession. I enclose the demand for current premium, & also notice re bonds ... In any case will you pay & forward notice to the company before 1 Sept, as I have not enough money at the bank & cannot get it out of the Post Office until I am fixed up somewhere. I shall send you some then.

Financial matters are becoming quite normal again & there is no occasion for panic masures. The bank rate is down to 5%.

130 Michael (Somerset House, London) to Mary (Tralee), 11 August 1914

It appeared from the Prime Minister's statement yesterday that we would get no civil pay while on active service. Today, however, the Adjutant went over specially to see Asquith, and as a result informed us that he had obtained a concession of full civil pay less military pay. He pointed out that in view of this liberal treatment it was our duty to volunteer for service abroad, & strongly appealed to us to do so. He said that we should simply be sent to guard the lines of communication between the Belgian coast & the army so as to keep a free passage for supplies, or if necessary, retreat.[50] Under the circumstances it would seem [an] ungracious thing to refuse, & in view of the trifling risk involved it would be a pity to lose this opportunity of taking part in historic events. Several of the Territorial regiments have volunteered in bulk, although none of them are being so well rewarded as the Civil Service. We should hope to come back covered with glory, & would have more to talk about than if we stuck the monotony here. Although it may seem cowardly not to volunteer, I shall, I assure you, not do so without your entire consent. Whatever my own feelings in the matter, I should take no avoidable steps which might cause you anxiety. You understand of course that the more men go out the greater the

chance of beating back Germany & ending the war soon. If you can wire
me early on Thursday evening, do so, if not I shall await a letter as on
Friday we shall be going to St Albans, or Abbot's Langley.

I am feeling very much the better for the training we have had so far. It
is vastly preferable to being stuck in an office. The weather is gloriously
fine; in fact too hot for marching.

*131 Michael (4th London Infantry Brigade, 2nd London Division, St Albans) to
Maurice (Tralee), 20 August 1914*

Dear Father,
Have just got your letter which was forwarded from Somerset House. We
are in many ways much more comfortable, as we get more and better
food, and straw is nicer to sleep on than hard boards, while of course the
conditions are very healthy. Our chief grievance is the strict discipline &
restriction of our liberty. We are not allowed to stir outside an area of
about 1/4 mile each way, except of course on the march. However, they will
probably relax a bit later on.

I have decided not to volunteer for service abroad. Under any circumstances I should have done so if only as a seeker after adventure, as I have
really no sort of feeling of 'duty' in the matter & am not an enthusiastic
opponent of German ideas, although naturally I should not like to see
either Ireland or this country overrun by Germans.

Things are dragging a good deal at the front. We hear of nothing but
victories, yet the Germans are all the time advancing in Belgium. Matters
must come to a head one of these days. With love MJM.[51]

*132 Photographic postcard from Michael to Hannah (Loreto College, Dublin),
2 September 1914*

I suppose you are nearly settled down now. Were you very lonely? Please
write me a long letter telling me all about your experiences.[52] Do you
recognise me on the back? It is not a very clear photo, as the sun was right
in our faces. It was taken at Harrow yesterday. We are back at Bedmond
again today.[53] Our ten days 'holiday' are over.

3. Michael with the Civil Service Rifles at Harrow 1 September 1914

133 'The March of Certain Men of London', a poem by Michael
(c. 1914 or 1915)

Men of London spurning glory
Heroes' page and epic story
Marching through the bloody war
Home service to the end
Away with irksome duty
Leave us home and beauty
Here we stand, with arms in our hand,
To meet the invader
Well we know he'll never come
Still it's a good excuse to some
And our mere presence frightens off
The daring German raider scared
Summer seasons have passed for us
Young & old have gone before us
But no bribes will ever part us
From our native land
Why be killed in battle
Like dumb driven cattle

When at home all careless you may roam
And live on clover
So we wait the blessed day
When all the clouds shall pass away
And oer the land the tidings spread,
At last the war is over

CHAPTER FIVE

Home Service, 1915

134 Michael (Dorking) to John (Tralee), 22 January 1915[1]

There was quite a pleasant little interlude today. We were to be reviewed by Lord Kitchener once more, this time on Epsom Downs. We had to be up at five, waking ourselves by auto-suggestion, & cook our own breakfast. When we started off it promised to be a fine dry day but presently it began to snow faster & faster, and when we got out of the train onto the Downs the land was clothed in white. However, the elements did not prevail against us, and after waiting for two hours in the blizzard we saw his Lordship come along in a motorcar, with some French officers. He did not get out of his car, & the formality was soon over.[2]

The afternoon I have spent in snowball fights. The snow is almost a foot deep already, more than I have seen for quite a long time.

I have noticed the name Weller over several shop fronts in Dorking. I do not know whether the owners are in any way related to Dickens' characters.

We are to be armed once more, this time with Japanese rifles which have been purchased by the British Government, probably ones that have been used in the Russian war.

There is, I fear, little doubt that the break-up of the Holy Roman Empire of Austria is at hand. That it will lead to a more settled condition of things in that part of Europe I very much doubt, however. On the contrary the multitude of races which despite their mutual antagonisms, have been held together in peace by the strong hand of the Habsburgs, will, when set at liberty, have no such restraining force, and everlasting strife is likely to be the result. Anyway, whatever may be said about the Austrian Empire, it has always been a great Catholic and monarchical force, and, more than any other state in Europe, preserved something of the atmosphere and traditions of the Middle Ages.

With several other Catholics of the battalion, I went to tea on invitation last Sunday evening to the house of Wilfred Ward, the writer.[3] He is himself away in America at present, lecturing on German 'atrocities', and we were received by Mrs Ward, who is a niece of the Duke of Norfolk. They were very nice to us and I hope to go there again.

By the way, Lord Gormanston, who is also a Catholic, is now lieutenant in our Company. I regret to say he does not seem to have inherited much of the military ability which, doubtless, won his ancestors nobility in the 15th century.[4]

135 Michael (Dorking) to John (Tralee), 13 February 1915

A word as regards my address. We have recently been re-organised on the platoon system and now there are only four companies, A B C & D, instead of eight. I am in C and the above is now the correct address...

Many thanks for copy of New Testament. I have also received Churchill's book.[5] By the way, last Sunday after Mass we were each presented with a copy of the *Imitation* [*of Christ*], so that I am now fully equipped for the study of the Gospel with the aid of the mediaeval and the modern interpretations. I have not yet started Churchill's book, and it is rather presumptuous of me to discuss or criticise it after merely glancing at one or two polemical passages. Both on the strength of these, however, and on theoretical grounds I take his reading of the Gospel to be that common to so many of his contemporaries and as indeed characteristic of the age. In other times Christianity was essentially interpreted as the Love of God, and, appropriately, its highest product was the contemplative monk. This version has prevailed from very early Christian times right down the ages, and has to a large extent determined the development of the church...

At present I am reading a book called *Barlasch of the Guard*, which deals with Napoleon's Russian campaign, the scene being chiefly laid in East Prussia.[6] It is interesting to read in these accounts of the old wars, the names of places which are now again the theatre of history. I shall send you the book shortly. I am also sending you some books which I have finished with and which you may care to read. In any case you can keep them.

It would seem as if the Allies instead of advancing into Germany, are finding themselves unable to keep their hold on the parts of the country which they had occupied. The Russian offensive in East Prussia has, indeed, collapsed very suddenly. If they fail to make a stand on their own frontier the threat to their own communications will be serious. Indeed, Russia's repeated failures to obtain any decisive results, whilst her ports are blockaded and her trade ruined must lead one to consider how long she will continue to wage a war which at present at any rate promises no advantage.

136 Michael (Civil Service Rifles, Dorking) to John (Tralee), 28 February 1915

I am afraid further reflection has not brought me much nearer to Churchill's and your attitude towards the Church and its work. I regard the organised Church as the greatest instrument and type of culture. If it has apparently whittled down the obligations of a Christian to a modest minimum, that is not the fault of the Church itself. It is due to the infirmities of human nature which make the highest reaches of Christian endeavour inaccessible to all but a few choice souls. If the Catholic Church was to touch the life of the common man at all it could only do so by allowing for his limitations. And in doing that it was really carrying out in letter and spirit the example of its Founder, to whom a sinner's repentance was more pleasing than a saint's sinlessness. People whose outlook is even unconsciously and unwillingly warped by a worldly or temporal point of view will of course, as Churchill does, look at morals mainly as a means of securing the greatest happiness of the greatest number. To them it is nothing if a man after having brought scores to ruin and misery during his active life, should at the last make peace with God. If the Church did not avail to keep him from crime, then the Church has failed in its mission. Such is their conception of its mission, an essentially false one, as I think. No amount of quotations from the Gospels, no amount of lip-worship of Christ, can conceal the real character of this new pseudo-religion, which has no real claim to be called Christianity. Christianity is a religion of mediation or atonement. Its object is not the betterment of social conditions, or the elimination of social evils. True, if everyone was capable of living as a perfect Christian these evils would cease to exist. But the Church has equally fulfilled its mission if, sooner or later it brings every soul to God, even though all the time every imaginable evil may rage upon the earth. Nor is it beside the point to add that all these evils are, according to the Christian teaching, sources of spiritual good. To the Christian then an Eldon Parr, dying and repentant, and his victim, patient and forgiving, are greater triumphs for the Religion than both men, honest though successful business men. Again and again it must be insisted against Churchill and every other modernist that the physical evil caused by sin is as nothing, counts for nothing at all in the reckoning. Whoever fails to grasp that fact does not understand the Gospels. The standards of this world must not be used to judge the Church and its work. The people must not, cannot, ask the Church to abolish war, trusts, sweating, poverty. If the activities of the Church tend in that direction that is an irrelevant circumstance for which the Church can seek no credit. But between conqueror and conquered, sweater and sweated, rich and poor, the Church is essentially neutral. One may be no better morally than the other, but even if he is, the Church cannot take sides, for the souls of both are equally objects of its solicitude. The Church's mission is not to save the vanquished from his physical sufferings, but to save the conqueror from his own moral blindness.

Looked at in this light the Modernist indictment falls to the ground, and is seen for what it really is, as an attempt to enthrone Positivism on the altars of Christ. And on the theological side, its trend is equally obvious, in the self-deception which tries to interpret old doctrine in terms of modern thought. Better far to deny these old dogmas root and branch than attempt to use them as the vehicle of a fantastic symbolism. It is not by such means that the Church can be rehabilitated in the minds of 'educated' men.

So long as such men persist in trying to modernise the Church, so long must they remain outside it. If they would seek peace with it, it is they and not the Catholic Church, that must make concessions, and the false pride which stands in the way of their submission is a far greater sin than any of Eldon Parr's...[7]

137 John (Tralee) to Michael (Dorking), 12 March 1915

Uncle Mick is gone, the one great example God has given us of the practicability of the injunction of Jesus – 'love one another as I have loved you'.[8] We sometimes thought it folly that he should give himself and all he had so unstintingly, that he should take the burthens of others on his shoulders; now it must seem to us very near the highest wisdom.

For over forty years he had endured sorrows that would have embittered any other man; they seemed to make him ever-greater hearted. He thought for others to the end, magnifying the little services they did him, making little of his own sacrifices.

And now we know that down the long vista of our future years we shall never see his face again, nor hear his voice nor grip his hand ... I suppose more than half the sadness of death lies in its dread finality; but there is something in the feel of the poor cold clay which changes, for a time at least, one's whole outlook...

I agree entirely 'that the physical evil caused by sin counts for nothing'. It is the attitude, the anti-Christian attitude, of which sin is the outcome that counts. The standard of Christ is the great thing; momentary lapses from that standard do not make a man un-Christian, so as the main trend of his life, of his desires and endeavours is towards the realisation of the Christian ideal which, probably, no one can arrive at a true understanding of life. And suffering arises out of sin. But the fact that good may come from the criminal greed of an Eldon Parr cannot make of him a public benefactor. He and his works are evil; and, in the almost impossible event of his repentance, that repentance is a condemnation of his life and, not less, of the church which countenanced that life and levied toll on its fruits.

You must surely see that it is at bottom a bad case, though you have, probably, made the best of it. Why not plead guilty and throw yourself on the mercy of the court.

I have read that *History of War and Peace*.[9] The action is too rapid and took my breath away.

I hope you have got those papers I sent you. I forgot to put in the no. of platoon in [the] address.

138 Michael (Dorking) to John (Tralee), 19 March 1915

With Uncle Mick indeed gone who was not only a great and true Christian but a great and true patriot, it is the passing of one who, while he lived, held up aloft the torch of an idealism rare in our generation. Many great and noble principles are poorer and weaker by his death. Almost the last was he of those men of old time in Ireland who, untainted by English sordidness, won the love and trust of the people by their tender charity, constant probity, public spirit and devotion. All those qualities which make the life of man beautiful were his in a surpassing degree, and our sense of irreparable loss is deepened by the too certain knowledge that in the rest of our journey through this stormy modern life we shall meet few if any, such perfect types of human character...

History is not a process of perfecting the human nature; once rid ourselves of the notion, and how futile do all reforms seem! Great War and Great Peace, Great Revolution and Great Expansion, come and pass, but who can say that they leave the world either better or worse than it was? Even the Church's mission, let me again remind you, is not to make this life an earthly paradise, but, sooner or later, after sins or sinless, to save the individual soul.

139 John (Tralee) to Michael (Dorking), 26 March 1915

But this is a most unsoldierly evasion! For months I have been trying to put clearly the case against the Churches, and owing to your evasiveness, I have had to repeat over and over the chief points in that case. You always write as if you had forgotten all my arguments and had retained only a general idea of the subject. Try to keep this letter until you have time to reply.

You have altogether misunderstood _The Inside of the Cup_ if you think of Eldon Parr as a sinner whom his[10] Church was striving to bring to penance...

I have no illusions about reformations. I know that in some sense all are doomed to failure. In the interior history of the Church we have plenty of evidence of this... And, yet, the world is a school where one may learn many a truth which one has seen but dimly; sorrow is a fire which may burn much of the grossness out of one. In God, and in these his agents of regeneration do I hope, not in myself where there is no hope.

Mother is daily expecting news of your coming. She sent a post card to Watford the other day thinking you would be there, and she would have written previously if she had been sure where to find you.

140 Mary (Tralee) to Michael (Dorking), 27 March 1915

I was delighted to get your letter today. I did not know where to write or send a parcel. I had a parcel made up & we used the cakes & sweets etc after getting your last letter. We were expecting you home every day for the past ten days. I hope you will be home for Easter Sunday. When you are coming you had better come at night as there is no connection to Kerry from Rosslare...

141 Michael (Dorking) to John (Tralee), 28 March 1915

We are leaving Dorking for Watford tomorrow, and I hope to be able to go home some day this week. I may then succeed in convincing you that my arguments are not evasive at all, but that, on the contrary, you make no attempt to answer them. This may be partly my fault, as perhaps I did not make clear that I was defending, not Christian 'Churches' in general, but _the_ Church of Rome...

4. Michael in the Civil Service Rifles, 1915

5. Michael with the Officer Cadet Brigade, Newmarket, 1917

142 Michael (Watford) to John (Tralee), 4 May 1915

I am afraid mother was very premature in taking it for granted that the
recent letter from the Inland Revenue means my release from the Army.
Although in the early months of the war there was a lot of talk about Civil
Servants being recalled to their offices, matters have now reached a stage
at which all probability of such a measure has vanished. On the contrary,
recruiting from the Civil Service has been opened again, after having been
stopped in the middle of August. The truth is that the Government are
straining every nerve to avoid or postpone conscription, although I fail to
see how it can be put off much longer. Recent news from the East and
West has revealed the character and present position of the war in a new
light, and people are beginning to realise that failing the intervention of
Italy or other neutrals, all the resources of the present Allies will not end
the war for two years more. There is a good deal of misgiving felt as to the
Dardanelles operations, which may, it is thought, prove a costly and irre-
trievable blunder. The casualty lists now appearing show that this new
theatre will eat up men as fast as the campaign in Flanders, and the objective is entirely subsidiary. It is only the Liberal press, indeed, which keeps
up any show of optimism now. All independent opinion attaches a sinister importance to the recent German victories.

I notice that the German submarines have got as far as Valencia [*sic*]
Island now. You are certainly nearer the war area in Kerry than we are
here, strange as it may seem.

What do you think of Sir Roger Casement as a candidate for the
College Green Division. If he is nominated, we may expect some lively
election scenes in Dublin.[11]

143 Michael (Saffron Walden) to John (Tralee), 24 May 1915

So Italy has declared war at last.[12] Our Prussian knight in shining armour
is now indeed fighting with his back to the wall, and doubtless the defeat
of the Empires is now an assured consummation. Nevertheless the first
result of this new complication will be to add an increased severity and
bitterness to the great fight, and the Allies may expect unexampled deeds
of ferocity on the part of their foe. The ethics of such deeds is not quite
so simple as you and the world appears to think. After all, as Clausewitz
said, there is nothing in the nature of war to limit the amount of violence
to be used in accompanying its end, and the sinking of the *Lusitania*, for

example, is a mere newspaper incident in the holocaust of millions.[13] Every act in war must, I think, be judged not by itself, but in the light of the object and ideals of the nation which sanctions it. If we think the cause of the Allies, the cause of peaceful commercialism and financial civilisation, is the good one, then anything they may do with a view to hurting Germany must obtain our approval, as being in every case overshadowed by the great end. On the other hand, if our sympathies incline us towards the romantic mediaevalism, the wild poetry, and the battle spirit of the Middle Age and the Middle World, then we must ignore all criticisms of the means employed to restore these things to their old supremacy in Europe. A war of civilisations knows nothing of ships or towns, or individual men and women. We may lament that they should suffer innocently, but then so have the many soldiers who have fallen.

I hope your Herr Professor of Economics will prove right in his forecast.[14] If the war puts a check on the disintegrating and subversive tendencies of the (late) modern world, it will not be the least among its many blessings. Lloyd George's taxing proposals, although defeated by the Irish, were a rather disquieting commentary on your teacher's notion. That the war should prove to be the means of bringing about far-reaching social revolutions would to me be a very unwelcome result.

The bringing of the Tories into the Government ought to hasten the coming of conscription.[15] That the new element will be strongly in favour of it there can hardly be any doubt, and now that the casualties are reaching a figure representing 60,000 or 80,000 a month, the necessity for decisive measures will soon become pressing.

You may be surprised to hear that I have been troubled by my old friend, or enemy, the Muse of Poetry, lately, and she forced me to put on paper the effusion which I give below, hoping it does not give you a nightmare.

> Outside the North wind rudely blows,
> Within a merry company.
> The last of Ireland's chivalry
> Drink to the memory of those
> Who, fallen in the German war,
> Will see their native fields no more.
> Where starlike shells light up the sky
> And war's wild music thunders high
> In lonely graves forever lie,
> The men whom Erin's bosom bore.
> A little life, a little love,

A little fight, then all is done.
To men of peace how tragic this,
But as for us we gladly miss,
Sad evening in the darkened grove
For glorious death in noon-tide sun.
Then fill the tankards high with ale,
'Tis not for us to weep and wail,
For peace or war it's all a game,
So here's your health, and mine's the same.

144 Michael (10 Platoon, C Company, Civil Service Rifles, Saffron Walden)
to John (Tralee), 10 June 1915

I was in London last week for two days, and after a bit of enquiry I succeeded in finding out the locality where the Zeppelin dropped bombs.[16] It is right in the East End in the neighbourhood of Shoreditch and Hoxton. A poor catch for the Zep, certainly, but by no means 'outer' suburbs as described in the official report. I saw one of the houses. The outer walls were standing, but within the place was entirely burnt down. I heard a rumour that damage was also done to Bishopsgate station, in the heart of the City.

We have in the past week begun to experience the intensity of soldiering in a greater degree than perhaps ever before. The great heat of 120 in the sun exceeded even the boiling days of last August, and a large number of men fell out on the march on a couple of days. When I came in on Tuesday I felt as relaxed as if I had been in a Turkish bath. The weather has now changed and last night the rain was coming in around the borders of our marquee, with the result that a lot of our things got wet, although we got off all right ourselves.

As far as present indications go, it seems that the Coalition Government will have greater difficulty in obtaining unanimous support than the old one did. The extremists on both sides, as well as the disappointed office-holders and would-be officeholders, seem bent on keeping up an attitude of more or less active hostility.

I am sending you some books to keep for me until less strenuous times. I have not succeeded in going far with *Inside of the Cup* as I find it difficult to interest myself in social or religious problems in these times. I am sending the books as owing to the very limited and insecure accommodation here, they would be liable to damage.

145 Michael (Richmond Park) to John (Tralee), 14 July 1915

We are now, at last, after eleven and a half months, enjoying what may be called a rest camp in the pleasant surroundings of Richmond. We are only doing just enough work to keep fit and have more time to ourselves than we know what to do with. The 'grousing', which used to be a feature of our regiment, has at last disappeared, everyone being apparently satisfied. This is expected to last until the end of September, when the coast defence work will begin.

The days that are passing now are, of course, interesting as being the anniversaries of those fateful days last year, when the issue of peace or war still seemed to hang on the formulae of negotiation and diplomacy, and the minds of all of us were looking forward with a certain apprehension to the future, sceptical though some of us were as to the possibility of war at all in our modern time. That illusion has passed, as has also the thrilled interest with which the outsiders witnessed the play of polity. The actual operations of war, the slow ebb and flow of great physical and moral forces, do not grip the mind much, even for the non-participant who can see them as a whole. Great and necessary, we know, is the part that war has to play in history, but the centre of interest has shifted from the field of battle, with its stories of individual heroism and sacrifice, to the future days of settlement when the political and moral results of this clash of ideals shall be unfolded. Of all these myriads of men who are fighting and dying along those great lines, how few, even among the fairly intelligent, have any conception of the real spiritual forces that play with their lives, or of the real outcome of final victory or defeat. The narrow patriot takes up arms for his country, and his soul is stirred by the popular catchwords of national hate or selfishness. But who is to tell the soldier whether the foe he has humbled may not have been the greatest hope of humanity and culture, or, on the other hand, the world's treasure-house of political experience and political wisdom? Most of these men, then, are dying for either fictitious or secondary causes, and this perhaps adds to the tragedy of their slaughter. Nevertheless we must not fall into the error of regarding this holocaust as useless or avoidable. The great questions must now, as always, be decided by blood. The destiny of mankind and the path of evolution are not to be decided by any judge or jury. The lawyer's compromise has no place here. Might, though it be not right, must prevail, until, at least, it be overcome by a better might. There is no other way but this. And vast though the scale of the suffering may be, it is not too vast in proportion to the magnitude of the issues involved.

Have you been reading anything lately? I see Churchill has published a new book in which he returns once more to the drab theatre of American politics.[17] I am at present engaged in Machiavelli's *Prince*. When I have finished I shall send it to you along with Professor Cramb's *Germany and England* an excellent book, worthy of preservation and remembrance.[18]

I hear our indulgent colonel here is trying to get seven days' leave for us, in rotation. He has my best prayers.

Have you heard what regiment our cousin Jim is in?[19] I suppose he has not yet been rushed to the front. Do you know if any of the Tralee men are gone out yet?

146 Michael (Tadworth Camp, near Epsom) to John (Tralee), 3 August 1915

I have just got your letter which was forwarded after some delay from Richmond. I rather envy you the idyllic conditions under which it was written. You can soon become a poet as well as a market gardener, under such genial influences of nature. I am myself writing just now under very difficult conditions. Picture a large marquee, with writing tables and benches ranged round, and the noise of many dialects never ceasing, while outside the pitiless rain drips, drips, as though during the past two days it had not made the ground muddy enough. Now and then, in the far distance, one can hear the thunder roll, like the growing cannonade of a new battle between the great guns across the water. You go outside and see the vast camp, dimly lighted, stretching over hill and valley, the resting place of the soldier since the beginning of the world. As I go back to that, I shall see the figures of the lonely sentries, like lost souls condemned for ever to wander through the watches of the stormy night. Such is the setting, gloomy but not altogether depressing, in which I write on this, the last day of the first year of the great war.

Who would have thought a year ago that the Germans would today be closing in on Warsaw and within cannon-shot of Riga? And what a change the lapse of time has made in the temper and tone of the English people. Instead of the loud bleatings about honour, and the paper partitions of the German Empire, that were so common in those August days, we see the unmistakable beginnnings of doubt and almost dismay at the task confronting them.

147 Michael (Richmond Park) to John (Tralee), 20/21 August 1915

I am glad that Cramb interested you so much. As you say, he is a frank disciple of what is called Russianism, which, in its turn, is a typical example of the Machiavellian statecraft, although containing many other ingredients, such as a heroic love of war and a historical and Imperial pride, which form the softer background to the teachings of the great Italian. But, of course, the policy of every large country, in all ages, has been guided by the axioms of self-interest and worldly wisdom which are tabulated in *The Prince*. It is only the greater strength of the spiritual element in Germany that makes for understanding.

It is worth while considering whether Machiavellianism is really deserving of the harsh words which you, in common with so many other 'divines', shower upon it. The duty of a statesman is to safeguard and further the interests of the community which is placed in his charge, and these interests are of a mutable nature, depending as they do on the material, moral and intellectual growth of the people, both absolutely, and in relation to other communities. By their very nature these interests must come into conflict with those of other states, and in the case of a rising community, the ruler is faced with the alternative of starving the national life of his subjects, or encroaching on the territories and possessions of his neighbours who are unable to protect themselves. It is to the constant acceptance of the second alternative that the whole progress of civilisation is due, there being, in general, no other means by which the higher civilisation can be made to supplant the lower. No infringement of the moral law is involved, because, in the first place, the state is not a moral entity, and, secondly, it is only acting in obedience to the same natural law which impels the tiger to prey on weaker animals.

It may interest you to know that the 'Eastern Counties' over which the last air-raid took place, on Tuesday night, include the eastern suburbs of London. It was the night of our return from Tadworth. The evening turned out very misty and still. I went to bed pretty early, but could not sleep even after lights out. A motor engine was throbbing somewhere in the park, but above this I felt sure I could hear occasional sounds of explosions. I was gradually dozing off when all of a sudden I heard a bugle sound in a far part of the camp. Of course no bugles sound between lights out and reveillé except the fire alarm or the general alarm. Soon the call, which happened to be the former, was taken up by the various battalions, quickly reaching our own. They started turning us out immediately, but before anyone was dressed the bugles blew 'no parade'. We turned in again, only to be roused ten minutes later by a repetition of the alarm, which was as quickly washed-out for the second time. The rest of the night was spent in peace, but a lot of us had no doubt that a raid was in progress almost over our heads. I believe quite a lot of damage was done in Walthamstow, Leytonstone, Dalston, and other parts of the Metropolis. The number of lives lost is probably grotesquely understated. Indeed, I think the reticence, not to say untruthfulness of the official reports on air-raids serves no purpose beyond mystifying the provincial public. Everyone in London knows the real facts almost immediately, and they must inevitably reach the German Government in a few days...

148 Michael (Richmond Park) to John (Tralee), 2 September 1915

Even granting the general truth of your remarks I still think that *The Prince* is, on the whole, a reliable guide to statesmanship and diplomacy. Of course it was written professedly with reference to the contemporary politics of Italy, but, allowing for the petty nature of its illustrations, its principle may be profitably extended to the relations between world powers. In their struggle for life, there is still the same necesssity for taking advantage of a significant weakness or difficulties, and the same charac-teristic weakness of treaties. Even the duplicity which you condemn is part of the game of skill in which a statesman ought to be adept. It is difficult to withdraw censure from a 'Prince' who deliberately enters into an engagement which he intends to dishonour, but even then you are trying to establish a standard which is not easily restrained within limits, and which is counter to the nature of things. It may be necessary to lull your neighbour with a false sense of security, in order to neutralise his greater potential resources. And, after all, once you admit the right to kill, in the struggle between communities, you cannot profitably attempt to retain any portion of the moral law in relation thereto. It is rather Pharisaic morality which regards double-dealing as a greater offence than the taking of life.

I am at present reading a short history of German literature, and am trying to persuade myself that I am interested in Goethe. In order to confirm or dissipate the impression, I should like you to send me on his *Dichtung und Wahrheit* (Poetry and Truth) if available,[20] also loan me Bell's catalogue.

Thanks for *Times* supplements. The articles you marked were very interesting. I should think that Ludovici's book, though entirely an ex parte statement, is a fairly valuable contribution to the subject.[21] Perhaps after the war people will again realise the value and necessity of leadership, in peace as in battle, and recognise also that the peace-leader, no less than the commander in war, must be a man fitted by training and character for the responsibility. There is abundant evidence that the requisite training and character are concentrated mainly, though not wholly, in one class. The worst that the democrat can say against that class is that, like every other, it is inclined to be selfish. Excluding this common factor it is, it must be admitted, immeasurably better equipped for the business of government than any other component of the state.

How are you getting on with your gardening? No doubt you find it a delightful recreation for week-ends. It is not likely to pall on you either, for all the year round it is full of variety and fresh interest.

149 Michael (Richmond Park) to John (Tralee), 18 September 1915

Many thanks for sending the volumes of Goethe. I have glanced at them, but have not seriously started to read the work, for the simple reason that I had just previously got *Wilhelm Meister's Apprenticeship*,[22] through which I am making my way famously ... As a novel it is unequal in interest and power, but through it all one can discern the pattern of this lofty and beautiful soul ... The book is more allegorical than realistic in form ... I can see nothing false or shallow or insincere in this man. He is a great teacher, with a message of vast import for the world, and withal a great poet, sweet of song. Germany and the world have, perhaps, indeed certainly, gone on their way and heeded him but little; yet, like all the highest things, he remains ever there, ever ready to receive us into his sanctuary, a haven of truth and rest to which we can always return at last.

When I have finished the book I shall send it to you ... I hope too that my, and your, opinion of him will be enhanced and not diminished.

The colossal taxation disclosed in the Budget is a stern reminder that a war is on. It ought to have a chilling effect on all classes in this country. The ruinous nature of the enterprise on which they are engaged will be brought vividly home to them. Personally I am not very enthusiastic at having to pay 1½d an oz. more for my tobacco, and about £1 in Income Tax.

150 Michael (Richmond Park) to John (Tralee), no date (c. October 1915)

I am afraid that in enclosing letters in Y.M.C.A. envelopes without an explanation, I too hastily assumed that the work done by the Y.M.C.A. people in connection with camps, which is so familiar to us, was at any rate not unknown to you. I may say then that in every camp and training centre both at home and in France, this association has erected huts or marquees for the recreation of the troops. In these places light refreshments are sold, facilities for writing, including free stationery, provided, and concerts held. They are a great boon, and we all appreciate the kindness of the ladies and men who give so much of their time gratuitously in attending to us. But it never occurs to any of us I am sure, to connect these places with the Y.M.C.A. clubs, as commonly known. There is no suggestion of the atmosphere of religion and moral fanaticism which rightly invites your ridicule when you mention this institution. They are simply convenient resorts for writing letters, reading, playing chess, or other sedentary occupations and amusements. I earnestly hope that this explanation is not too late to overtake the horrible rumour that I had become a member of the Y.M.C.A.[23]

Although Goethe's autobiography is, no doubt, a very famous and important document, yet to judge him as a poet or a teacher by it is as impossible as it would be in the case of almost any other writer. The record of facts, experiences, emotions, friends &c which form an autobiography, however valuable, is, at the best, but an imperfect account of the formation and working of the mind whose creative genius as shown in his works of imagination, commands our homage. If we are interested in *Poetry and Truth*, it is, broadly speaking, because it tells us so much of the author of *Faust* . . .

If I must define my conception of Goethe's 'culture' I should call it 'the education of man's mind in the perception and pursuit of beauty'. In other words the development of man's highest religious, moral and artistic instincts.

151 John (Tralee) to Michael (Richmond Park), no date (c. October 1915)

. . . I have read *Wilhelm Meister*, and any dislike of Goethe was supplanted by keen pleasure before I had got through half the book. The analysis of Hamlet's character shows rare discrimination and Goethe's views on dramatic representation interested me very much. But far more than these things – though critics seem to insist that the book is not to be regarded as a novel – the story itself delighted me. The author is continually springing surprises on one; all his characters have just such a mystery about them as many, or most, men have in real life...

I hope you will let me know in detail how *Poetry & Truth* impressed you and whether it left on you such feelings towards Goethe as I described when sending the book.

You mention that you are reading a good deal, tell me if I may send any books.

152 Michael (Wimbledon) to John (Tralee), 20 November 1915

I have not yet quite finished *Poetry & Truth*, but can say that the book has in no way diminished my opinion of the author. It is a bright and interesting narrative, showing on every page traces of the strength and depth of Goethe's character, and full of charming and affecting passages. To a certain extent it is marred by a soupçon of egotism which hardly conforms to our taste, although I suppose we must now regard it as more or less inherent in the German mind...

Well, it is a far cry from the influence of Ancient Greece on the literature of the ages to that of modern Greece on the politics of the present hour. Doubtless you are following those brief telegrams from Athens with as much interest as I am, seeing that the fate of the whole war probably depends on the issue there. The strongest misgiving prevails here as to the outcome of the negotiations, but it is no easy matter to pierce through the veil of the Greek and British censorship. I think myself that Greece will not intervene on the German side. It is difficult to see how she could hope to be compensated for her sacrifices, in the event of victory. That she can remain neutral much longer seems, however, altogether impossible. The imminent prospect of the Serbian army being driven back on her frontiers will raise a problem which can only be solved in a sense hostile, and most directly hostile, to one or other of the belligerents.[24]

Meanwhile, we have the cheering news that the Allies have placed large munition contracts in the States, for delivery up to December 1917. It ought to be possible for Mr Asquith to make up his mind about conscription by that time. That there is any likelihood of his introducing it in the near future I can assure you nobody thinks for a moment, apart from some 'eligible' young men who are hypnotised by fear...

153 John (Tralee) to Michael (Wimbledon), 24 November 1915

...Events have, so far, borne out your remarks about the attitude of Greece, though I doubt if Tino[25] has yet said his last word. At any rate, it is encouraging to see that our Government is determined to compel Greece to help vindicate the right of small nationalities to stand aloof from the quarrels of their greater neighbours.

You will have seen, from the paper father sent you, that John McGaley has not learned to appreciate the cause for which we and our allies have drawn the sword.[26] Clearly success in the Intermediate does not necessarily imply a grasp of those 'cosmopolitan considerations' referred to by the Most Rev. Dr O'Dwyer in his recent much discussed letter.[27] It is up to the Intermediate board to see that the children of the rising generation are instructed in the principles of international politics and imbued with a spirit of imperial patriotism.

154 Michael (Wimbledon) to John (Tralee), 1 December 1915

...So John McGaley has been trying to revive the glories of the martyrs. Well, in his enforced idleness (or is it hard labour!) he will have time to meditate on the folly of trifling with arbitrary power. Who knows but when his three months are up, he will go straight to the recruiting office and join in the fight for liberty?

Having finished Goethe and Sophocles, I shall send them on to you shortly.

155 John (Tralee) to Michael (Wimbledon), 5 December 1915

No man bathes twice in the same stream, least of all do I. So the mood in which I last wrote has passed, for ever perhaps; I have bathed in quite other, holier and more purifying waters. After years of intellectual anarchy and blindness, it has been given to me, at last, to submit to that 'sweet yoke' and that 'light burthen' which I had so long refused. With a completeness which I could never have foreseen, when last writing to you, I have been able, through God's grace, to adopt the Catholic outlook on life and to accept, without reservation all Catholic dogmas. It is not that no doubts now come to one: it is rather that I am able to examine these doubts from the Catholic point of view. And all this is not the result of any strain imposed by any will; I did not force myself to accept the Catholic truths, in fact I resisted them almost to the last; the force came from some power outside myself. I have been allowed to see many things more clearly in these days. I see now that in so far as I differed from the Church I was a materialist. I thought, for example, that the Catholic teaching regarding the Eucharist was a materialist interpretation of the word of Our Lord whereas, as a matter of fact, it is one of the many Catholic doctrines in which is emphasised a vital principle of religion viz: the utter subjection of matter to its Creator. My denial of this doctrine was, in effect, a denial of the power of God over the matter which he made. It is so, I think, with all the Sacraments, apart from, and as a condition of, their effficacy as channels of grace, they demand that we should believe that God, working through His Church, can and does give to matter or to ritualistic forms certain powers of which our senses give us no evidence and on which our reason throws no light. I think that this is, in itself, a strong argument in favour of the identity of the Catholic Church of today with the Church founded by Him who said 'Blessed are they who have believed though they have not seen', 'unless you become as little children (i.e. in faith, surely) you shall not enter into the Kingdom of Heaven' and 'Blessed are the clean of heart (who are they but those who are unpolluted by material-ism); for they shall see God'...

156 Michael (Wimbledon) to John (Tralee), 7 December 1915

I was very much interested in your confession of faith new-born. I can scarcely say that I have any definite standpoint from which to discuss the matter, but there are certain reflections nevertheless which occur to me. For instance, if you hold that works of art are to be judged by their influ-ence in promoting beautiful actions, how much more does this apply to religious dogmas? Judged by this test, your own, many of the doctrines to which you now so passionately cling appear devoid of value and, accord-ing to the strictest use of your own terminology, lacking in external harmony. The practice of praying for the dead, for example, whatever may be said in its favour, cannot by any stretch be held to strengthen the springs of moral action. The doctrine of the Trinity itself is, from an ethi-cal point of view, entirely indifferent. In suggesting this contradiction between your religious views and your theory of art, do not think I am defending the latter. Rather should I put it before you as a proof of the weakness of your case in regard to aesthetic values...

157 John (Tralee) to Michael (Wimbledon), 10 December 1915

...You think I make a fetish of action. It is a thing I am utterly incapable of doing. The Church, whose standards I unreservedly accept,
values all things only in so far as they tend to bring men to God. She
fully recognises the value of contemplation, but she regards good as an
active principle which cannot confine itself to contemplation alone.
Beautiful actions are, if one may put it so, a projection of beautiful
thoughts which, at once, make the beauty of these thoughts evident to
others and re-act on the mind of the doer. I think you are wrong about
the attitude of the Church towards this question. The idea of pure
contemplation as a means to the great end of life is entirely Buddhistic;
it has no place in the teaching or example of Our Lord. The Church
by explicit command and by the implications of many of her tenets
imposes a life of active good on her members. The doctrine of the
Communion of Saints, for instance, places on believers duties towards
their fellow Catholics which can scarcely be fulfilled in a purely contemplative existence...

   ...Do you yet retain your expectations of Greek aid? It seems to me
that, if King Constantine had any positive policy at all, it is to range
himself beside the Germans at the first favourable moment and drive
the French and the British into the sea, and the British are doing their
level best but to ensure that he'll have his people behind him.

158 Michael (Wimbledon) to John (Tralee), 14 December 1915

I am more than ever convinced by your last letter that there is a real
difference in our opinions, but I still hope to convince you that you are
in the wrong. You have not met my point as to how to explain the artistic or aesthetic imperfection of a work which is morally irreproachable
or beneficial, as for example La Fontaine's *Fables*. There must be an
aesthetic sense or criterion different from the ethical. The case in which
you find your difficulty, that of a work which is acclaimed as artistically
faultless although it is morally reprehensible, is not insoluble. I have at
present got Schiller's aesthetical works in hand. In one of his essays he
discusses the influence of culture or taste on conduct. He maintains
that a man of taste who avoids certain immoral actions because they
are disgusting or vulgar to his taste, is not, to that extent, under the

influence of conscience at all. His aesthetic sense acts in this instance before his moral judgment, and the latter is, to use a military term, held in reserve. Apply this to criticism, and you will see that a really true sense of beauty will condemn such as Maupassant's, as artistically false, without regard to their influence on conduct ...

With your strictures on modern art of all kinds I am in heartiest agreement. When I see the *Times Literary Supplement* of last week discussing modern 'poetry' and quoting under the heading the most nauseous string of words I have ever seen or heard, I begin to think that those people who encourage our young 'poets' by buying their works deserve all they get. We are complacently told that the romantic movement is dead. So is poetry it would seem. But we must not be unjust. Even today there are in this country men with a true gift of expression, and something worthy to express. Rupert Brooke was such a one and his death was a real loss.[28] But if the modern poet in general starts off with the charming principles laid down by the *Times* reviewer, it is obviously waste of time to look for beauties in his work ...

I have not yet seen any reason to change my opinion about Greece's ultimate attitude and action. I sincerely hope that I shall prove to be wrong and that your diagnosis of the position, which is undoubtedly correct as regards the *inclination* of the chief actor, will turn out equally just as a forecast of future *events*. Should Salonica be invaded by the German Armies, the temptation to the Greeks to join them will certainly be very great, but naval power may even then prove an effective check. However that may be, we are sure to witness a series of most desperate struggles on Greek soil in the near future, and it is likely to be the chief theatre of war throughout the winter.

159 Michael (Wimbledon) to John (Tralee), 28 December 1915

Many thanks for the *Iliad*, which I received on Xmas Eve, just before going away on observation post. It is a fine translation, and gives one a fresh and vivid interest in these ancient stories ...

I am not in the least surprised at what you tell me concerning the Censor's display of curiosity. Censors are always chosen, it would seem, for stupidity, and the man who peeps through your keyhole, and tells you he is doing it, requires no other qualifications for the job. But perhaps I had better not say hard things about these good people, or they might not allow my letter to reach its destination.

My leave is due to start on the 8th January, but as that day is a Saturday, I shall try to get away a day or two earlier.

I wish you all a very happy New Year.

CHAPTER SIX

The Rising and the Somme, 1916

Thanks very much for copy of *The Odyssey* received today. Since first I knew of this translation I have wished for a copy of it.[1] I love those old voyages in unknown seas, those strange adventures, those interventions of the ever-watchful gods and that fine heroism which broods over the whole, warming every thing it rests on into a beautiful life, like the noon-day sunlight. I have read Kingsley's *Heroes*[2] once more and its appeal is stronger than ever; there is something in those tales of the youth of the world that makes the heart young again, something more potent than Medea's charms.

I am sorry that I was so voiceless while you were here, but there are times when I lose utterly the power to say anything I want really to say.

Have you yet applied for that commission?

You received the *Odyssey* rather late. I ordered it in time for you to have it by the 19th. I went to a retail bookseller, and I suppose he was slow in getting it. If you like it as well as I like the *Iliad* it will indeed be a treasured book. I must say that previously the idea of reading Homer was rather repellent to me. I thought that his great reputation as a poet rested more on flowery rhetoric and what are commonly called 'heroics' than on those other qualities which make a poet beloved. I find on the contrary that he surpasses all I have read in tenderness of feeling combined with truth and dignity. Where I looked for nought but the glory of barbaric war and the bareness of a primitive time, I find a replica of the modern world, the world of all time, differing from our own only in non-essentials, while through the human tumult one has, ever and anon, glimpses of ever-dear nature, wild mountain streams and sacred groves, rich meadowlands and the sounding sea. One feels as though the soul of the World is singing, the Genius of the whole human race, with all life the burden of the song.

On further consideration, I do not think that applying for a commission would be a suitable way out of my difficulty. I believe that my insurance premiums would be largely increased if I had to go abroad, and of course my total income as a subaltern would be no greater than it is at present, as my civil pay would be reduced to practically nothing, while on the other hand I should have to keep myself & have increased expenditure generally. I think the most straightforward course is to sign on in a few weeks time, before the Act comes into operation,[3] and go to the 3rd Battalion Civil Service Rifles. From what I hear, I can rely on the training in that Battalion to break me down in quite a short time, even if I pass the doctor first.

162 John (Tralee) to Michael (Wimbledon), 30 January 1916

I share fully your feelings about Homer. Beside his *Odyssey* how incredibly tawdry and vulgar appears the vast bulk of modern literature, mean as a self-made sausage king beside the goodly Odysseus...

... What a glorious re-birth when Europe rises up newly born of blood and fire, purified of all the dross that has clung to it! What vigour and beauty, what dignity and holiness shall grace the new lives which God shall give us!...

I suppose the course you are adopting about the Commission is the wisest. Your expectation of breaking down under the training reveals a pessimistic mood. I wish the whole thing were over; some American astrologer, who foretold the war, says peace will come by June 12th – a Wilsonian no doubt, that is a Wilsonian before ... the conversion. The President however will feel annoyed at the curtailment of his time for exchange of notes preliminary to the venting of his new found ire.

163 Michael (Ewell, Surrey) to John (Tralee), 9 February 1916

Many thanks for Plutarch's *Lives*. I have long thought of having a complete copy of them. I am still jogging along in the company of Homer. Since coming here I have done scarcely any reading. Our daily programme is somewhat as follows. Get up at 10 a.m., then breakfast, go down into the village and have a game of billiards. Dinner at 1 p.m. after which we may go for a short walk, or play a game of draughts or otherwise charm away the time until 4 when we have tea. At 4.30 p.m. we go on duty, and remain on, doing an hour on guard and two hours off, until we are dismissed from headquarters which is usually about 11 p.m. but may be much earlier or much later according to circumstances. Not a very strenuous life is it?

We are going before a Medical Board on Friday to be examined re fitness for foreign service. I shall write home when I hear the result.

I have long been inclined to the opinion that life and the real world must be made the criterion of moral systems, not vice versa. The attempt to erect particular affections and the actions they inspire into general laws of conduct is bound to prove a failure ... The complexity of human relations is infinite, and can as little be compressed into a universal law of love as into a law of irreplaceable struggle. Love and hate, killing and saving, heroism and baseness, are all phenomena that despite their apparent contradictions are really inter-related, and form necessary parts of the one huge process of life...

164 Michael (Ewell) to John (Tralee), 15 February 1916

Before you have time to reply to this I shall probably be back in Wimbledon, this time in huts, where the Battalion is going on Friday. My address will then be as before, leaving out Springfield Road.

The points I try to make against the Christian ideal are not that it fails to recognise the role of evil. I say that in the first place, it sets up as a law of conduct a human feeling which cannot be forced but is always spontaneous and is therefore useless as a guide to moral action. To ask that a man shall love all his fellows equally is to ask too much . . . On the other hand I know that moral indignation is never so keen as when the affections are also engaged. As we agreed when I was at home, the experience of the war shows that injuries done to our friends seem to be the height of wickedness against God and man. But I see no hope of extending this susceptibility so as to embrace the human race. Even if it were it would not help us much, because the very same feeling causes us to think lightly of, and gloss over, the most palpable crimes committed by those to whose side we are attached.

I am convinced then that if there is a possibility of any moral standard at all, it can only rest on cold, impartial reason, the basis on which pre-Christian philosophers tried to rest it . . .

Send me the *Irish Catholic* by all means. I am sure it will be interesting.

165 Michael (Wimbledon) to John (Tralee), 12 March 1916

At last we are beginning to know our position a little more definitely. This 105th Battalion is going to be entirely disbanded in a short time. Tomorrow those who signed for foreign service at the last moment are going down to Warminster to join the 2nd Battalion, Civil Service Rifles. The remainder of the battalion, which includes unfit men, married men, and those, like me, who are appealing, will soon after transfer to the 107th Provisional Battalion, stationed near Lowestoft on the East Coast. If my appeal is heard soon, and, as I expect, it goes against me, I shall doubtless have to sign foreign and go down to Warminster.

We have, I think, seen the last of the snow now, and today is quite mild and springlike...

166 Michael (Wimbledon) to John (Tralee), 29 March 1916

...We had the worst and, I hope, the last snowstorm of the season last evening. The blizzard stopped about 11 p.m., and this morning we awoke to a beautiful clear day, with a touch of warmth in the sunshine.

167 Michael (Wimbledon) to John (Tralee), 6 April 1916

Thanks for sending the Irish papers. The financial grievance of Ireland, accentuated by the war, is, of course, one which mainly affects the pockets of the taxpayers. If they are not sufficiently alive to their own interests to insist that their representatives in Parliament shall press their claims, it is waste of breath for a minority to cry about the matter. In other countries oppressive taxation is resisted by the whole weight of the class affected. In Ireland apparently, the people who have to pay look upon those who would champion them as traitors and factionists.

Apart from this, it must be borne in mind that, if ten millions a year represents the wastage of Ireland's wealth owing to the war, it is but a small proportion of that of G[rea]t. Britain, or any other of the countries involved. It would be misleading in my opinion to look merely to the place where munition contracts are placed. Even though G[rea]t. Britain made all her munitions, and consequently kept the *money* in this country, the loss of wealth would still exist in the same enormous degree. Furthermore, the probability is that Ireland's share in financing the war, as represented by loans, is relatively very small. I think it well to mention these facts, which have no relation whatever to the higher question of Ireland's position in the war as a combatant, and the general issues of patriotism and principle involved thereby.

Fr. Kane's lectures in the *Irish Catholic* make very good reading. I should like to have them in a more permanent form.[4]

168 W.K. Moonan (Assistant Secretary, Board of Inland Revenue) to Michael (Wimbledon), 22 April 1916

I am directed by the Board to inform you that they have been pleased to promote you to a Surveyorship of the 3rd Class, at a scale of salary commencing at £200 and rising by £15 annually to £350.

I am further to inform you that under the Treasury Regulations it is provided that 'where a civil servant would in the normal course have been promoted to a higher post but for his long absence on military duty, that post should be kept open for him on his return and in the meantime he should continue to receive the former scale of salary less the prescribed deductions'.

It has also been laid down by the Treasury that on return to civil duty, such civil servant 'will enter at the salary which he would have attained if he had been placed on the scale of the new post on the day (to be certified by the Head of the Department) when, but for his departure on military service, he would have taken up his duties'.

Your promotion to a Surveyorship of the Third Class will be dealt with in accordance with the above regulations...

169 Michael (Wimbledon) to Mary (Tralee), 7 May 1916

I got your letter, and cannot understand how it is that you have not received mine. I have written three or four in the time you mention, and one to John also.[5] In case you do not get them at all, I had better tell you again how I stand at present.

I was before the Appeal Tribunal on Saturday week, and, of course, they could not grant me any exemption or extension. So there was nothing left to do except to sign the foreign service form or become a conscript. I did the former on Wednesday last, and have already been formally transferred to the 2/15 Batt[alion]. County of London Reg[imen]t (Civil Service Rifles). I leave here on next Wednesday, for the headquarters of that Battalion at Warminster. The Battalion itself is supposed to have gone to Ireland, and if that is so I hope to join them shortly.[6]

There appears to be still a chance of getting a month's leave when I go to the 2nd Batt[alio]n. At any rate, a number of men who signed and went there after the order cancelling this leave came out, have managed to get it.

I shall let you know anything further when I get to Warminster...

I hope to have better news of father when next I hear from you...

170 John (Tralee) to Michael (Wimbledon), 21–22 May 1916

It is full time for me to reply to your letter. I find it is dated over six weeks ago – 6 Ap[ril]. – but it might well be six decades ago, so many changes have occurred in the interval. The old problems have been swept rudely into the background, if not out of existence altogether; the old ways of thinking have been changed. Ireland is no longer the Ireland of six, of four, weeks ago; the political attitude of our people has radically altered; their passivity in the hands of politicians has passed, & I hope for ever; even the politicians themselves have not been immune from change, their bellies have been pricked by the bayonets of our Volunteers, and the great stove of wind retained therein has been considerably, though, of course, not permanently reduced. Perhaps you distrust these lightening [*sic*] changes; so should I had they not been purchased with the noblest blood in Ireland.

I do not know what view you take of the rebellion. Probably if you did not condemn it on other grounds you would do so on the grounds of hopelessness. And yet was the rebellion a blunder? No doubt, from a practical point of view, it was. No doubt the calculations of the leaders were falsified. It is clear that they counted on a German landing, and that when they had actually started the fighting they still believed that German aid was at hand. It was, then, a blunder and it has cost the lives of over a dozen of the best men that even Ireland has ever brought forth, and the freedom of many more. It may cost us a decade of oppression. But Pearse and McDonagh, Plunkett and McDermott are not really dead; the men who sought to destroy them only succeeded in giving them a power over the hearts and minds of men greater than ever they had before. They shall live while Ireland lives. As to the possibility of oppression it appears to me that in dealing with us, while we remain a subject people, there are two policies open to England viz: oppression and bribery. Of the two the former is the least dangerous for us. Our enemy has tried oppressing us for vastly the greater part of seven hundred and fifty years and has never attained more than a faint and fleeting semblance of success. The second method has received but scant attention from our rulers. Apart from isolated measures, like Catholic Emancipation, and the land acts, it was not, I think, seriously tried till the English Liberals came to power ten years ago. Then commenced a campaign of corruption which engaged first the representatives of the people and having conquered them, engaged in turn almost every other class of the community meeting with a success far greater than that of any other campaign undertaken against us by England. So successful was it that the Government in Aug[ust]. 1914 thought Ireland the 'one bright spot' – the one place where slaves enjoyed their slavery. That the hopes of Sir E. Grey have been frustrated we owe first of all (in point of time) to Carson and the Covenanters who re-intro-duced physical force methods into Irish politics; secondly to Eoin MacNeill, Roger Casement and to that gallant band of knightly-hearted men who have laid down life or liberty in the service of Ireland; thirdly, perhaps I should have said firstly, to John Redmond and his accomplices who have given the country a surfeit of constitutionalism and loyalty; fourthly to the mad recruiting policy of the Government, with its 'economic pressure' and to the lying pretence (as it seems to me) that the Volunteers were conducting an anti-recruiting campaign; fifthly to the talk about liberty and small nationalities, the absurd hypocrisy of which grated on the nerves of many Irishmen and which made many wonder if Ireland was not entitled to share in the 'liberties of Europe' and the 'rights of small nationalities' for which her people were expected to fight. But there is another cause deeper than all these, it is that, down through all the vicis-situdes of the ages of bondage, God has kept alive in the breasts of some, at least, of our race the soul of the Irish Nation. He has given us, from time to time, down through the generations, prophets of nationhood who have kept us from too long forgetting our Jerusalem.

The prospect is one that troubles many; but, if I interpret rightly their spirit, our Volunteers are undismayed. They are leaderless, disarmed, disorganised and yet they are united in a spirit of unchangeable fidelity to the holy cause in which so many of their comrades have suffered. As for me, I have never been so proud of Ireland, never so hopeful about her future. Come what will, I know now that she will be faithful to herself, to the high destiny for which God has preserved her. And surely God has saved her for a high destiny. You know her glorious services to God in the past, how in an age of darkness she was a light to the world; you know too her unswerving fidelity during the centuries of persecution. It is not for us to claim the credit of these things; I believe that, but for our loss of freedom and the persecutions which we have suffered, we too should have gone the way of the rest of Europe. Yes, I believe that God allowed us to be delivered into the hands of our enemies because He knew that the things we should suffer at their hands would fortify our faith and prepare us for the glorious labour of the future. Despite all that has happened, I believe that God has preserved us for this hour, that, in the reconstruction of the world, Ireland may be, once more, a light unto men that, as is my prayer, she may bear aloft a cross now in triumph, that cross which she has borne so long in agony, raising it before the eyes of all men, bringing them to do reverence unto Christ, to take up their Cross and follow Him, so that, at last the Cross may rule the world, that the Kingdom of God may come.

It is, perhaps, a far-fetched hope, and yet it is such a hope as the history of Ireland suggests. Does it not seem as if we had been kept in a state of suspended nationhood that we might be restored to full national life when the world would have most need of us? Was ever the need so great as now? But even if the time is not yet, I shall know that it is only a postponement, that some day our country will take her place amongst the free peoples of the world and as the noblest of them all. And Ireland is, even in bondage, a great nation, though hundreds of thousands of her own children dislike and despise her, and these are the basest of humankind. But, then, there are the others in whom the soul of Ireland lives, men like Pearse and McDonagh and Casement who soar above the petty Mammon-worship, the mean prudence of the world and commune with the highest heavens. It is in virtue of these men that Ireland is great and holy.

Less than twelve weeks ago I heard Pearse lecturing here. He spoke, as I should say he always did, like a Hebrew prophet, recalling men to a sense of their high duty. Even had he been alone in the good fight it would still be a grand thing to belong to the same race as he. <u>May 22.</u> It was a remark he passed on that occasion that convinced me of the imminence of an insurrection.[7]

It will be of some melancholy interest for you to know that Frank Fahy is among the sentenced Volunteers. He was sentenced to death, but the sentence was commuted to ten years penal servitude. He was a captain in the Volunteers, and was one of the officers in command of the Four Courts during the rising. A British officer, or ex-officer, who was detained at the Four Courts for some days, has paid a fine tribute to Frank Fahy and to Edward Daly, another Volunteer captain who has since been shot.[8]

You have probably seen Nathan's effort to implicate the Gaelic League in his evidence before the Hardinge Commission.[9] I don't think his statements are quite true, that is to say I don't believe the G.L., as such, was directly involved in the rebellion. But the men who made the Gaelic League were the men who made the Irish Volunteers; and the Irish revival was one phase of that revolt against English dominance of which the rebellion was the outcome. 'Not only would he have Ireland free, but he would have Ireland Gaelic.' So wrote Pearse of O'Donovan Rossa ten months ago, and so may we write of Pearse and of those who have fallen with him. Indeed, it is on this issue, more than on any other that I would judge and condemn the present parliamentary representatives of Ireland. They do not realise that Ireland to be great must be truly herself, that she must bear upon her the authentic marks of her descent from that great Ireland of the past, that she must speak the same language, that she must be cast in the same mould, and that all the things that come to her from other hands must also be shaped in that mould becoming truly part of her and entering into her living tradition. To me, political freedom is desirable mainly as the means by which this re-transformation may be accomplished; and these men, who have led Ireland for some decades past, would substitute for all this a mere semi-self-governing province.

The spirit of this indictment is that of Pearse's charge uttered last February in Tralee, and it seems to me that the words are largely his, which must have lain in the background of my mind these last months. Another point – a hopeful one – is worthy [of] note, viz: that the recent rebellion, more than any similar movement since the flight of the Earls, more even than the '48 movement, was dominated by the Gaelic spirit. It would seem that we are getting more into line with the traditions, nearer to the centre.

There is much that I would say about the immediate political prospect, but the probability that you will not read down to this point deters me. Enough to say that no probable, pacific settlement between Ireland and England can have any finality; and that, in any case Lloyd George is not the man to effect such a settlement. But, let the worst come, and even though our higher hopes be frustrate [*sic*] I still look to the day when Eoin MacNeill, the Odysseus of the Volunteers, shall take the place from which John Redmond has fallen.

Written, mostly, a week ago, I have kept this letter doubting, fearing, wondering whether it were wise to send it. But 'what matter if for Erin dear we fall?' Should I be charged with seeking to cause disaffection amongst his majesty's forces I shall be repaid by a sudden, if transitory, renown ...

P.S. What think you of the King St[reet] atrocities? How finely they would illustrate the inventions of the Bryce Commission! ... [10]

171 John (Tralee) to Michael (Warminster), 28 May 1916

Evidently, if that rumour, of which you have told mother, is true, the decision to send your battalion to the front must have come sooner than you expected. It would be well if you could get that leave before going. But we feel, and even mother, notwithstanding her fears, feels that in any case you will be safe. I have an impression that you are not the sort of person to die young, and, in addition, a curious confidence in such instincts.

I enclose an inflammatory and seditious document, which bears a German-looking signature.[11] It would seem, on this ground, to be the production of an uninterned Hun, and on other, internal evidence, to be an effort to draw a namesake of yours from his allegiance to the king and his duty as a soldier. Would it be worthwhile bringing this man's treasonable actvities to the notice of the *Daily Mail* and the Rebellion Commission?

P.S. You will probably be especially interested in that portion of the evidence produced before the Hardinge Commission which deals with Kerry.[12] County Inspector Hill stated that the Kerry Volunteers mobilised and then in consequence of some arrests got nervous and went home. This is, to say the least, misleading. The fact is that on Good Friday Austin Stack and Collins, a Post Office official, were arrested;[13] following the arrests which were effected by stratagem, the Tralee Volunteers mobilised and spent some hours parading the town armed and at times proceeding at double pace and, I believe, giving other indications that they were eager for fight. They were not interfered with in any way and dispersed late that night, presumably tired of their manoeuvres. On Easter Sunday there was a general muster at which there were present according to my reckoning from 800 to 1,000 men. This was part of a general scheme of Easter manoeuvres all over the country. The manoeuvres were cancelled at the last moment by Headquarters, but were carried out in Tralee owing to the presence of a number of country Volunteers who in some cases marched 30 or 40 miles to be present. During all Easter week the county was on the verge of an outbreak but partly [due] to the wishes of Casement which had been conveyed to the local leaders, partly to the impossibility of communication with Headquarters and to the uncertainty of what was going on in Dublin, partly to other causes, nothing happened. But no further arrests were made until May 9th (I think), after the Volunteers had delivered up their arms and when there were between one and two thousand soldiers, including artillery-men in town.

J.M.

P.S. (Still another.) If you still wish to get the *Irish Catholic* I shall send it to you. I have given up the rag; its politics always objectionable are utterly insufferable under present conditions. If I were to continue reading there is a danger that I should develop a definite homicidal tendency.[14]

As to Dr Kane's lectures I have no doubt they will be published in book [form] later on. I shall have a look out and get them for you.

This last P.S. was a happy thought; in these times it would be madness and highly dangerous to the realm to allow so much paper go waste. Had it not been for the Summer Time Act I might have spent another hour filling in the margins and the spaces between the lines. As a law abiding subject I will let you off for this time.

172 Michael (Warminster) to John (Tralee), 20 June 1916

I am writing these few lines just before we leave for France.[15]

Although we are going away to take part in the greatest adventure of the ages, and into a sphere of action totally different and alien to the past experience of all of us, it would be hard to find a trace of anything approaching excitement or even interest in anyone. The English character finds no room for an emotional outlook on even the gravest things. And sees all in a matter-of-fact light. So we go forth without rejoicing or depression, thinking chiefly of the journey and the food and the load we carry on our backs. The latter, indeed, is not unimportant. The most pressing problems of the moment are, how to get all our kit into our packs, and, when in, how to carry the colossal burden.

I hope you will excuse the shortness of this epistle, but there is so much odd work to be done that one has no time to collect one's thoughts.

You had better take charge of enclosure, in case of accidents.[16]

173 John (Tralee) to Michael ((BEF), 2 July 1916

At last you have reached France, that land to which our people have so often turned, not in vain, for aid, that France which has stood for so much in the history of Europe and the world – at one time for chivalry and romance, at another for luxurious and, more or less, incompetent despotism, again for wild revolutionary frenzy and, latterly, for mere putrescence. And yet, perhaps, one should not judge France by these things; one knows how often, how almost invariably, in nations the dregs come to the top. The state that was Louis XIV or, at later dates, Marat or Robespierre, Napoleon or Talleyrand, Clemenceau or Briand may perhaps have not been the true France, may have been, in some way, divorced from the spirit of the nation. That there was, and is, something in France which these men did not suspect and could not express, I have no doubt, though I should find it impossible to express what it is clearly. The thought of France impresses me as that of a bright light shining out from the world steadily, unflickering, through the storm of revolution and counter-revolution, bringing to my mind that wistfulness and glad melancholy which come upon the wanderer who sees, across the last mile of ocean, the flickering lights of home. It is a strange example of the association of ideas that the name of France, in certain moods, brings to my mouth a taste bitter-sweet, yet wholly pleasant and quite wholesome. You will recognize that these impressions are based more on imagination than knowledge, and I shall expect you to correct them on your return or before it when your experience shall have been more extensive.

The Lloyd George proposals have already resulted in the resignation of Lord Selborne, and the position of W. Long and Lord Lansdowne is regarded as still uncertain.[17] The scheme has aroused strong antagonism amongst the unionist members of Parliament, and no enthusiasm in any quarter. Diplomatic considerations will probably overcome the unionist opposition and it should be a simple matter to rig a convention in this country to endorse the decision of the Ulster conference. There is however a point which will probably carry weight in Ireland viz: the question of an amnesty for the political prisoners. Devlin has represented to the country that an amnesty would form one of the provisions of the settlement; the Prime Minister has denied this statement and the temptation has passed.

The trial of Sir Roger Casement has concluded, the prisoner being found guilty and sentenced to be hanged.[18] The fact that Sir F.E. Smith, the notorious ex-would-be-rebel, conducted the case for the Crown imparted a touch of irony to the proceedings. It threw an interesting sidelight on modern society to see Lord Reading – Rufus Isaacs of Marconi fame – pronounce sentence of death on the unhappy criminal.[19] Well might Casement exclaim that he had rather lie in the dock than fill the place of his right hon. accusers! History will deal kindly, even reverently, with the man, now so much abused, who brought down fire and brimstone on the society in which the Smiths and Isaacs, Redmonds, & Devlins, Carsons and Lloyd Georges live and thrive. The pity is that these men are not bound and delivered to the tender mercies of the Huns; the wrath of God would then cease to fall on Albion.

Fostered by the press, the feeling has grown on one that the critical months of the war have come. It appears to be assumed that the cannonade along the British front foreshows a big offensive. Perhaps before winter, if the war is not over, at least it may be less difficult to predict the final issue. No doubt from your closer view-point, you can see the struggle more clearly and estimate more fairly its immediate possibilities. But, I suppose, expert evidence from the front might not pass the censor.

174 Michael (BEF) to John (Tralee), 6 July 1916

I was glad to get your letters, and have also received papers. I do not think there are any others I particularly want.

I came out yesterday after several days in the trenches. It has been a mildly exciting time I need not say. We got one or two hefty bombardments, but the first nervous shock of hearing a shell come along, whizz —— and then BANG, was already allayed by one or two big fellows that had come over to the village where we were billeted a few nights before. Our life in the trenches consisting chiefly of heavy work, done night and day, except when we were in the front firing line, where we were in closest contact with the Hun. Very little sleep was obtainable, but somehow one seemed to be able to do without it, whilst the excitement of dodging shrapnel seemed to lighten the weight of our dreadful labours. In spite of the serious and tragic element in the situation, one could not help laughing at times at the grotesqueness of it all. Life, at a certain minimum, went on as usual. One ate (and groused about the coldness of the tea or the prevalence of bully), chatted, wrote, read, admired the sunset, or cursed the rain, almost forgetting about the war, or even slightly incredulous of its existence, except when the rattle of a machine-gun reminded one of the deadly work that went on increasingly.

Well, the night before the battalion was to come out I was warned of my appointment to a clerical post in which my knowledge of French will come in useful. So I am now detached from the battalion, and billeted in a once fine old chateau, now alas the worse for the wear of the war (excuse alliteration). As soon as I become proficient in my duties I expect to have plenty of work to do, but one wants that out here where the ordinary pleasures of life are almost entirely absent.[20] There are practically no inhabitants left except some of the poorer classes, whose means of livelihood, almost without exception, seems to be giving the British Army an insight into the mysteries of French wine. It is not French life at its best, in any sense. Nevertheless, one can see enough to be able to rebut the charge of decadence, so often levelled against a people that now, as often before, has shown itself virile and full of energy. The people hereabouts are no more decadent in any sense than the people in similar places at home. They have shown themselves a match for evil fortune, nor have they lost their old loyalty to their country and to religion, I feel sure.

Thank mother for cigarettes and tobacco which I received today. We are now given an issue of tobacco and cigarettes, and mother need not send any out in future.

I hardly know what books I should like. Could you send out the following two? *Honoré de Balzac* by Brunetière,[21] Nelson 1/- *Faust* Goethe, Everyman's.

175 Mary (Tralee) to Michael (BEF), 9 July 1916

It was a great relief to get your letter yesterday. It was written on the 2nd July & received here on the 8th. That is the third I got since you went to France & two mail cards.

I was in an awful state on account of the rumours that you could not write at all for this month.

Do not worry at all. I am feeling better now as I am confident we will have good news in the next week or so. Leo Casey is away & will be home this evening. I shall see him as soon as he arrives.[22]

John has written to Mr McQuade.[23] The Party will be in London on Monday & I will go on Tuesday & see what I can do. I know I will succeed with God's Holy Help. Father had a letter from Tom O'Donnell today saying he will do everything possible. Mr Flavin engaged to do the same.[24] I shall get more help in London.

J. Baily whose son has a Commission as you know will give me all particulars.[25] He told me to go to him on Monday. John is sending your papers and will write tomorrow.

Did you get parcels & papers already sent?

I wrote to you almost every day since you went out.

There was Mass on the First Friday for you & will be for the next nine First Fridays.

Pray to the Sacred Heart every day for your speedy & safe return to us.[26] I shall write to-morrow again & give you fresh news I may have. Do not be downhearted. We will have a happy meeting sooner than you expect my loving boy.

If this horrible war was over I would face anything. May God remove it soon. Father is improving…

176 Note by Major P.T. Chute (officer commanding Tralee Depot, Ballymullen, Royal Munster Fusiliers), 10 July 1916[27]

I know Mr Michael Moynahan [sic] of the Prince of Wales' Civil Service Rifles, now serving in France to be a most respectable & well educated young man. His people are well known and well connected. In civil life the bearer Mr Moynahan is a surveyor of taxes.

177 Mary (Tralee) to Michael (BEF), 18 July 1916

What a joy it was to hear of your appointment to a clerical post, on my return from London yesterday. I feel now as if I had not a care in the world. The last two years since the war started were awful for me. It was well I did not know you were in the trenches. I would have gone crazy altogether. As it was I did not stop crying since you went to France only for the days I was away. You will I am sure be sent back to office work in a few months. I was at the War Office and the Inland Revenue. I met [the] Superintendent of Taxes not Mr McQuade but the Head & he was very nice. I met also one of the chiefs Mr Crowley.[28] He wants you in Somerset House with himself. He was very kind and sympathetic.

I also met the Secretary of Mr Lloyd George. He will certainly do his part. I would give you more information but I am not so sure if my letter will go safely. He Mr McPherson told me [to] write to your O.C. & put my position before him.[29] He will then communicate with the War Office & the rest will follow. When I have made the application for your return as I mean to do this evening you can go to your O.C. I know you want to fight for your country & I do not wish you would feel otherwise, but you know well my unfortunate circumstances as I told Mr McPherson and Mr Crowley. Your Father is dying. John suffering, as he is from the spine & all my young children wholly dependent on you. If I had gone before you went to France there would not be the slightest doubt of your being brought back to the Office. You of course would not hear of my doing that & hence all this worry & fearful trouble. Goodbye now my boy & may God grant you will be safe until we meet again ...

178 John (Tralee) to Michael (BEF), 23 July 1916

Long though I have taken in answering it, I was delighted with your letter. The news it contains is excellent, and has raised mother's spirits prodigiously.

Your experiences in the trenches must have been sufficiently thrilling, though, it would seem, you were at a relatively quiet part of the line. I have made a feeble, and vain effort to imagine the sound of shell-fire. How could I succeed here in the fading light of this particularly quiet summer evening when the most awe-inspiring sound is that of a distant train, shunting, or of children playing in the town. The very birds are silent, asleep, though but now I heard a swallow, under the eave, gently chiding her young, and, again, over by Quinlan's, the jarring notes of a frightened jackdaw and a momentary snatch of song. As I sit on, all other bird sounds cease, while, to the East, there arises the rasping of a corncrake. It is hard, indeed, to think that under that same kind heaven, breathing such gentle, caressing, rose-scented air as this, men are desecrating the more than Sabbath stillness of nature with the sounds of murderous hate.

24 Jul. Would it be desecration, too, to introduce into such an atmosphere the unsavoury subject of partition? The Government, characteristically, has not yet made up its mind, rather, is not of one mind, on the Lloyd George proposals. This time, at least, I have no mind to curse this indecision, for everyday the opposition to exclusion grows stronger in all parties. Whatever chance the proposals would have had if rushed when first mooted is, I trust, gone. Whatever their fate I [have] no notion of despairing of the future, though partition is bound to cause bloodshed sooner or later if it goes through. Radical changes are impending in Irish politics. The bishops have practically thrown over Redmond, a fact which much though I distrust episcopal politics, I welcome. It is hardly an exaggeration to say that none but placehunters will now do reverence to the 'party', and there are signs that even they are ratting. An anti-partition organisation has been formed in the North and, with capable leading and a sufficiently broad programme it ought to spread over the whole country, preparing the way for the next election.

I wrote to Dent's some time after receiving your letter ordering them to send on *Faust* and Pascal's *Pensées*. I hope you have rec[eive]d. them. In giving your address I left out the Platoon, Co[mpan]y. and batt[alio]n. A letter addressed in the same way by mother has come back, so I have been afraid the books might not reach you.

Not knowing Nelson's address I have ordered that book about Balzac through Eason's. I shall send it on receipt.

179 Michael (BEF) to John (Tralee), 3 August 1916

Thanks for Pascal's *Pensées*, which is the only book I have received so far. Dent's did not have *Faust*, so I wrote for another book which I am expecting to receive from them in due course. I am reading Pascal, and am impressed by the depth and truth of his thought. He has to be read slowly, like every writer whose books are really worth reading. I have also got through a good deal of *Le Pape*, by Joseph de Maistre, a great Catholic and Conservative writer whose books I had long wished to see.[30] 'Après la guerre' I hope to get a copy, if they are still in print. I doubt if there is any English translation. This book maintained Papal infallibility years before the Vatican Council.

I do not think I should be much interested in Samuel Butler.[231] He hardly had the universality which makes a great genius.

The Irish political outlook is not very cheering. How could it be in our time, when (as, indeed, in all times) force is the only law, and sincerity and idealism can only speak with the voice of the spirit. Perhaps it is better so, for when they can speak with the voice of the sword they quickly lose their distinctive character. When the spirit tries to work in material ways it is up against a contradiction. The spirit aspires to heaven, matter grovels on the earth. Thus it is that the enterprise may be glorious, but the worker is not conscious of the glory while he is working. The statesman as a statesman making war, the soldier as a soldier fighting, are simply workers, conscious only of their task, which to them seems, must seem, just as commonplace as any other task. And all the material work, however, inspired, will shape for itself material ends. Hence to give an idealist ways and means is to shatter his ideals.

You should put the short address, which I gave to mother in my last letter, when writing in future.

If you want to form some idea of shell-fire, imagine the buzzing sound of a rapidly revolving wheel, continued for about five seconds as the shell approaches through the air, suddenly ceasing and followed by an explosion similar to that heard in the blasting of rocks. Picture this happening 200 times a minute and you have a moderate bombardment. I should say the 2nd shell is the worst, so far as the nerves are concerned. The first you ever hear, you do not know what the buzzing is, and the explosion tells you. The second time you hear the thing coming, you know, and a funny feeling creeps down your spine.

180 John (Tralee) to Michael (BEF), 9 August 1916

I am glad you admire Pascal, though he was identified with the Port-Royal quietists. Have you found the taint of heresy in him? I believe his *Lettres provinciales*[32] are a crushing attack on the Jesuits; if I remember rightly Emerson does not recommend them.

I have heard of Jos. de Maistre too. I rather envy your access to books like his, though my ignorance of French would make it useless to me. By the way, if you can get at Montalembert's *Monks of the West*, read it. I believe it is a magnificent book.[33]

It is a pity Dent's hadn't *Faust* in stock. I have just found that it is also included in Bohn's Pop[ular]Lib[rary] I shall have it sent to you. With regard to the other books you asked for – Brunetière *Balzac* – Nelson's don't appear to give their address on any of their books so, I got Eason's man to order it on getting your first letter. About a week later he asked me for further particulars as the book could not be traced. I told him all I knew, but again the result was the same. I shall write now to Nelson's, with 'London' for address, for a catalogue, and if I can make out the book I shall send it. By the way, I don't like Balzac. He seems to me a man without vision; is it not enough that, when he had settled to prosperity after a long struggle, it was said to him, as to the man in the Parable 'Fool this night –'? However you shall see for yourself. To help your judgment I will send two volumes of him; one in French, containing *La Peau de Chagrin, Le Curé de Tours* and *Colonel Chabert*; the other, a translation of *Eugenie Grandet*.[34]

Wouldn't it be a good plan, if I sent a deposit to Dent's or Bells' so that you could order books according to your requirement?

The political outlook in Ireland is, indeed, uncertain, but not wholly gloomy. At least one gleam of light pierces the darkness – John Redmond can never stand on his feet again. He has been so battered and kicked while on the ground by the Press, the Cabinet and the Bishops that he is a hope-lessly bruised and broken man. We may doubt the chivalry of some of those who have turned on him – Most Rev. Dr Walsh's letter, which you will have seen in the *Weekly Freeman*, should have been the most potent possible stimulant for Redmondism – but we cannot doubt the net result.[35] The sore of Redmondism opened by the Rising must, indeed, remain open for the present. It is best so, for all the poison that has threatened the life of Ireland will pour through it.

I suppose I agree with your remarks about use of force by idealists though there are circumstances in which it is not only justifiable but necessary. And what more potent expression can the voice of the spirit receive, in this world, than that which is given it by the mute victims of materialism dying on the scaffold or in the barrack yard? The political and religious history of the world will answer.

P.S. May I send you occasionally a paper called *Irish Opinion?* It publishes rather freely the opinions of its readers and, therefore, (this is my reason for asking permission before sending it) sometimes contains articles which, though not seditious or inflammatory – we may trust Gen. Maxwell and Lord Decies for that – are perhaps disloyal.[36]

181 Mary (Tralee) to Michael (BEF), 8 August 1916

I did not write since Friday the 4th as Father is very bad ever since. He is nothing better today. I am sure it is the great heat is the cause of the state he is in. He got up blood on Friday morning & never improved since. I shall write tomorrow again & let you know how he is getting on. I am enclosing a letter Mr O'Donnell got from Mr Crowley yesterday. I told you we made some efforts to get you back to office work in London & although I know you desire to be in France doing your part still you can imagine the state I am in with your Father so ill & you cannot blame me for doing all possible to have you home. Han did not come back yet. I am writing to her this evening to come home.

I hope you are not worrying about us. We are writing to Mr Crowley again...

182 Thomas O'Donnell MP to Maurice Moynihan, no date (c. 7 August 1916)

Dear Maurice,
This was here before me today.
TOD.

183 *John Corcoran (War Office, Whitehall) to J.P. Crowley (Somerset House),* 19 *July 1916*

After full consideration of the case of Private M.J. Moynihan, the Adjutant General's Dept have decided that they cannot agree to discharge him. He is a fully trained soldier in Category A1 and in present circumstances the Military requirement of such men is held to be paramount.

184 *Mary (Tralee) to Michael (BEF), 9 August 1916*

Father is improved to-day. If the weather got cooler he may continue to improve. I went to Great Ormond St. when in London, to find the house vacant. I know nothing of Uncle John since he wired from Dublin in May.[37] I wrote then & got no reply. Mamma is at B.[ally]Velly at present. Uncle Pat was laid up & she was sent for. Mrs Power is in Dublin consulting a doctor for the past three weeks.[38]

How are you. I shall send tobacco & cigarettes in my next parcel on Friday. Did you get the last one. I sent biscuits, chocolate and a tin of Chivers Army Provisions. I would like you to tell me what you require. Do you want socks or shirts.

Leo Casey is still in Castletownbere although he expected to be sent out before this. Jim Murphy is in the trenches for some time . . .[39]

185 *Michael (BEF) to John (Tralee), 22 August 1916*

I am afraid that book on Balzac is causing you more trouble than it is worth. It is a volume in the same series as that book by Balzac, *Le Peau de Chagrin*, which you have. I have got *The Chouans* from Dent's instead of Faust. It is a not particularly brilliant picture of revolutionary times in Brittany.[40]

As a matter of fact I am reading very little lately. In the place where I am now I have to run about a good deal all day. Besides I am no longer tempted by the library of the chateau. The house I am now in was quite empty and unfurnished when I came into it, and there is nothing sumptuous about it as an office now.

I have run across a man in another battalion out here who was a journalist before he joined the Army, and knew Uncle John slightly in London.

Any Irish papers you like to send out I shall be glad to have.

186 Michael (BEF) to John (Tralee), 18 September 1916

Thanks for the trouble you have taken over those two books, *Faust*, and the monograph on Balzac. They have both come and are welcome additions to my 'library'. As regards your suggestion about sending a deposit to Dent's, I think you had better leave it alone, as I have quite enough literature now to carry me on for an indefinite period.

I am afraid that no re-arrangements that can take place in Irish politics will lead to any fruitful result while the war lasts. Until normal conditions are restored in Great Britain, it is vain to hope for any tangible gain from fresh agitation. There is no means by which any movements of Irish opinion can reflect themselves at the polls, still less in Parliament itself. The policy of inaction adopted by the Government, which, it must be admitted, has its justification in the force of circumstances, can only be met by a corresponding policy of waiting on the part of the Irish people. They have really lost nothing by the failure of the attempt at a temporary settlement, and they should not be led by their chagrin at that failure to beat their heads against a stone wall, before peace reopens the door to free discussion and rational negotiation. And in this interim period, it must not be forgotten that even under a semi-hostile military regime, they suffer far less inconvenience than the inhabitants of belligerent countries on the Continent have to put up with from their own war-administration. Apart from the suppression of opinion, there is no restriction in Ireland of the free exercise of ordinary avocations. The citizen of Ireland is far better off than the citizen of independent Greece. And the war, which has brought desolation and ruin to so many of the richest parts of Europe, has, in Ireland, brought, if anything, increased prosperity...

187 Michael (BEF) to John (Tralee), 20 October 1916

Your letter, describing your adventures on the borderland, was very interesting. Such a severe illness as you have gone through does indeed, no doubt, give one a close view of death, and spiritually and mentally one ought to be the gainer by the experience.[41]

There is, as you say, a difference between such a glimpse of the End, gained in what I suppose we may call the tranquillity of sickness, and the stormy and lowering aspect of the thing as it is witnessed on the fields of combat. In the former case one may truly say 'nullique ea tristis imago', it comes as the last act of a satiric comedy. But here it is 'atra pallida mors'[42] stalking through the tumult of a tragedy, becoming at last familiar, and, to some degree, despised, but never friendly. It is nevertheless in many ways a great experience, although we find it hard to realise it now, we who are living out here in the midst of wars such as Scipio never knew, and cast about in a play of human forces which all man's will and rational purpose cannot master.

To the population too who have lived close to the great guns through all the unending strife, this will one day seem a gigantic and monstrous time. They have, indeed, settled down long since to a humdrum life in the midst of the noise of death, but many amongst them have had experiences the terror of which can never be effaced from their hearts...

Well, we have had today, after much rain, a typical autumn day, bright sunshine but very cold. The hastening winter seems to bear with it, like all winters, the promise of a new spring. Let us hope that before that spring passes it will have brought this troubled earth into peace and rest, at last, from all its wars.

I told mother in my last letter to address in future to the company and battalion. I should add that no mention of the brigade is allowable.

188 Michael (BEF) to Mary (Tralee), 23 October 1916

I got your letter a day or two ago, and note that you are sending on the lace collars. You need not think that there is anything serious in my wanting them. It is just to encourage Irish industry, you know. Still I shall be glad if the young person for whom they are intended is pleased with them.[43]

I send you enclosed a prayer which a pious lady here presented me with to-day. I hope Han may be sufficiently advanced in her French to understand it.

As regards winter clothing, I do not want any singlet, but you can send me a pair of pants.

Have you heard from Dunne yet? I have not had any letter lately, but no doubt he is getting on all right.[44]

I hope John is by now completely better and that everybody else at home is well.

189 Maurice Moynihan (Tralee) to Officer in Charge of Records, 11 November 1916

I duly received your report No 15.6723 of 6th inst. to the effect that my son, Pte M.J. Moynihan., no 530231, 2/15 Bn. London Regt. P.W.O.

Civil service Rifles was ill from fever at No 6 Stationary Hospital, Frévent.

Previous to that I had a communication from himself stating that he had been transferred to the 3rd Canadian Hospital Bologne [*sic*] but telling me not to write him as he did not know what his future movements should be. I have got no information since.

I shall be obliged if you will let me know his condition as soon as possible.[45]

190 *Michael (Le Havre) to John (Tralee), 21 November 1916?*

I daresay you have written long ere this, but if so I have not received your letter, nor indeed have I had any correspondence from any quarter for a month now. It is not a pleasant experience, I can tell you, to be thus isolated from home. I am expecting day by day to have my letters re-directed here but they do not come, and I am beginning to give up any hope of getting anything written during that time.

It is not easy for you to imagine nor yet for me to describe, the feelings and thoughts to which one is subject under the strain of these stupendous and terrible times, surrounded always, whether in the fighting-line or in these quiet back-waters, by the 'crested walls of war'. Looking in front one sees a vista of trials hard indeed, relentless, but which can and must be faced with firmness of soul, and endured unto the end. But looking behind, one is oppressed by those anguished longings of the heart … It is the call of that far-off little town, with all that it contains of peace and solace for the spirit, that makes one wish passionately to pierce through the intervening spaces of time, and see the end. Only by shutting one's eyes to these things, and forgetting all the dear associations and the trea-sured brightness of past times, one can face with equanimity the death which also, in its grim way, brings peace to the fighter. And yet how is it possible to forget, when their very remoteness only makes them nearer and more vivid. One can only hope, and trusting to the kindly indulgence of fate…

191 *Michael (Le Havre) to John (Tralee), 25 November 1916*

My correspondence is getting down here gradually. There must be a good deal still in arrears, however. The latest I have received is your letter written to the Detail Camp, posted on the 17 Nov. That is prompt work, is it not?

I am glad to get John Power's address, and shall most certainly write to him without delay. I remember hearing of his ordination a long time ago, but was quite ignorant of his whereabouts. It is about seven years now since I saw him, and I shall be very pleased to get into touch with him again.[46]

I am not in need of anything in the way of literature at present, excepting, of course, papers. I can get all the books I want in the town. There are, however, two dictionaries which I should like to have, if you could possibly procure them. They are Jäschke's *Conversational Dictionary*, English–French English–German. They are 2s/6d each, and the publishers are W. Lockwood & Co, 75 Charing Cross Rd W.C., assuming the books are still in print.

I left a number of books behind me in the place where I was clerk to Town Major, in the hope of being able to recover them after the war.

At present I am reading Balzac's *César Birotteau*. Superficially, the most striking thing I notice about it is the extraordinary similarity of plot to that of Wells's *Tono Bungay*. The hero, or protagonist, is a perfumer instead of a chemist, but, like Ponderevo, he makes his tidy *bourgeois* fortune by the sale of proprietary articles, which are 'pushed' in the most approved modern style. Not content, he launches out into the field of speculation, taking the land as his arena instead of the Stock Exchange. He falls into the hands of financial sharks, and is ruined. The story, like Wells', ends with his death. There can be no doubt about Balzac's skill in giving a fascinating and lifelike picture of the life and manners of his contemporaries. There is little of the sublime about his work, nor is there anything of the quality called humour. But on the other hand there is no exaggeration either in the drawing of the characters or in the action, if this book may be taken as representative. It is just a slice of life, a tragi-comedy such as has been enacted in the modern world thousands of times. In this respect his admirers may justly claim Balzac as a pioneer of the novel as it is understood today.

192 Michael (Le Havre) to John (Tralee), 29 November 1916

Yours of 25 November, containing the news of the death of Larry Quinlan, came as an unexpressible shock and sorrow.[47] For he was the sort of man whose death comes as a personal grief to all who knew him, a man who combined high spirits and an outward carelessness with the deepest sincerity in friendship, and trueheartedness rare in a man, a type of that 'jovialité française, grave et légère tout à la fois',[48] which is Irish no less than French. Give my humble and heartfelt condolences to his family in their irreparable loss.

I am afraid the letter which I sent you a week or so back was one which I ought not to have written. It represents a mood which is not new or infrequent and certainly gives a true aspect of the catastrophic convulsions of the time, as seen by one who is taking part in them, yet it is only one of several aspects. There are times when I feel inclined to laugh at it all, and with an overweening and monstrous egotism, ask what grotesque trick of fate it is which has made me the sport of these vast animate but unintelligent forces. I think, how can these material storms reach or ruffle the spirit, which is occupied with its own and proper business. In such moods the whole drama recedes like some legendary war, fought over again by fancy in the darkness and solitude of the great hills, a visionary cycle, with its Achilles, sacker of cities, or Cuchulain, the slayer of men, or Siegfried with his old German sword. So unreal does it seem, and impossible, after thousands of years of religion and civilisation and culture, that this thing should happen in the 'perfect flower of human time'.

Perhaps this mood is less justified, for what illusions should we have left about the peace that preceded the war, and will doubtless follow it? It was a peace in which all the elements of human discord were present, except the spilling of blood, a peace equally destructive of the soul, and poor in charity. A peace so strong in its evil that it still lives in all the warring lands. In other words the peace of commerce, of finance, of profit-seeking of every kind. Well these things are all necessary in their way, and the world has got to be lived through and not reformed, and perhaps for all who could swim with the tide those times were better than the present. But it is well to remember that famous peace meant misery and disaster for as many as does the present war. This is not socialism or any -ism, but merely commonplace fact with no suggestion or hope of any remedy . . .

193 Michael (Le Havre) to John (Tralee), 8 December 1916

I got your letter of 3rd inst a day or so back. Thanks for sending those dictionaries so promptly. You need not send that French–German one you have. You may find it handy at home, and in any case my carrying capacity as regards books is very limited.

I do not know that you are altogether fair to Balzac in criticising his *Eugenie Grandet*. I have not read the book, but accepting what you say regarding the principal figures, you surely will admit that there are persons whose character is not developed or ennobled by suffering. In some cases it is hardened, in others it is undermined and breaks down. Others there are again who after trouble remain much as they were before, while those who are really purified by it are a minority. It all depends on the individual nature. And I have no doubt that in Balzac's wide stage you will find some of every kind. Indeed I think if you read *César Birotteau* itself you will change your opinion on this point.

Personally I go to Balzac with the assurance that I shall find depicted by him the best, the staunchest the most vital and the most healthy side of French life, intermingled it is true, as it should be, with the other sides, but always retaining its superiority and its interest. It is free from the Realism that paints everything black, and from the Romanticism 'couleur de rose'. In a sense, one might call his work an apology for life. And it is a convincing one, which leaves one more satisfied with the world, as well as more appreciative of the unshakeable foundations of true virtue in man.

I am shortly going to start his *Médecin de Campagne* which appears to be less a novel than a series of dissertations on religious and political questions.

By the way, please refresh me with your views on the Fall of Asquith and the Fall of Bucharest.[49]

194 John (Tralee) to Michael (Le Havre), 14 December 1916

I have received your letter of 8th inst.

I notice you have answered some of my questions in your last letter to mother. The replies are not such as we had hoped for, but we are confident that all will be well with you...

It may be that I am unfair to Balzac; certainly one novel scarcely affords a sufficient basis for criticism of his entire attitude towards life. I don't object to *Eugenie Grandet* on the ground that suffering never does affect men and women in real life as it affects Eugenie and her mother. The most casual observation will show us that it may have a narrowing effect. But I think that Balzac exaggerates that effect; and, in *Eugenie Grandet*, his men and women lack the complexity of mind and diversity of mood which seem to characterise humanity...

In Mr Asquith's fate one welcomes the downfall of a particularly shifty politician, while sympathising with the humiliation of a very weak man. The effect of the change on matters relating to the war, it would be difficult to forecast. It may bring nearer an effort – whether prudent or otherwise – to force a decision in the war, and an attempt – of whose madness there could be no doubt – to enforce conscription in Ireland. On the other hand, whether it be significant or not, it is, at least, surprising that ministerial reconstruction in the three chief Entente countries should immediately precede the German offer to discuss peace. Someone has suggested to me that the Germans are afraid of Lloyd George. Two other possibilities suggest themselves to me viz (1) that it is a move to embarrass the new ministries committed to the more vigorous prosecution of the war, and to increase the growing strength of the peace parties in the Entente countries; (2) that it is a serious offer, and that the ministerial changes in England, France and Russia, if at all connected with it, were a preparatory measure, whether by way of offering stronger resistance to 'German Peace', or of removing men committed to definite peace terms now recognised as impracticable. In short the only certain thing is that the Entente Governments can't afford to give a non-possumus reply...

195 Michael (Le Havre) to John (Tralee), 14 December 1916

Please note change of address above. I received today the three books from Burns & Oates. It is very good of you to send them. I only hope I shall have time to read Canon Sheehan's work before I rejoin the first battalion. I have so many books now that I don't like to part with that it will be a difficult job to pack them when the time for moving comes. A certain amount of scrapping will be inevitable.

I have started reading a book by Prof. Holland Rose on the Development of the European Nations, 1870–1914.[50] It is well worth studying, as bringing clearly before one's eyes the historic ambitions of the European states, and the workings of policy and war. The logical sequence which has brought the present two groups of hostile powers into being enables one to see the true bearings of the struggle and therefore incidentally to weigh the prospects of peace. Personally the impression I get is that there is nothing in the actual situation to warrant the expectation of an early end to the war, despite the German overtures, and that until a crushing decision is obtained, or exhaustion steps in, the warring nations can come to no agreement regarding the violently opposite interests which are urging them on. It is not a squabble over nothing, which might be settled by a calming of tempers and a re-born spirit of goodwill. Whether the objections of statesmen are really of vital importance to their people's lives and prosperity is indeed a question; but at any rate these objectives are similar to those which have given birth to war in all ages.

196 Maurice Moynihan (Tralee) to Thomas O'Donnell MP, 19 December 1916

My Dear Tom,
I have a letter this morning from my son Michael who is now at Le Havre after recovering from fever. He has no idea of his future movements, but says there is a possibility of his being sent back to England. In that event it would be as well to see Mr Crowley of the Inland Revenue but Michael owing to his proficiency in languages, thinks his services would be made available in the Intelligence Corps if the War Minister could be approached. He gives the following references: Lieut. Tyler of the 2/18th London Regt. and Capt. David-Devis late of 2/13th London Regt. under both of whom he served as Town Mayor's clerk.

If anything could be done in this direction it would be best to do it while he is still at Le Havre...I hope this letter will overtake you in London, and thanking you for all the trouble you have taken in the past and in connection with this and other matters.
I am, My Dear Tom
Yours sincerely
Maurice Moynihan

197 Michael (Le Havre) to John (Tralee), 19 December 1916

I have now had time to look through the books you sent. I have read *The Hound of Heaven*, which is a short poem, and have nearly finished *Triumph of Failure*.[51] I must say it would be difficult to choose three books more linked together in community of theme and purpose. One might say that St Francis' book is the science, Canon Sheehan's the history, and Thompson's the poetry of the same subject,' namely the struggle between the higher and lower elements in man, culminating in the triumph of the former with the re-discovery of the Christian religion. It would be difficult to resist the emotional appeal of these books, and the first and the last leave no more to be said, though, alas, much to be done. In Father Sheehan's book, however, there is much that I find unsatisfying, I cannot help saying. His conception of the very minor value of pagan and lay culture does not appeal to me. I see much more in the art and letters of ancient Greece, and eighteenth century Germany, than a mere hollow sepulchre, covered on the outside with pretty flowers which may without sin be plucked to deck a convent refectory. It seems to me that all beauty in thought and form has a certain divinity, and an inherent depth of meaning.

His conception of a religious reformer in the modern world is hardly happy. It invites comparison with the realities of our time which are not to the advantage of the great organisation of the Church. It forces one to doubt the possibility of a moral stimulus in any institution, as such, and to wonder what would happen if the Church gave up being a political state, swayed by diplomacy, and faced the world as an uncompromising upholder of Christ's teaching and of nothing else on earth. I fear that day will never come, and the thought fills me with doubt. Today no Henry goes to Canossa to the feet of Hildebrand. Hildebrand instead goes to Henry, and frames his actions, or inactions, to suit Henry's imperious will. And there are so many Henrys and they all want to be pleased. The result is that there is no spiritual or moral unity in the church, and no moral authority in its ministry. It has compromised with the world in a thousand ways. Were it not better far if all the ambassadors at the Vatican were dismissed, and all the Governments in the world made hostile, even though the Church as a consequence were hunted and persecuted all over the earth...

198 Michael (Le Havre) to John (Tralee), 23 December 1916

...The novelist who depicts the life of man in all its variety, and the wondrous complexity of human society, satisfies an artistic need, and we can ask nothing more of him. To perform this task he must have that sense of proportion which you require. To draw the pictures of a dozen social *milieux*, and to give each its own proper place and importance, as Balzac has done, requires more than the qualities of the photographer.

I have now finished *Triumph through Failure* [*sic*], and have found it, especially in its closing chapters, a very beautiful book. As I wrote to you in my last letter, the introduction of an imaginary Revivalist crusade is not a *motif* which appeals to me. It is too remote from the real world, apart from its suggestion of hawking sacred things in the market-place, and exposing them to the mockery of the multitude. But the appeal of religion to the individual soul, which is the closing note of the book, must touch a responsive chord in the deepest impulses of man. And the eloquent expression of love and reverence for the Church must fill us with pride.

The Hound of Heaven is a most beautiful poem which, judging by the quotation, must have been often in the mind of Canon Sheehan when he wrote.

199 John (Tralee) to Michael (Le Havre), 24–25 December 1916[52]

A little while ago, on returning from a walk on our beloved hills, I got your letter. Curiously enough, the question you raise – that of the relation between the Church and secular powers – had entered into my thoughts while walking … The Church must so far compromise with the world as to accommodate herself to the ever-changing conditions in which she has to pursue her mission … I don't know what was in your mind when you wrote, but I presume you were thinking of the Pope's failure to condemn acts of injustice and outrages in the war. Well, the war is an outcome – like most wars – of materialism and irreligion and, whatever may be said of the incidents by which it was precipitated, or of the methods of conducting it, it is impossible to say on which side the real root evil exists in the greater degree. So the Church, when one group cries out for the condemnation of the other simply writhes on the ground and when appealed to again , says, with her Founder, 'Let him that is without sin among you cast the first stone'. Meanwhile she does her utmost to mitigate the evils of the war and to bring back peace to the world…

You little thought when you wrote those, perhaps, unpremeditated words what a dread vengeance you were calling down upon your head. Lest I should never end I spare you any opinion of Canon Sheehan's attitude towards Greek and German culture. Of his book, I shall only say that I should like to hear what you think of it *as a novel*. For the rest, I reserve some remarks of a personal nature and, perhaps, some of a political for a more favourable condition. And so … I send forth this thing, rambling, ill-connected, inorganic – which, meaning to be a letter has become a pamphlet or booklet, earnestly hoping that you won't be charged excess postage thereon.

200 Michael (Le Havre) to John (Tralee), 30 December 1916

…I repudiate as much as you do the hypocrisy of those who though themselves professed unbelievers or heretics, yet have the presumption to call on the Church to 'speak out' and exercise a moral authority to which yet, according to their tenets, it has no claim. Nothing could be more abhorrent to me than the idea that the Church should be the vehicle of a diplomatic victory for the apostles of a self-interested pseudo-morality.

When I wrote I had in mind something more than merely individual incidents of the time. Distressing though some of these may be, they possess no assignable importance relatively to the cataclysm itself. It was the attitude of the Church towards the latter that I felt inclined to question. I will not enter now a statement of the nature of these questionings. The attitude of the Church towards war in general, and indeed the attitude of the universal human conscience towards war is, I cannot help seeing, too complex a problem to be discussed, much less defined, in the brief pages of a letter. Therefore you were right in calling my few words hasty. Blinded as we are now by the magnitude of the struggle, it is difficult for us to realise that there [is] really nothing in the moral order at stake or in jeopardy in this war any more than in the smallest tribal contest. It does not mean the end of either vice or virtue, truth or falsehood, religion or scepticism. Our civilisation itself will, at its close, no matter how long it rages, be much as it was before; certainly not dimmed in any degree. Though we may think so, we are not really at the close of an epoch, except in the political sphere. For these reasons alone, to ask the Church to condemn the whole proceeding, root and branch, would be as irrational as, in your instances, to anathematise any particular crimes. Even more so, perhaps, for while the morality of a single action may be clearly definable, that of the war as a whole, is, as I said, open to argument. Only human weakness prevents us from seeing it in its character of a splendid, though terrible event, as in an earthquake, or the crash of worlds in space. And for my part, however little I appreciate it now, or shall in the near future, I shall, if I come out of it whole, look back upon this as a glorious and an epic time, and congratulate myself that I have lived to see it, and take part in it. I hasten to admit that this is not how one feels amid the screaming of shells, and the mud of the trenches, and the sights and sounds of death. But what is horror in the present becomes magic to the memory. And memory is, perhaps, the higher arbiter in such a case.

The thing that arouses such favourable emotions cannot, therefore, be altogether evil, and the individual man who takes part in it is hardly a criminal or an evil doer. The mainsprings of policy which direct it, however, give rise to considerations of a different order, and without going into the matter at length now, I should like to express my conviction that the attitude of the Church to them is only defensible by the frank adoption of the Machiavellian thesis of the distinction between public and private morality. What the ecclesiastical attitude to that doctrine is, I do not know, perhaps you can enlighten me. Anyhow it is an ethical point of no little importance, and cannot have escaped the attention of moral theologians.

I think I, too, had better avoid any further topics at present, having to consider both your patience and that of the censor as well.

CHAPTER SEVEN

Officer Training and the King's Liverpool Regiment, 1917–18

201 Michael (BEF) to John (Tralee), 11 January 1917

Thanks for papers which are coming pretty regularly. We are now in a better position to get recent English papers, so you need not in future include these.

The war position at the moment is very involved & every day seems to provide a fresh surprise. The general attitude all over the world seems to be one of expectancy & this will tend to paralyse, in the case of Germany, any great offensive which she may have intended to open on the west with the possibility of general negotiations being opened, her leaders are not likely to risk the enormous fresh sacrifices which such a move would involve, & consequently I rather anticipate a period of quiescence.

Meanwhile so far as I personally am concerned I can hardly complain of the time we are having. With a decent, comfortable, billet, in easy reach of civilised life, excellent rations, & pleasant company, there is little ground for depression. When I consider that the public at home are hardly able to obtain meat for their Sunday dinner, I think that we, with porridge & bacon & eggs for breakfast every morning, a 4 course lunch & a four course dinner, are almost having the best of the bargain.

I am hoping to have better news of father.

I should be glad if you would include such papers as *Public Opinion* & the *New Age* in papers now & then.

Fr. Caulfield[1] is gone up to the trenches for a walk this morning. It will be his first time in the line, & I am anxiously waiting to know what he thinks of it. Tonight we are all three going back to a village for dinner. Bon, Hein?

How has the stoppage of butter affected you? I presume that Shanahan's will find a ready market in Dublin for what they can no longer send out of the country.

202 John (Tralee) to Michael (BEF), 12 January 1917

. . . If you specified what the Pope ought to have done with regard to the war, I might be able [to] offer some defence of his actions. With regard to particular offences and acts of barbarity, I think the Pope has always protested. If I don't mistake he has condemned the invasion of Belgium, the Russian outrages in Galicia, the submarine and Zeppelin outrages etc. In an allocution delivered on Dec. 4, the Pope said: 'In the general convulsion now prevailing we behold in one place sacred persons and things maltreated, even those of high dignity, though both are inviolable by divine right and the laws of nations; and, in other places, numberless citizens dragged away from their own fireside, followed by weeping mothers wives and children; elsewhere, unfortified cities and undefended populations made the object of attack, especially by aerial incursions; everywhere, both on land and sea, such crimes are committed as fill the soul with horror and pain.'

This is, of course, in addition to diplomatic action. I may say that I have read of many cases in which Belgians or Frenchmen, condemned to death by the Germans for espionage and such offences were saved by Papal intervention; while I have heard of only one case, that of Roger Casement in which the Pope intervened on behalf of a man condemned by the Entente Governments, and then the appeal was refused. Nor was it the Germans [who] refused the appeal for a Christmas truce in 1914. These little incidents show that the people who are most anxious for papal condemnation of Germany are most impatient of any Papal interference with themselves, and have apparently done their best to damage that influence they want to use on their behalf.

So all the peace talk threatens to come to nothing. Germany's attitude resembles very much that of a card-player who having got on well in the first hours of play, is anxious to draw out before the luck turns against him. It is hard yet to estimate the effect, or even the motive, of these tactics; but, I imagine, the Russian avowal of lust of conquest is playing Germany's game. On the other hand, the revived reports about economic distress in the Central Empires, and of dissension between them, may have some substantial basis of truth. We may not, after all, be so far from peace.

I am more optimistic than you about the conditions after the war. There may, indeed, be no historical justification for my optimism: the last great war seems to have left things little better than they were before; but somehow I believe it will be different now. Some years ago, the late Fr. Benson wrote a novel, called *The Dawn of All²* in which he forecasted what Europe might be like in sixty years or so if the Church-ward tendencies of our time were to conquer, England and France are Catholic monarchies, the Pope is universal arbiter, Germany alone is a hotbed of socialism, the Emperor (for if I remember well the dignity of the Mediaeval Empire is revived in his person) is a sceptic. In the book, which was written some years before the war, there is a reference to the 'European war of 1914', which left France bereft of some territory, but with the monarchy restored, and which was the starting point of all the great changes. Ireland, I must add, is represented as a sort of monastic enclosure. Save, perhaps, for the last point, it is for such things that I hope.

203 Mary (Tralee) to Michael (BEF), 23 January 1917

It is time for me to write again to you. I am expecting a letter from you. I am glad you got the parcels. I hope you have received the one posted on the 20th. Have you anything new. It would be splendid if you got home if even for only a short time. Denis Baily was at home last week & had only two days.[3] It is said here that all the fellows will get leave in their turns. All here are well. The weather is awful. There is a heavy frost for the past fortnight. I hope it is finer with you. I shall send Treasury notes tomorrow. With love from all and your loving Mother.

204 Michael (1/15 Battalion, London Regiment, 15 Camp, 8 I.B.D.) to John (Tralee), 24 January 1917

...I saw the General the other day, so have advanced another step towards my commission. It will take some weeks still probably before the papers go through. In the meantime, I shall have to go up the line and join the battalion while I am waiting. So in a few more days I shall probably have a new address to give you. Of course any letters sent here will be forwarded all right.[4]

The weather is intensely cold here at present.

205 John (Tralee) to Michael (BEF), 22 January 1917

I got your letter this morning.

I must apologise for my recent letters, and my ever-recurring preachiness. It is only an outcome of that pharisaism which has always characterised me. I believe, indeed, the things I said but, as my vain pre-occupation with style, when writing of them, sufficiently proves, I fear I hold these truths but lightly. And even were it not so, since they are mere intellectual convictions whether they arise logically from religious belief or not I have no right to press them so eagerly.

Catholicism surely is wide enough for all men and no one man can grasp all its significance, nor feel all its beauty, nor understand all the implications of its truths. If you think that I have tried to reduce an universal faith to the limits of a narrow, personal or sectarian creed, you are perhaps right, and I am sorry. In truth, my life for the past fourteen months has given me no right to pose as a teacher. At the beginning of that period, I found myself suddenly, contrary to all my expectations, and not as the result of any reasoning process, restored to Faith. Then for a time, though in a very incomplete way, Faith coloured my life and thoughts and was the motive of my actions ... Before I could never believe it possible for me to feel really convinced of the truth of Catholic dogmas, and, whenever I contemplated the possibility of submitting to the Church, I always thought of it as an act of the will, an act of self-compulsion, a locking-up of my infidelities in a secret chamber of my mind, and leaving them there as a skeleton in the closet, always threatening my security and peace; yet, when the change came, there was nothing of that kind in it; there was no self-compulsion only a glad yielding to an almost irresistible force, no locking-up of infidelity but a dissolution in the tide of Faith.

That is what happened to me, and you will see how unexpected, unmer-ited and wonderful it was. Yet that state lasted less than five months: the events of Easter week marked its end. At that time my thoughts were turned almost entirely to politics, and bitterness ousted charity from my heart. And in the nine months since then I have never recovered what then I lost, though, happily, thank God, I have never been seriously tempted to infidelity. It is some consolation to learn that some especial grace and joy come to confirm revised Faith or Love and it then withdraws leaving men to face life and prove their sincerity. But, though the memory of those first months remains to me as proof of the truth and gracious power of Catholic Faith, there comes at times a feeling that I am but toying with holy things, that my assertion of faith in God is little but a mockery.

I am writing this ev[enin]g. to Burns & Oates to send you a little book, an appreciation of which I read in last week's *Irish Catholic*.[5] I hope it will not be an unwelcome addition to your luggage; though I almost changed my mind about it when I learned that you were to be on the move again.

Wishing you – if it seems not ironical – a very happy birthday.

206 Mary (Tralee) to Michael (BEF), 4 February 1917

I wrote to you on Friday the 2nd but forgot to put your number in the address. I sent a parcel last evening containing biscuits, tobacco, & sweets. I hope you will get it alright. How are you. I am anxiously looking out for a letter. I was very much disappointed at not having one this morning. Did you get the parcel sent on the 27th & the Treasury notes I sent in a registered letter. Do write soon to me. I hope you will be able to get leave before long. James Murphy got another month. He is at home since the 1st of October. Leo Casey arrived home in time for his father's funeral. It was lucky, for the girls were so lonely. Oh Michael I am longing to see you ... May God grant you will be here soon. All are well here except Father. He is only middling. The weather is still very severe. I hope it is not so bad with you...

I told you in my last letter it was only the day before Feb. 1st, I got a letter written to you on the 20th October. I also got back the first letter I wrote to you after hearing you are laid up in hospital in Boulogne.

207 Mary (Tralee) to Michael (BEF), 8 February 1917

Your two letters to John & me gave me great pain. You must be suffering terribly but have courage and patience & God will bring you home safe & sound to us. There will be Mass tomorrow morning at the Dominicans for you & two Masses at the Parish. I know the Sacred Heart of Jesus will listen to me & send you home safe.

Pray to the Sacred Heart yourself & place yourself under his Holy protection. Did you get the parcels sent on the 27th & another on your birthday. I also sent out Treasury notes on the 27th. I am sending you another parcel tomorrow. Do not be a bit despondent. You will be at home before long & perhaps to stay. It is terrible to think of us here comfortable, if not happy, & you as you are. We will with the help of the Sacred Heart of Jesus be together soon & not to part again. What about Commission have you heard anything. Goodbye Goodbye my boy with love from all & your own loving Mother.

208 Michael (BEF) to John (Tralee), 15 February 1917

It was only today that I received your letter written on the 28th Jan., along with two others from home of about the same date. The book you ordered has not yet come. I spent my birthday, by the way, in marching into the front line trenches, and immediately taking up post as sentry to look over the parapet.

I too, like you, have been more perplexed by the problems of politics and war, as they affect religious faith. I sometimes feel that either the moral dictates of religion are impossible, or else the wickedness and uncharity of man is inexcusable. Either conclusion is upsetting to the soul striving to love good and find it in the world, and see God in the world. Yet the doubts and trouble of the intellect are always combated by the aesthetics or moral impulses of the emotions, which find such ineffable beauty in the teachings and traditions and ritual of the Church. And no amount of scepticism could shake me in my conception of the religious life, combined with humanistic culture, as the highest ideal of earthly existence. At the very least, I could hope for happiness in attending the Catholic service and keeping Catholic practice. The body is weak and easily tempted, we know, yet now at any rate it seems to me that I could ask for no greater pleasure when I get home again than to go to Benediction in the little church of our childhood, and live in the freedom and spaciousness of Catholic society. That is one of the strongest aspirations which call me home, and I only hope that if this grace is granted to me I shall not turn my back on it.

Thanks for papers dated 8 Feb. received today (16th). Roscommon election result very interesting.[6]

209 Michael (B Company, 13 Officer Cadet Brigade, Newmarket) to John (Tralee),
21 April 1917

It is quite strange to be in a place like this after three years of the ordinary regimental life. Of course in some disciplinary points it is still the same. For example one has to fold blankets in a regulation manner quite different from the various ways one has learnt before; books must be in a particular spot on the shelves, with the edges in a straight line; a large part of our precious time has to be given to cleaning equipment and rifles &c. But in other respects it is more like school life than army life. The business of the officers and N.C.O.s here is simply to impart knowledge, as best they can. They are not perfect at their job indeed, very far from it. Most, if not all, are here simply because having been wounded at the front they are unfit for further service. Some are veterans of Mons and the Marne. The captain of B Co[mpan]y, for example, went out with the Lincolns in the original expeditionary force, was wounded in a fortnight, and has never smelt powder since, scarcely the ideal way of selecting teachers, and the methods in vogue betray this hand of the amateur. A lot of time is given to lectures, and rightly so. But unfortunately the lectures are seldom anything more than an unskilful rehash of the text-books, and it is largely waste of time taking them down. Then they are as slow in getting things going as a cumbrous engine in starting. After a fortnight we have scarcely touched the fringe of any of the subjects we have to learn. It is not surprising in consequence that they have a large number of failures at the exams.

I was of course rather glad that as a result of the recent British advance, the villages in which I worked are now well out of the danger zone, although I imagine they must have got it pretty hot at the time of the attack.

210 Michael (Newmarket) to John (Tralee), 11 May 1917

I need hardly say that I was very pleased with the result of the S[outh]. Longford election.[7] Coming after the Bishops' manifesto it has made a profound impression on English opinion, as represented by the Press. The Liberals especially seem very angry. I think the two events, at any rate, spell the doom of any kind of patchwork scheme which the Government may have had in view. I hope the advantage so gained will be followed up and that no stone will be left unturned to eradicate what remains of Redmondite influence in the country.

What between the U-boats and the Russian crisis it is hard for people in this country to feel very optimistic just now. Events in Russia are still so confused that it is difficult to imagine what the ultimate outcome will be. It will take some time yet before the various parties and shades of opinion find their natural level, but it seems certain that Miliukoff[8] is the advocate of a lost cause, and the issue lies between a 'war for democracy' and out and out pacificism.

211 Extract from Maurice Moynihan, 'Reflections on Longford', in the Kerry Sentinel, *19 May 1917*

...It is impossible that the Party of which Mr Redmond is the titular leader can find any crumb of comfort in the result of the South Longford election. They had various excuses to offer for their defeat in Roscommon

... In Longford, however, nothing was left in doubt ... The Party regarded South Longford as one of the safest constituencies in Ireland ... That they were beaten under these circumstances is a sure indicator of what will befall them in at least four-fifths of the constituencies which they misrepresent...

The minor planks of the Sinn Fein platform must be left in the background for the time being, and all efforts concentrated on a repudiation of England's claim to make laws morally binding on this country. So long as Ireland sends representatives to the British Parliament so long will the Irish question be treated as one of domestic politics ... By abstention from Westminster the fact is brought home at once to other countries that Ireland is a separate and distinct Nationality and that she aspires to have her claims allowed by her sister nations of the world. Sinn Feiners are not out to smash the Redmondite Parliamentary Party merely: they are determined to smash Parliamentism [*sic*] as a National policy .. . Sending Irish Nationalists to the British Parliament is placing them in the way of temptation, and it is A HISTORICAL FACT that no Irish Party since the Union withstood the temptation or escaped the process of disintegration...

The Irish Party in the British Parliament may be compared to an army attacking a hostile fortress. If the officers of that army are accustomed to enter the beleaguered stronghold to breakfast and dine with the garrison, and to discuss their plans over the coffee and rolls and the wine and walnuts, they can hardly be expected to retain an adequate warlike spirit for hurling explosive bombs against the enemy whose hospitality they have been enjoying...

Let them [in the Irish Party] ask themselves the question, 'Are we inferior to the Belgians ... Serbs, Roumanians [*sic*], or Montenegrins...?' The war which is devastating Europe is ostensibly waged on behalf of small Nationalities ... My own impression is that the age of monarchies is rapidly passing into history and that after another generation a reigning king will be a rare curiosity. The United States did not join in this war for the purpose of re-establishing on a firmer base the tottering thrones and effete monarchies of Europe ... Then there is the great Republic of France, and what will, in all probability, be the still greater Republic of Russia, both of which will throw their preponderating influence into the scale with America for the discontinuation of the monarchical form of government in Europe. So it looks as if the abolition of kingships would be made a *sine qua non* at the Peace Conference which will assemble after the war. Ireland will, therefore, have no need to look up ancient lineages...

212 Michael (Newmarket) to John (Tralee), 17 June 1917

The release of the prisoners has come with startling suddenness after the previous adverse change in their treatment. It will have a profound influence on impending events in Irish politics, though hardly in the sense which the Government anticipate. The Sinn Fein movement is bound to receive a tremendous impetus from the fact that its most potent living advocates are again at liberty to use their eloquence and influence on its behalf. Their first utterances in public will be awaited with the most intense interest, as on them depend[s] the fate of the coming Convention. It is safe to say that unless that Convention has their support or toleration it is fore-doomed to failure. I wonder if the Government have any realisation of this. Probably, with their usual total misunderstanding of Irish political tendencies, they have not. I have never yet met any Englishman capable of grasping the point of view of any country but his own. This national failing will always prove the greatest obstacle to any of even the most well-meant endeavours to settle the Irish question.

Thanks for the papers, which I got this morning. I shall be glad to get them fairly frequently in future.

The heat is terrific here at present. One is in a state of perspiration all day even when sitting in the huts. Fortunately there are swimming baths not far away, which are very popular on Wednesdays and week-ends.

There is another exam. on Wednesday next, and probably one more the following week.

213 Michael (Newmarket) to Mary (Tralee), 19 June 1917

I only got your letter of 15th June this morning. I am very sorry to hear that Sister Bernardine is dead.

I suppose Maurice's exam is over by now. I hope he has done well right through.

We are having another one tomorrow. It may be the last before the final. I hope so, as we are pretty sick of them.

Have you heard anything of Uncle John since?

Have Austin Stack and F. Fahy arrived home yet? No doubt a great reception awaits them when they do.[9]

214 Michael (Newmarket) to John (Tralee), 7 July 1917

So the date for the Convention is fixed at last.[10] It is still being boomed by the Press here, and great expectations are founded on it. This, of course, is part of the obvious game of throwing dust in the eyes of the world. The onus of settlement is now ostensibly thrown on the Irish *people*, and the responsibility of failure rests on them and them alone. Such is the theme. Has there ever been such a travesty of the idea of representative institutions? A convention, heavily weighted and rigged from top to bottom, is to meet behind closed doors to, at the best, debate and register a decision which will have no moral or political force, and in all probability will only be the prelude to new and more embittered controversy. And this council of political hangers-on is represented as the authentic voice of Ireland. The clumsy attempt to deceive the public opinion of the whole world must fail, and its authors stand exposed as tricksters of a very low order, who [have] not even yet learned their trade properly, in spite of assiduous practice.

The vast underhand influences which are at work on behalf of the same bluff in Petrograd have not yet borne the fruits of success. The revolutionary masses in Russia, visionaries though they be in many respects, are not likely to be taken in by smooth phrases and insincere formulae. Their aims are clear and definite enough and if they show the necessary persistance they will even yet administer a rude shock to the intriguing diplomatists. It is an intensely interesting drama, this, even though for us it is being played chiefly behind the scenes. The spectacle is that of the first contact of crude but straightforward democracy with old-fashioned statecraft and political cunning. On the one side is the impetuous and inexperienced strength of Titanic youth; on the other all the guile and dexterity of a thousand years' experience in government. Which is going to win?

215 Michael (7th (Reserve) Battalion, King's Liverpool Regiment, West 1 Camp, Park Hall, Oswestry) to John (Tralee), 12 September 1917[11]

I am getting inured now to the new conditions of life in the Army as an officer. They are of course much easier in ever so many ways, at present anyhow, and one is relieved of a lot of physical labour which falls to the lot of a private. More comfortable conditions, and a large amount of freedom from petty restrictions and bossing, also make [for] a more cheerful outlook on life possible. We are not yet finished with a certain amount of elementary training, but it is undergone in a very different spirit. Still there

6. Michael commissioned as an officer into the King's Liverpool
Regiment, September 1917

7. The last group family photograph, summer 1917

is always the tendency to grouse at work, and any idea we have had that an officer's chief pleasure lay in ordering men about and correcting them is quickly dissipated.

As regards the time I am likely to be here, it is not at all likely to be long. Orders came from the War Office today for eight officers to proceed overseas. Some of them had been here less than three weeks, and were still attending the School of Instruction. They go on leave tonight, and report to Folkestone on the 18th inst., Tuesday next, at 10 am. If I receive instructions similarly, I shall probably be leaving here in say a fortnight from now and will have about 4 clear days at home.

I had a very interesting talk with Jimmy McElligott in Dublin. He is not going back to the Civil Service, but is making enough out of journalistic writing.[12]

216 Michael (Oswestry) to John (Tralee), 21 September 1917

In the atmosphere of this place one is very much out of touch with tendencies and movements both at home and throughout the world. No one ever discusses the possibility of peace; the general attitude is one of implicit acceptance of the war as the normal medium of human activities, and the military life, with its pleasures & pains, as the perpetual life of man. As for the turmoil of political life, it is beyond the ken of those amongst whom I am now living; events in Russia and Ireland (though the latter is never mentioned) would be equally met by the eternal 'Englishmen cannot understand' these strange peoples and their peculiar ways. Under the circumstances it is only natural that I too should give up speculation and simply live through our narrow circle of events as they happen, without endeavouring to pierce the veil of the future.

I am expecting marching orders at the end of next week, though in any case it will probably be a month from now before I reach my unit in France, owing to delay at the Base & so on. The 8th Liverpools were fearfully cut up in August at Ypres, coming out with 2 officers and 50 men left. You may have seen in the paper that the West Lancashire Territorials, which comprise the Liverpool battalions amongst others, has also been in the latest show. After these hammerings the Division may get a rest for some time. They have been in the Ypres sector for 12 months, since leaving the Somme. I certainly hope they get shifted south, as I do not like Belgium in winter.

I hope father is getting better. I did not hear from mother this morning.

217 Michael (BEF) to John (Tralee), 26 November 1917

I am getting settled down with my Batt[alio]n. now, and where we are at present at all events, it is much more pleasant than fooling about in England. Splendid billets, a nice small little mess consisting of the company officers, and a general free-and-easiness, all conduce to make one feel very satisfied. Practically all the parade work is done in the mornings, and the rest of the day is free except for odd jobs, such as censoring letters, looking after the issue of rum &c. The evenings are usually spent playing auction. It is quite different from what I expected I assure you. I have only been within sound of the guns for a couple of nights, and now even that does not disturb our slumbers.

There is a nice little church here, & in this respect we score over the Protestants who hold their service in the open air. We have a Catholic chaplain in the Batt[alio]n., although the actual number of Catholics is not very great.

I have had no letters yet, although I have written several. But I suppose there has hardly been time for one to reach here in reply so far.

We are having the C.O. to tea this afternoon. Before he comes I shall have to study the French names of various birds and beasts. That is his pet fad, and I want to go one better and put him some posers.

218 Michael (BEF) to John (Tralee), 10 December 1917

...We have now moved to a place where we can hear the artillery going night & day. Apart from the surroundings we are not uncomfortable. I find I sleep very warm at nights and we still can get civilised food.

I have nearly been getting into trouble again. The day before we moved I went on leave to a certain large town. The train back was to leave at 7.25. I got to the station at 7.30 and found it had gone. So I put up for the night at an hotel, and next morning caught the first train at 7 a.m. When I got to our village I found the whole battalion had gone and left not a wrack behind. So I walked to the main road hoping at least to get a motor lorry which would be going in the same direction as they were to take. Happily I found they were all on the road in a fleet of lorries and had not yet started the journey. So I rejoined them, and have escaped with a mild ticking-off.

Lord Lansdowne's letter ought to have a deep influence on public opinion regarding the future of the war.[13] In spite of press efforts to belittle it and its author, it expresses more closely than is publicly admitted the feelings and thoughts of the masses of every country. As time goes on, the sentiment is bound to grow, and must sooner or later react on policy. The out-and-outers will have a heavy reckoning to pay in the end.

I wish you success in connection with that position.

I hope father keeps well.

219 Michael (BEF) to John (Tralee), 26 December 1917

I got your letters of 16th and 19th inst.

Well Xmas is over now, and it may interest you to know how we spent it. We got a barrel of beer for the men, & there was plenty of plum pudding. For ourselves, our dinner consisted of soup, tinned lobster, tinned rabbit and peas, plum-pudding, and cheese savoury. Not so bad for this place, eh? We have done no work of any description for the past 3 days. We lie in bed until 10 or 11 a.m., and spend the day & evening playing cards between meals. There is a little excitement now & then when a German plane comes over. I saw one brought down in flames the other day.

So you see though the war is all around us we are fairly comfortable & cheerful. Of course the tremendous business obtrudes itself into all our thoughts and talk, but apart from that one begins after a time to look upon it with some degree of philosophy.

We have seen no newspapers for over a week, & do not know how the world is going. All sorts of rumours reach us in consequence, great naval battles, peace negotiations, &c &c.

The country about here is a howling wilderness. Ruin reigns supreme; imagination cannot picture this spectacle of levelled masonry, shattered cemetery, & blasted trees, with the great shells sighing & shrieking on their fell mission. And in the midst of it all men are living and eating and working, & it seems like the normal and established way of life.

I wish you a happy & prosperous New Year.

220 Michael (BEF) to John (Tralee), 29 December 1917

I am giving this to a friend going on leave to post.

It is to tell you that I am at present stationed at BOESINGHE, north of Ypres, see *Daily Mail* Map. I work up near Houthulst Forest, past LANGEMARCK.

We expect to move down south in a day or two near Armentières (Ploegsteest).[14]

Let me know whether you receive this but mention no names or places. Cheer[i]o, M.

221 Michael (BEF) to Maurice junior (Tralee), 4 January 1918

Thank you for your letters and good wishes for Xmas.

I suppose Xmas holidays will be over by the time you get this. Hope you will work hard for the next exam.

To say that I am quite comfortable in my new abode would be rather an exaggeration. Still I have a civilian bed & there are chairs & tables left in the house. The great trouble is to keep warm. These French stoves are all right with coal, but they give very little heat on wood. Besides the former owners had hot water pipes which are now alas! for ever cold.

Well, c'est la guerre, as our *Allies* say, and it is no use grumbling.

Write again soon. Good bye for present love Michael.

222 Michael (BEF) to Mary (Tralee), 10 January 1918

I am sorry to learn from your last letter that father's condition is so serious. I pray that in spite of appearances he will recover and be well when next I see him.

We continue to have a quiet uneventful life here. There is scarcely any fighting activity at the moment. The weather is against it for one thing. Yesterday there was a heavy fall of snow but during the night it thawed.[15]

Fr. Caulfield is now staying with us as regards meals. He sleeps in his own billet a couple of miles away but braves the fury of the weather to come & dine with us. We all get on splendidly in our little mess. After dinner every evening the affairs of this world & the world to come are thrashed out, & as we all have very different points of view the argument at times becomes pretty warm.

The situation as regards peace looks at the moment more hopeful. Lloyd George's speech opens the door for a conference, & there is little doubt that the German people will, now they see peace approaching in the East, insist that it shall be general. Everyone out here is optimistic about the prospect and there is an undoubted feeling in the air that the war is coming to a close.

223 Michael (BEF) to John (Tralee), 15 January 1918

I got your letter of 7th the other day. It is terrible to think of father being so bad. One's anxiety is doubled when, as out here, news is only received four days late, and getting home is so difficult.[16]

You may have noticed that our pay is to be increased by 9/- a day. This will wipe out my civil salary altogether. I shall therefore have to pay N.B. & M. insurance premiums direct instead of by deduction as hitherto. Will you please write on my behalf to the company, explaining the circumstances, and asking what arrangement they wish to make as regards payment, so as to keep the benefit of the reduced premium. Quote the number of the policy. The Civil Service will also, I expect, come down on me for over-payment of salary as the increase dates from 1st October. I shall not pay them however until I get the back pay from the Army. The change leaves me better off to the extent of about £17 per annum, which is a consideration in these times.

So according to Mr Churchill the storm will soon break over our devoted heads. Well, we are keeping calm so far, but if it does come I daresay we shall not altogether enjoy it.

Your West Wind has brought the rain over from Kerry today. It is a downpour, and as our ceiling is full of shrapnel holes, & the upper storeys are ruined, the winter is coming in to our sitting-room & we can have a shower bath at any time in some corners of the room.

I wish you many happy returns of your birthday. I am sorry I can send you nothing to mark the event, as the shops in this town are now only inhabited by ghosts. Fuit Troja!

224 Extract from the Kerry Weekly Reporter, 19 January 1918

Death of Mr Maurice Moynihan.

The announcement of the death of Mr Maurice Moynihan ... will be received with feelings of profound regret, not only in Tralee, but throughout Munster, where he was so well known as a true-hearted sterling, consistent and uncompromising Irish Nationalist. A strong believer in the liberation of his country by force of arms, he like many others of the extreme wing of Irish Nationalists, threw in his lot with Parnell and Davitt in the constitutional movement and was a tower of strength to that organisation during the strenuous struggles of the early eighties for the land for the people. He was one of the victims of the coercion regime and suffered imprisonment for the high crime and misdemeanour of 'laughing at a policeman'. The charge against him was one of threatening language, but the Sergeant of police who brought the charge, could not push the case further against him than that what he did was 'a contraction between a booh and a laugh' and nobody in court laughed more heartily than did Maurice Moynihan. But the notorious Cecil Roche and another Removable bound him to the peace for the 'crime' and refusing to give bail, he spent a month in Tralee Jail.[17]

At the time of the Parnell split he stood solidly by the side of the Irish Chief. He stood on many a platform in support of the candidature of the late Mr Edward Harrington against the Federationist candidate Sir Thomas Esmonde and in later days fought vigorously for Mr Thomas O'Donnell when he was opposed by Mr Julian.[18] The latter at the time had the support of the 'Prince Merchants' of Tralee ... In the town everything seemed uphill work for the then democratic candidate. He could not even get a friendly house in the town from which to address a meeting. The 'mob' was against him and his supporters but Maurice Moynihan, who never faltered where his conscience bade him do and dare, defied wealth and all the influences it was able to procure and addressed meeting after meeting from brakes in different parts of the town and had the extreme satisfaction of seeing his man carried to victory at the polls. The victory was a striking vindication of the principle of right against might. But, alas, Maurice Moynihan was doomed to taste the cup of bitter disappointment in later years, when the former opponents of Mr O'Donnell became his friends and admirers, and the aspirations of the people who stood by him were cast aside by the Party of which he became a member. It was little wonder then that Mr Moynihan gave his whole hearted support to the Sinn Fein movement when the barrenness of the results of the Parliamentary machine became apparent. If there are Irish Nationalists who differed from him in that decision none worthy of the name will ever dare assert that his actions were not always dictated by a conscientiousness and pure souled desire for the freedom of the land he loved so well. Were Maurice Moynihan a man who placed self before country he could have attained wealth and power. He had all the education, the gifts of oratory, the power of pen, the force of character, which would easily have lifted him to fame. But his pure burning love for the upliftment of his motherland blotted out all selfish considerations and no taint of self advancement ever sullied that noble soul in the pursuit of its grand ideal. He was a leading figure in the Gaelic Athletic movement, and indeed there was no Nationalist movement ever started in Ireland that did not find in him a powerful advocate by voice and pen, in word and work. He had been in failing health for some time and his death was not unexpected. We join with his legion of friends in tendering our respectful sympathy to his sorrowing widow and family in their great bereavement.

225 Michael (BEF) to John (Tralee), 12 February 1918

I am writing this in what used to be the parlour of the convent. The change from the other billet took place the day before I got back, and was due to the fact that our people were receiving unwelcome attentions. This is much better, and we are sleeping on the ground floor instead of a cellar. However in a few days we shall (D.V.) be better off still, and in a place where there are civilians, and some kind of life going on around.

When we move I shall be detached for a time, and billeted with one of the R[oyal].E[ngineers]. officers. My address will, of course, be the same.

Things are very quiet here at the moment but you can judge for yourself from the papers how long that is likely to continue.

I have no work at all to do at present as the R.E.s are employing all our men. I was up the line the day after I came back, but since then have been vegetating in the billet. I hope to be a little busier when I go back.

The officers of our batt[alio]n. who, I told you, were lost last December, have now, I am glad to say, been officially reported as prisoners.

226 Michael (BEF) to Mary (Tralee), 22 February 1918

I got your letters of 15th & 16th I wrote to Uncle Pat very soon after I left home, either from Dublin or the French port, I forget which. I did not get any reply, but I suppose he received letter all right. However I shall write him again very soon … I hope your visit to Ballylongford will do you good and restore you to health. You will have to take good care of yourself and cease from worrying.

We are enjoying our rest pretty well. Our chief job is riding around to visit our various sections. We are not much troubled by the Germans here. The other day an aeroplane dropped some leaflets in English addressed to Irish soldiers, & exhorting them to throw in their lot with Sinn Fein. It was written by an Irish woman resident in Germany. The next day they sent down bundles of a French newspaper published under German direction … At night a bomb was dropped in the neighbourhood.

227 Michael (BEF) to John (Tralee), 2 March 1918

I am afraid I have been rather slack in replying to your last letter. As a matter of fact, there is nearly always something to prevent me writing in the evenings here, and the morning is a most uncongenial time for settling down to correspondence.

Situated as I am over here, it is impossible for me to follow Irish affairs with the same knowledge or the same perspective as when at home. The events of world-importance amidst which we live must of necessity over-shadow everything else in our minds, not only because of the personal interest we have in them, but also because their meaning and their gravity are more immediately obvious to us than anything else. The humblest private here understands and thinks more about international, than he ever did about domestic politics, so it comes about that I see Ireland at present only, as it were, through the wrong end of a telescope. My impression of the permanent features remains as vivid as ever, but of passing events and the ever-changing tableau of contemporary forces I can keep no account. Thus in my numerous discussions and arguments on the 'Irish question', I always come down quickly on first principles, an inevitable thing when one is think-ing of a far-off, historical entity, and moreover trying to combat essentially alien points of view. You in Ireland who have to deal with politics, which is the wisdom of the passing hour, need never trouble with those fundamen-tals, which are always implicitly assumed in the free political life of every nation. To be more concrete, the question that agitates you in Ireland is as to the wisdom of alternate policies of Sinn Fein, Parliamentarianism, or Unionism, from the *Irish point of view*. I, on the other hand, have to endeav-our to justify the existence of an Irish point of view at all. You, in other words, are engaged in making history, while I can only try to interpret it. It is not a useful or a fruitful occupation. It is the least indeed one can do, but really it amounts to nothing more than, as it were, keeping the flag flying. For where difference of opinion is due to opposition of interests, no argu-ment will ever bring about agreement. The premisses on either side are wholly irreconcilable. There is only one potent argument in such cases, and that is the law of the strongest. It is sad, from a human point of view, that it should be so, but the matter is hardly in doubt.

I am glad to get the February *Catholic Bulletin*. I hope you will continue sending it, as it is always intensely interesting, and I regard it as perfectly invaluable.

March has come in in the orthodox manner, with biting east winds and sleet. We do not envy the lot of the men in the trenches just now.

228 Michael (BEF) to Father (John) Hyacinth Power, 12 March 1918

I was very glad indeed to receive your letter of 28 Feb. I need not say how much I appreciate what you say about my father. It will take my mother a long time, I fear, to get over the shock of his death, which up to the last she could not believe was so imminent.

It is now well over a year since I wrote to you before from France. I believe you wrote back but I never got your letter. I am glad to renew the correspondence, to build a bridge over the relentless years and recall with you the happy spirit of past times. We little dreamt in those far off days of the great events that were impending over the world, and how they would affect us nationally and individually. Yet, if we only knew it, all this clash of races and interests existed even then in embryo, and this present tremendous conflict has only given greater vehemence and meaning to principles and forces which were always subconsciously present in men's minds. 'War', the Germans say, 'is a continuation of policy', and in the case of our own dear country the new time has brought a change in methods, not hoped for some years back, but the ideal of a free nation remains the same, or rather has gained enhanced strength. A new hope, born of martial self-reliance, has arisen in the land, and it is sustained by the broader principle of international justice which, though as yet mere words, have still gained an ever-increasing acceptance, as the sole means of restoring peace to an anguished world. Believe me, I have nothing but the fullest sympathy for the new men and the new (or 'old but ever new') teachings, and I should be sorry that you should ever think or expect otherwise. One does not part willingly with early loyalties or early traditions, and indeed the rolling years do but confirm them.

For myself, I accept the lot which I imposed on myself before ever the war started, and I hope some day to be able to give you a better justification of it than is possible now.

When do you expect to be going home?[19] I hope to be on leave again before very long, and to see you then.

With sincere regards and best wishes, I remain, Your affectionate cousin, M.J.Moynihan.

229 Michael (BEF) to John (Tralee), 18 April 1918

Well, the fat is in the fire now I suppose so far as Ireland is concerned, and all the troubles of the past three years will come to a head.[20] It is hard to know what the people can do against the colossal forces against them but I do not expect they will submit quietly. I should like your views on the situation.

I suppose the tremendous events that are taking place out here are absorbing a good deal of attention in Ireland, as now indeed they interest her in a more direct and wholesome fashion than before.

I have been on the move for the past three weeks, marching & countermarching. Now we are stationary for the moment, living under canvas in bad weather.[21]

230 Michael (BEF) to John (Tralee), 22 April 1918

I have just heard that my name has been put forward as a 'fluent French speaker'. I do not know what it is for exactly, but fancy it would be as liaison officer with the French Armies. In that case, my dictionary of French military terms, which I left at home, would be useful, so I should be glad if you will send it on.

Hoping to hear from you soon about the Irish situation.

231 Tess & Cis Power (Rock Street, Tralee) to Michael (BEF), 11 May 1918

Ever so many thanks for your letter.

I was delighted to get it. I hope you have not had too bad a time of it since, it is a good thing to be in the line anyway.

We must thank the Gods for small mercies!

When do you expect to get home, Michael?

For goodness sake try to get a holiday soon.

We are expecting John home in June,[22] so perhaps the two of you would be home together. That would be great! Conscription is the talk of the day here. When the bill was passed first, it created a great panic everywhere; but people are taking things much cooler now. I wonder will they enforce it?

We must only hope for the best anyway. I suppose you heard A. Stack and a few more of the leaders were arrested.

Austin was down here for a week and he was arrested outside the Police Barracks. He is in Belfast now.[23] (Jo's address is Loreto Hall, 77 Stephen's Green.) Outside conscription gossip there isn't very much news here at present (as usual)!

Did your mother tell you about the the shots they heard in Ballyard the other night. The shots were accounted for in a very simple way, but they got an awful fright as they thought a *Rebellion* had started! They were quite surprised to find everything as usual in the town next day. Old Mr Downing of Bohercanny was buried to-day, one of his sons also died a fortnight ago...

Now I think my dear boy I've given you all the news of this dull unnewsy town in a nut-shell...

Love from Tess and your affect[ionate]. cousin Cis.

232 Mary (Tralee) to Michael, 25 May 1918

I am expecting to hear from you for the past few days. I hope there will be a letter this evening. U[ncle] John is still here & is evidently not in touch with his wife as she has not written to him since he came here this day week ... J[ames] Murphy is in Fermoy in Hospital suffering from some kind of skin trouble, common after trench fever. He is very lucky... Try & let me know about yourself & what you are doing. I hope you got the two last parcels I sent ... there will be a public Procession on Sunday week the 2nd of June in honour of the Sacred Heart & for peace. Let us hope we shall have peace & that you will be at home soon & safe with us...

233 Mary (Tralee) to Michael (BEF), 28 May 1918

I got your letter & two Field Cards. I judge from the letter that you have been in the trenches. God help me if I knew it what a state I would be in. May God bring you back safe to me. I shall send you the parcel tomorrow.

There is no account of Leo Casey for the past two months, at least as I heard in town yesterday. They must be in an awful way...[24] U[ncle] John is still around & is better than he was for a long time. I do not know what he means to do. Maurice is killed from hard study. He says he may get an ex[hibition]. I think you ought to ask for leave now you will be four months gone the first week of June. We are all well here & praying for you to come back soon. The weather is lovely. It would be grand to be in Fenit now & to have you there.

234 Field Service Post Card from Michael, written 2 June 1918, postmarked 3 June 1918

I am quite well.[25]

235 Mary (Tralee) to Michael (BEF), 3 June 19181

It is only this evening I am posting the parcel. I was waiting for a barm brack & they did not get them in. I am just sending a cake & butter, but shall send cake & bacon on Friday. U[ncle]. John went to Limerick. I think he must be sure of getting something there. He is fairly well. The weather is lovely now. You were never in Ballyard in fine weather. Pray hard to Our Lady of Perpetual Succour to bring you soon. It does not matter whether it is raining or the sun shining while you are where you are now. It will not be long however when we will be able to look back & think all this trouble a horrible nightmare.

We had the Blessed Sacrament Procession yesterday. It was even more impressive than last year. I never prayed as fervently as while we were marching, asking the Little Infant Jesus to bring you home safe and unhurt to me . . .

Everyone here sends love & the most from your loving Mother.

236 Telegram from the Keeper of the Privy Purse, Buckingham Palace, to M. Moynihan Esq. [sic], Springmount, Ballyard, Tralee, 18 June 1918

The King and Queen deeply regret the loss you and the army have sustained by the death of your son in the service of his country. Their Majesties truly sympathise with you in your sorrow.[26]

237 G. Bellwood (RC Chaplain, 46 G.C.S. BEF) to Mary (Tralee), 21 June 1918

Your letter has been forwarded to me. I am the R.C. Chaplain 46 G.C.S. and was attached to the Canadian Hospital at the time your son was admitted. First, let me convey to you my deep sympathy in the loss you have sustained. Your son, as he was so seriously wounded, received the last sacraments of the Church. He did not speak much to me, or give me any messages as, when I saw him, he had just come from the operating theatre, and wanted to sleep.

And after he had died, he was buried with Catholic rites in the military cemetery R.I.P. I wrote to you after his death, but as I was given an address in Lancashire, I presume you never received my letter. No doubt the field postcard you received was posted for him on his admission into hospital. I am afraid this is all the information that I am able to give you . . .

238 Private Patrick O'Hara (BEF) to Mary (Tralee), 10 July 1918

It is with deepest regret that I l[e]arnt of the death of your son Lieut. Moynihan from wounds which he recieved [*sic*] during the excetution [*sic*] of his duty. He was sent out in charge of a reconnoitiring [*sic*] party in no man's land on the night of the 2nd & 3rd & was about to return when the Boche opened fire, & wounded the whole of the party, two of whom died including your Son. During my time with him as his servant, (which was since he came to the Batt[alio]n.) I always found him very considerate. Also I may say that there is not a man in the Company who could truthfully say any thing against him in any way. Neither would he ask any one to do anything which he himself could not do. And all those who knew him, were very sorry indeed to hear of his death. Whilst writing this letter, I may at the same time convey to you their united sympathies & condolences. It was my good fortune that I was not with him at the time of the mishap. I was sent by the company commander with other men to get rations, otherwise I might have shared the same fate. But I suppose it was God's will that it should be so. But dear Mrs Moynihan you may rest contented that he recieved [*sic*] the rights [*sic*] of the Church before he faced his Creator, as the priest who is attached to our Batt[alio]n. informed me of the fact, also he was intered [*sic*] well behind the lines so he is sure to have had a respectable Burial, which thousands of poor lads out here have not had. I have said all that it is possible for me to say at the same time doing my best to console you in your sad bereavement. Though no words of mine can heal the wound which his death has made in your heart. Still it is the only thing that is in my power to do for the present I will conclude at the same time my deepest sympaties [*sic*].

   Remaining your's very sympat[h]etically, Patrick O'Hara
P.S. I would have written before but I did not have your address. But our priest who has just returned from leave gave it to me. If you are answering this letter, my address is Pte. P. O'Hara 308875 C. Coy 8th Irish Battn. Kings Liverpool Regt. BEF France.

239 Extract from the Kerry Sentinel, 6 July 1918

Travelling Without a Permit. Mr John Moynihan Arrested
Mr John Moynihan, commercial traveller and butter buyer, Ballyard, Tralee, was arrested on Wednesday evening and detained in custody charged with having travelled outside the Tralee Special Military Area

without a permit. It appears he applied for and was refused a permit. He is son of the late Mr Moynihan, the well-known Tralee Nationalist, and brother of the late Lieutenant Moynihan who was recently killed in action in France.

Mr John Moynihan was brought before a Military Court on Thursday and charged. He was left out, but he will live in Listowel to enable him to perform his duties.[27]

240 Official report on injuries to 2nd Lieutenant M.J. Moynihan, War Office[28]

Report on Accidental or Self-inflicted Injuries
Number, Rank, Name and Unit of injured officer
2nd Lieut. MOYNIHAN, M.J. 8th.(Irish) Bn.K.L.R. Date of Casualty. 2-6-1918
1. Nature, Location and Severity of injury
   G.S.W. left groin. Severe.
   (Sgd.) A.H.Falkner Capt. R.A.M.C.T. M.O. i/c 8 Kings Liverpool Rgt.
2. Short statement of the circumstances of the case
   On the night of June 2nd/3rd. 2nd Lt. Moynihan took out a patrol from No.1 Post at 10.30 p.m. The patrol sustained heavy casualties & returned about 11 p.m. via listening post on No.1 Post. 2nd Lt. Moynihan proceeded down trench at the double to fetch Stretcher Bearers. He was challenged by sentry over trench on No.1 Post, twice, he disregarded the challenge apparently not hearing it & was shot by the sentry at close range.
   (Sgd.) W.G. Lofthouse Lt. 3/6/18 O.C. 'C' Coy.
3. Commanding Officer's opinion as to whether the officer was:-
   (a) In the performance of his military duty. Yes.
   (b) To blame. Yes.
   (c) Whether any other person was to blame. No.
   (Sgd.) J.F. Jones Major. Commanding 8th (Irish) Bn. 'The King's' (L'pool. Rgt.) Date 4.6.18
4. Opinion of G.O.C. Brigade
   2/Lt. Moynihem [*sic*] was wounded while returning to a Front line Post, through not hearing the sentry challenge. No disciplinary action to be taken.
   (Sgd.) F.J. Longbourne Brig.-Gen. Commanding 171 Inf.Brigade. Date 5.6.18.

Epilogue: The Moynihans, 1918–99

It is uncertain whether the Moynihan family ever learned of the circumstances of Michael's death, although his younger brother Maurice may have suspected that the official report was not all it seemed. He once mentioned having received another letter from Private Patrick O'Hara (see Document 238, in Chapter 7) after the war. By the time the official report came to light in 1998 both Maurice and Denis, the last surviving members of the family, were in frail health, and it seemed impossible to ask them about such an upsetting subject. In 1996, however, Maurice had been able to recall, painfully but clearly, the terrible day the telegram arrived in Tralee: 'We were playing in the field near the house when we heard screaming. We rushed to the house and found my mother running around in circles just screaming, with John trying to calm her. But for John she would have gone mad.'

The deaths of Maurice and Michael were not the only tragedies faced by Mary and the family. Her father-in-law, also named Michael Moynihan, died later in 1918 and in February 1919 her beloved twin brother John Power died in Limerick of tuberculosis.

In the general election of December 1918, Mary and her uncle 'Pat the Rock' were listed among those electors assenting to the unopposed election of Austin Stack in the West Kerry constituency. During the War of Independence Tralee experienced serious disturbances, particularly at the beginning of November 1920, when attacks on the RIC led to the destruction of the County Hall as a reprisal. There were also attempts to set the Technical Schools and the Carnegie Library on fire.[1] Another casualty of the war was Michael's battalion, the 8th Liverpools, which was disbanded because of fears of political disaffection.[2] When Dorothy Macardle was researching her book *Tragedies of Kerry 1922–23* (Dublin, 1924) she stayed for a time with the Moynihans.

Mary lived with John in Clontarf, north Dublin, from 1926 until her sudden death, following a heart attack, in December 1949. It is said that on the day before her death she told John that she had seen a soldier dressed in khaki standing at the garden gate.

John had been thinking seriously about entering the priesthood, but as he had become the mainstay of the family after Michael's death this was impossible. He remained active in the Gaelic League, and became a Sinn Féin member of Kerry County Council and Tralee Urban District Council, as well as Chairman of the Tralee Sinn Féin courts. In 1922 he became editor of the *Kerry Leader*, which was suppressed in August that year in the wake of the Civil War. When the Free State's forces arrived in Tralee he was arrested and interned in Tralee, Limerick and Gormanston for fourteen months. After he was released from internment he was appointed editor of the *Kerry Reporter* and the *Kerry News*.

In 1926, however, John moved to Dublin with the rest of the family and was appointed director of information for the newly founded Fianna Fáil party. In 1929 he became secretary to its leader, Eamon de Valera, and accompanied him to the United States in 1929–30, when de Valera was setting up the *Irish Press*. John worked as a leader writer and assistant editor of the new paper from September 1931 to March 1932 when Fianna Fáil first came to power. John was appointed Secretary to the Government, a post he occupied until 1937, when his brother Maurice succeeded him. John went to the Department of Finance as assistant secretary in charge of Establishments. He was actively involved in the Legion of Mary, which brought him into conflict with the Archbishop of Dublin, Dr John Charles McQuaid. After Mary's death in 1949, John lived for some years with Maurice, his wife and his children, to whom he was a much-loved uncle. In June 1952 he took early retirement and some years later went to live with his sister Hannah in Glasgow, following the death of her husband. He remained active in the Legion of Mary and died in Glasgow in December 1964. He was buried near his mother in Clontarf.

During the upheavals of the Civil War, Hannah ('Han'), who had become active in Cumann na mBan, was interned in Kilmainham and the North Dublin Union, along with her cousins Cis and Jo Power. In 1927 Hannah married Patsy Keane from Knocknagoshel and moved with him to Glasgow. The couple had three children, Simon, Maurice and Sheila. Hannah died in May 1992.

Maurice, the fourth of Mary's children, was a student at University College Cork when he was shot in the thigh by a Black and Tan while walking down Washington Street, sustaining an injury that troubled him for the rest of his life. Maurice, who tacitly supported the Anglo-Irish Treaty, graduated from UCC with a first class honours degree (B.Comm.) and went back to Tralee to teach at the Technical Schools. Maurice did not remain a teacher for long, however. Michael's old friend James McElligott, a distant relative of the Moynihans, had stayed in Great Britain after the First World War to work as a financial journalist on *The Statist*, before becoming a financial adviser to the Irish delegation during the Treaty negotiations. In late 1922 he had returned to Ireland on being appointed assistant secretary in the Free State's Department of Finance (he was to become its secretary in 1927). It was McElligott who urged Maurice to sit for the new Civil Service examinations and, despite his family's political reservations, Maurice did so. In 1925 he became one of the first six successful applicants. McElligott subsequently appointed him his private secretary. He often talked to Maurice about Michael.

In 1932 de Valera invited Maurice to tea in the Dáil's restaurant and, to Maurice's great surprise, asked him to be his private secretary. When he told de Valera that he did not agree with some of his policies, de Valera replied that it did not matter. He was de Valera's private secretary for a year before returning to the Department of Finance. He married Mae Conley in August 1932, and they had five children, Mary, Maurice, Martin, Anne and Joan. His daughter Mary married Hannah's son Simon. In the spring of 1936 Maurice transferred to the President's (subsequently Taoiseach's) Department to supervise the drafting of the new Constitution. In 1937 he succeeded John as Secretary to the Government and Secretary of the Department of the Taoiseach, a post he held for nearly twenty-four years. Then, in 1961, he succeeded James McElligott as Governor of the Central Bank, a post he held until 1969. (McElligott died in January 1974.) After his retirement Maurice worked on two books: *Currency and Central Banking in Ireland 1922–60*, published in 1975; and *Speeches and Statements by Eamon de Valera 1917–73*, published in 1980. Maurice died in August 1999.

Denis, the fifth Moynihan sibling, studied medicine briefly at UCC, but gave it up to join the Civil Service. He worked for a time in the Department of Industry and Commerce, under the redoubtable Thekla Beere and then became, like Michael, an assistant inspector of taxes. In 1930, however, he entered the Dominican Order, taking the religious name of Father Anselm. He was ordained in 1937 and served as master of novices in Cork from 1942 to 1953. He became a founder-editor of the journal *Doctrine and Life* in 1951. He served two terms as Prior of San Clemente in Rome from 1962 until 1968, when he returned to St Saviour's in Dublin. He remained there for the rest of his life and served for a time as official assistant to the Provincial and Sub-Prior. He was deeply involved in the beatification of Edel Quinn of the Legion of Mary and was her literary executor. His booklet, *The Presence of God* (1948), was often reprinted. Father Anselm died in January 1999.

The youngest child, Thomas, who had been only five years old when Michael was killed, became the focus of Mary's maternal love and concern. Like his older brothers, he joined the Civil Service, working in Customs and Excise. He married Teresa Lyons, and the couple had two children, Denis and Anne. Thomas died in 1996.

Notes

Notes on Introduction

1   Canon Sheehan, *My New Curate* (Boston, 1900), pp.13–15, 50–1.
2   Tom Garvin, *Nationalist Revolutionaries in Ireland 1858–1928* (Oxford, 1987), p.13.
3   S.M. Hussey, *The Reminiscences of an Irish Land Agent (being those of S.M. Hussey compiled by Home Gordon)* (London, 1905), pp.60–5.
4   James S. Donnelly, Jr, 'The Kenmare Estates during the Nineteenth Century', *Journal of the Kerry Archaeological and Historical Society [JKAHS]*, 21 (1988), p.17.
5   Hussey, *Reminiscences*, pp.179–80.
6   Donnelly, 'The Kenmare Estates', pp.61–98.
7   William L. Feingold, 'Land League Power: The Tralee Poor Law Election of 1881', in Samuel Clark and James S. Donnelly, Jr (eds), *Irish Peasants: Violence and Political Unrest 1780–1914* (Manchester, 1983), pp.285–310.
8   The Land War, crime in Kerry and the Parnell Commission are all discussed in a stimulating study by Margaret O'Callaghan, *British High Politics and Nationalist Ireland: Criminality and the Law under Forster and Balfour* (Cork, 1994), particularly Chapters 5 and 6. I am also grateful to Dr O'Callaghan for letting me read her unpublished article on RIC Reports and their political uses, 1879–91.
9   Frank Callanan, 'The "Appeal to the Hillsides": Parnell and the Fenians 1890–91', in Donal McCartney (ed.), *Parnell: The Politics of Power* (Dublin, 1991), pp.148–69.
10 Paul Bew, *Conflict and Conciliation in Ireland 1890–1910: Parnellites and Radical Agrarians* (Oxford, 1987), p.1.
11 In a letter of support for O'Sullivan, published in the *Kerry Sentinel* on 15 January 1910, Maurice Moynihan paid tribute to O'Sullivan's work for tenants evicted from the Kenmare estate and other estates, 'who, now, after years by the roadside, are able to hug their own fireside'.
12 James S. Donnelly, Jr, 'Cork Market: Its Role in the Nineteenth Century Butter Trade', *Studia Hibernica*, 11 (1971), pp.130–63; Paul Bew, *Land and the National Question in Ireland 1858–1882* (Dublin, 1978), pp.10–11.
13 Document 127, 5 August 1914. John Revington was described by his great-nephew as 'a staunch Unionist' who stood for the town council on occasion. His unionist views were stronger than those of his two brothers, whom he enjoyed annoying by claiming that he had purchased the Freedom of the City of London. A third brother, Harry Revington, 'was almost eliminated from family records for marrying a Boer woman and fighting against the Empire'. Information from Gordon Revington, Tralee.
14 PRO CO904/18/50 List of Suspects.
15 *Kerry Sentinel*, 9, 12 and 26 January 1895. The case is recounted by Pat Lynch in

They Hanged John Twiss (Tralee, 1982), but Lynch evidently did not know who Power and Moynihan were. The incident is also mentioned in J. Anthony Gaughan, *A Political Odyssey: Thomas O'Donnell MP for West Kerry 1900–1918* (Dublin, 1983), p.23, n.1. Twiss was hanged on 3 February 1895. The South-Western Divisional Police Reports for January and February 1895 state that Twiss 'was well known in the County Kerry & the adjoining portion of County Cork E[ast]R[iding] to have been organiser as well as a perpetrator of serious crime for many years past. Several persons who are well known to have been in the conspiracy to murder the caretaker Donovan have already fled the country. Since the conviction of Twiss, particularly when approaching the date of execution, a reprieve was vigorously got up, but it is noteworthy that the organisers were almost exclusively confined to the Parnellite party.' The agitation was 'a miserable failure'. PRO CO904/64.

16 PRO CO904/65 South-Western Division Monthly Report, December 1896.

17 NAI CBS 'S' 3/716, 15200/5. My thanks to Dr Maura Cronin for this reference.

18 PRO CO904/68,69, Inspector General's and Kerry County Inspector's Monthly Reports, 1898. The foundation stone for the monument in Tralee, which commemorated not only the rising of 1798 but also the risings of 1803, 1848 and 1867, the imposing 'Pikeman' statue in Denny Street, was laid in September 1902 during a ceremony at which Maud Gonne was guest of honour.

19 In a letter of support for Moynihan, published in the *Kerry Sentinel* on 3 May 1899, James Bunyan declared that 'every Nationalist in the county who admires Mr Moynihan's manly political record – and surely their name is legion – should use whatever influence he may possess to procure his election, and thus show that Kerry men are not unmindful of the services of one of the most sterling sons of their historic kingdom to the National Cause'.

20 In February 1902, in response to being asked for longer reports, the Kerry County Inspector wrote in irritation to Dublin Castle: 'I cannot write about nothing & practically at present there is nothing to write about.' PRO CO904/74.

21 This was a review of Thomas F. O'Sullivan's *Story of the GAA* (Dublin, 1916). It was reprinted in the *Kerry Sentinel* of 25 November 1916. Maurice also wrote a letter to the *Kerry Sentinel* on the subject of Hecate.

22 Document 12, 29 March 1909.

23 *Inis Fáil*, April 1906.

24 John J. Horgan, *Parnell to Pearse: Some Recollections and Reflections* (Dublin, 1948), p.56.

25 Senia Pašeta, *Before the Revolution: Nationalism, Social Change and Ireland's Catholic Elite 1879–1922* (Cork, 1999), p.55

26 John Hutchinson, *The Dynamics of Cultural Nationalism: The Gaelic Revival and the Creation of the Irish Nation State* (London, 1987), pp.255–66.

27 On this point see Eunan O'Halpin, 'The Civil Service and the Political System', *Administration*, 38 (1990–91), pp.284–7.

28 Moynihan Family Papers (MFP).

29 Document 26, 24 June 1909.

30 These general themes are discussed in Hew Strachan, *The First World War: To Arms* (Oxford, 2001), pp.103–62; Robert Wohl, *The Generation of 1914* (London, 1980); I.F. Clarke, *Voices Prophesying War 1963–1984* (Oxford, 1966); and, in the Irish context, Garvin, *Nationalist Revolutionaries*, and Pašeta, *Before the Revolution*.

31 Document 67, 21 July 1912.

32   Document 68, 24 July 1912.

33   Document 58, 7 March 1912.

34   Document 43, 12 August 1910, in which John mentions 'that wiliness which you and I were taught to regard as a distinguishing characteristic of Roman ecclesiastics'.

35   Document 34, 8 July 1909.

36   J.J. Heaney, 'Modernism', *New Catholic Encyclopedia*, vol.7 (New York, 1966), p.994; Anne Fremantle (ed.), *The Papal Encyclicals in their Historical Context* (New York, 1956), pp.196–213.

37   Garvin, *Nationalist Revolutionaries*, p.128. Among Ryan's papers there are two draft autobiographies that include accounts of these years: 'Quests and Comrades' (1938) and 'Golden Decades' (1941), UCDAD LA 11/A/1. He was unable to find a publisher for either of them, to his disappointment. However, his son Desmond Ryan (1893–1964) wrote an elegiac memoir that deals to some extent with this part of his father's life: *Remembering Sion: A Chronicle of Storm and Quiet* (London, 1934), pp.23–62.

38   The Catholic hierarchy believed that Irish colleges, which students could visit in the holidays, were preferable to compulsory Irish in the new National University. Sir Bertram Windle, President of University College, Cork, told Archbishop Walsh in June 1909 that the Gaelic League would 'wreck the whole higher education of Catholics by driving boys and girls into Trinity and Belfast' (quoted in Pašeta, *Before the Revolution*, pp.23–4). The most recent account of the O'Hickey controversy is Lucy McDiarmid, 'The Man Who Died for the Language: The Reverend Dr O'Hickey and the "Essential Irish" Language Controversy of 1909', *Eire–Ireland*, XXXV, 1–2 (2000), pp.188–218.

39   Document 69, 7 August 1912.

40   Document 11, 23 March 1909.

41   O'Donnell to Dillon, 15 October 1914, quoted in Gaughan, *A Political Odyssey*, p.97.

42   See Wallace Martin, *The New Age under Orage: Chapters in English Cultural History* (Manchester, 1967).

43   Lord Hugh Cecil, 'white with rage . . . his gaunt Elizabethan frame shaken with ludicrous passion, would stand up and scream [at Asquith], "You've disgraced your office!"', according to George Dangerfield, *The Strange Death of Liberal England* (London, 1936), pp.52–3.

44   The complex relationship between Ireland and the monarchy is explored in James Murphy, *Abject Loyalty: Nationalism and Monarchy in Ireland During the Reign of Queen Victoria* (Cork, 2001).

45   Lord Hugh Cecil, *Conservatism* (London, 1912), pp.240–2. His views on Ireland mirrored his late father's, Lord Salisbury.

46   H.G. Wells, *The New Machiavelli* (London, 1911), pp.354–5.

47   This also seems to have been the case in Kerry. In his monthly report for April 1912 the County Inspector of the Kerry RIC wrote that the Home Rule Bill 'has not caused excitement or very keen interest but the measure is generally regarded with satisfaction and a feeling of assurance that it will become law'. PRO CO904/86.

48   Document 77, 9 November 1912.

49   W.B. Yeats considered Ryan's play to be 'excellent . . . really an astonishing piece of satire', and wanted to revive it. Only the second scene has survived: it can be

found in Robert Hogan and James Kilroy (eds), *Lost Plays of the Irish Renaissance* (Newark, 1970), pp.10–37.

50 Canon Sheehan, *The Intellectuals: An Experiment in Irish Club-Life* (London, 1911), pp.227–8.

51 Quoted in Gaughan, *Political Odyssey*, p.93.

52 Documents 95 and 96, 17 November and 6 December 1913.

53 Document 106, 30 March 1914.

54 Documents 95 and 105, 17 November 1913 and 23 March 1914.

55 Peter Simkins, *Kitchener's Army: The Raising of the New Armies, 1914–1916* (Manchester, 1988), p.18; see also Ray Westlake and Mike Chappell, *British Territorial Units 1914–1918* (London, 1991), and Peter Dennis, *The Territorial Army 1906–1940* (London, 1987).

56 Documents 109 and 110, 26 April and c. 28 April 1914. Hew Strachan's observation (*First World War* p.147) that 'the recreational appeal of part-time service became the means by which a Nietzschean anxiety to test one's courage was transmitted into action' is apposite to Michael's explanation.

57 Keith Jeffery, *Ireland and the Great War* (Cambridge, 2000), p.2.

58 Document 112, 10 May 1914.

59 Ibid.[roman]

60 Document 130, 11 August 1914.

61 Document 133, poem entitled 'The March of Certain Men of London'.

62 *History of the Prince of Wales' Own Civil Service Rifles* (London, 1921), p.230.

63 PRO CO904/94, Kerry Monthly Report, August 1914.

64 Ibid. Kerry Monthly Report, September 1914.

65 O'Donnell was also instrumental in setting up the *Kerry Advocate*, which was started in July 1914 and became a pro-war newspaper. It supported Redmond, and opposed Sinn Féin, MacNeill and the Gaelic League. It ceased publication in May 1916. Gaughan, *Political Odyssey*, pp.103–5.

66 Thomas Neilan Crean, 'Labour and Politics in Kerry During the First World War', *Saothar*, 19 (1994), p.27. Low levels of recruitment from agriculture were widespread throughout western Europe: Strachan, *The First World War*, pp.139–40.

67 Document 134, 22 January 1915.

68 Document 145, 14 July 1915.

69 Neilan Crean, 'Labour and Politics in Kerry', pp.27–39.

70 PRO CO904/95-99, monthly reports for 1915.

71 It is worth noting, regarding both this meeting on 27 February 1916 and the labour rally in October 1915, that the Kerry County Inspector failed to mention in his monthly reports the presence of Connolly and Pearse in Tralee.

72 Billy Mullins, *Memoirs of Billy Mullins: Veteran of the War of Independence* (Tralee, 1983), pp.45–7; Mannix Joyce, 'The Story of Limerick and Kerry in 1916', *Capuchin Annual* (1966), pp.338–9; T. Ryle Dwyer, *Tans, Terror and Troubles: Kerry's Real Fighting Story 1913–23* (Cork, 2001), pp.73–90.

73 *History of the Prince of Wales' Own Civil Service Rifles*, pp.232–5.

74 Document 192, 29 November 1916.

75 Document 190, 21 November 1916.

76 Document 209, 21 April 1917.

77 Document 211, extract from Maurice Moynihan, 'Reflections on Longford'.

78 Document 212, 17 June 1917.

79 *Kerryman*, 6 October 1917.
80 Michael's father, among others, would have been less impressed by the fact that Lord Kenmare, son of the 4th Earl who had dismissed his estate workers at the start of the Land War, was the battalion's Honorary Colonel.
81 Document 227, 2 March 1918.
82 Document 228, 12 March 1918.
83 Document 171, 28 May 1916.
84 In 1924, the year after the end of the Civil War, 500 ex-servicemen paraded through Tralee: Peter Malone (ed.), *Images and Chronicles from the Archives of* The Kerryman *Newspaper. A Portrait of Kerry in the 20th Century* (Tralee, 2001), p.71.
85 Kerry County Library in Tralee has typescript statistics listing the names of Kerry servicemen who died in the war and their geographical origins. These were compiled by an anonymous author. In St John's Church in Tralee there is a roll of honour of men from the Church of Ireland parish served by this church who joined the British armed forces during the war.

Notes on Chapter One

1 Michael had just started at UCD, where he was studying French, Latin and Mathematics. He had lodgings at 37 Waterloo Place. His mother clearly had reservations about the other lodgings he mentions, Whelan's. At the beginning of 1909 he moved to other lodgings on the north side of the city, at 4 Sybil Terrace, Drumcondra, where he stayed for the rest of his time at UCD.
2 Dr John Molyneux was the Moynihans' family doctor in Tralee.
3 James McElligott and James Enright were friends of Michael from Tralee. James McElligott (1893–1974) was a distant relative. He studied classics and economics at UCD.
4 Dr Denis Coffey (1865–1945), Dean of Medicine and President-elect of UCD, was from Tralee.
5 The *Irish Nation and Peasant* was a shortlived but influential radical weekly, published from 1909 to 1910, and edited by W.P. Ryan (1867–1942), a socialist journalist and enthusiast for the Irish language. Ryan had been a prominent member of the London Gaelic League, where he got to know John Power, one of Michael and John's uncles. The *IN&P* succeeded the *Irish Peasant*, also edited by Ryan, which had been started in 1905 but had been forced to close in 1906 because of clerical pressure. 'On the People's Service' was a regular comment column in the *IN&P*. The one that Michael refers to here is probably that of 6 February 1909, which discussed the meeting of the new Senate of the National University of Ireland and the attitude of the hierarchy to the thorny issue of whether the Irish language should be a compulsory subject for matriculation at the NUI. This topic was to dominate the columns of *IN&P* for most of 1909: the journal was robustly critical of the Catholic hierarchy's opposition to compulsory Irish.
6 *The Plough and the Cross: A Story of New Ireland*, a novel by W.P. Ryan, initially appeared as a serial in the *IN&P* and was published in book form in 1910. The title of the present volume, *Their New Ireland*, comes from the closing sentence of the novel.

7 J.W. ('Joe') O'Beirne was the business manager of the *IN&P*. He had been active in the London Gaelic League and was another acquaintance of John Power. He had also worked with Ryan on the *Irish Peasant*. P.S. O'Hegarty recalled Joe O'Beirne spending many a morning in the outer office 'tearing his hair and asking where he was to get money to pay the printers': P.S. O'Hegarty, 'W.P. Ryan', *Dublin Magazine*, XVIII, 3 (July to Sept. 1943), pp. 72–3.

8 The Maynooth Movement figures prominently in *The Plough and the Cross* as 'a crusade which the bolder professors are entertaining' and that would 'give new life to Ireland – of all creeds – [and] must be based on a grand, unmistakably spiritual issue' (p.4). See also the Introduction to this volume, pp.xxv–xxvi.

9 The issue in question was compulsory Irish: see Document 2.

10 Dr Michael O'Hickey (1860–1916), Professor of Irish at Maynooth, had found that his support for compulsory Irish brought him into conflict with the Irish hierarchy.

11 Immanentism is 'a philosophical position maintaining that human experience is the only ultimate source of verification', according to the *New Catholic Encyclopedia*, vol.7 (New York, 1966), pp.388–9. Immanentism was closely linked to Modernism and both were condemned in the encyclical *Pascendi* (1907), the longest ever published until the 1980s. Priests had to take an oath against Modernism every year. The *IN&P* was strongly pro-Modernist. See also the Introduction to this volume, pp.xxiv–xxvi.

12 Elsie O'Kennedy is one of the leading characters in *The Plough and the Cross*, much of the action of which is set in the Boyne Valley.

13 Stephen Gwynn (1864–1950), MP for Galway City from 1906 to 1918, and Sir Bertram Windle (1858–1929), President of University College Cork, were both members of the senate of the new National University of Ireland. The Coiste Gnotha was the executive committee of the Gaelic League.

14 Father William Delany, SJ (1835–1924), President of UCD, had forbidden students to debate the subject of compulsory Irish.

15 *Evening Telegraph*, 24 February 1909.

16 *T.P.'s Weekly* was a literary and political journal edited and owned by T.P. O'Connor MP (1848–1929), one of the leaders of the Irish Parliamentary Party. He appears thinly disguised as Terence O'Connellan in *The Plough and the Cross*, which satirises his journal as 'Terence's Terse Tattle'. The review of H.G. Wells's novel *Tono-Bungay* was anonymous.

17 *The New Age*, edited by A.R. Orage (1873–1934), was a socialist weekly published in London that became a prominent forum for cultural and political debate. See also Introduction to this volume, p.xxvii.

18 Leonard Brannigan, manager of the *IN&P*, was another member of the London Gaelic League and a friend of John Power.

19 The *IN&P* had published a prospectus in the issue of 27 February 1909, which stated that the lack of working capital was 'crippling', and asserted that the paper was 'far in advance of its time, and though it avowedly stimulates Irish thought and mind of the better kind, it can only become popular in the broad sense slowly, such are the peculiar and abnormal circumstances of present-day Ireland. That would be so, even were there no active forces and personages working against it, which is the case especially in country places.' Although Mary Moynihan withstood Michael's pressure to buy shares, there exists among his papers a certificate for the purchase of five shares in the company, dated 22 March 1909.

20 Dr MacEinri (Seán Pádraig MacÉinrí, 1862–1930), a doctor and author of several Irish grammar books, was another member of the London Gaelic League and friend of John Power. 'On the People's Service', *IN&P* 6 March 1909, reported at length on a meeting in Tuam of the committee that ran the Irish-speaking Coláiste Chonnacht. The purpose of the meeting was to elect a new principal, but the Catholic Archbishop of Tuam, Dr John Healy (1841–1918), refused to allow MacÉinrí to go forward for election as they had clashed on previous occasions over compulsory Irish. Healy's decision was opposed by other members of the committee, including Colonel Maurice Moore and Father Bernard Crehan, a curate at Riverstown, County Sligo. Healy subsequently stated that 'the bishops of Ireland have spoken [on compulsory Irish], and their decision binds'. When Moore pointed out that the bishops had actually said that it was a matter for fair discussion, Healy replied that 'it was a matter for fair discussion before they spoke, but not since'. Healy attracted considerable coverage in the *IN&P*. In his memoir *The Pope's Green Island* (London, 1912, pp.171–2), W.P. Ryan describes Healy as 'a big man in more ways than one; the most towering, vital and irrepressible personality amongst the Irish Catholic episcopacy'. Walter MacDonald (1854–1920), in his *Reminiscences of a Maynooth Professor* (London, 1925, pp.82–3), has a more jaundiced view of Healy: 'As a Conservative, he was out of place. He should have been a mob orator, and he seemed to know it.'

21 Father Augustine O'Quigley was Prior of the Holy Cross (Dominican) Church in Tralee from 1907 to 1913.

22 John Power (1892–1956), a cousin of the Moynihans, was a student at the Jesuit college Clongowes Wood, in County Kildare.

23 There are two pamphlets to which Michael might be referring – *An Irish University, or Else* and *The Irish Bishops and an Irish University* – both of which were published in the spring of 1909.

24 The idealistic editor Fergus O'Hagan and his sister Maeve are two of the leading characters in *The Plough and the Cross*.

25 A series of articles, 'Belfast and its Industries', appeared in the *IN&P* from April to June 1909.

26 The Countess was the wife of John Campbell Gordon, the 7th Earl of Aberdeen (1847–1934), a Liberal politician who was Lord Lieutenant of Ireland in 1886 and again from 1906 to 1915.

27 According to *The Clongownian* (June 1909 pp.193–4) John Power supported the motion for compulsory Irish 'in a really good speech, which suffered somewhat in the delivery'. The motion was carried by 44 votes to 31.

28 John had been working in Cork for some months, at Shanahan's, a butter merchant's. He was staying with his great-uncle Mick Power, who was a pig buyer.

29 In 'A Shriek of Warning', G.K. Chesterton (1874–1936) had attacked the views then held by his brother Cecil (1879–1918) and by H.T. Muggeridge (1864–1942), arguing that their socialism was too abstract and too reliant on a political oligarchy: *New Age*, 29 April 1909.

30 This play by 'A Patriot' (Guy du Maurier, 1865–1915) was being performed to packed houses in London and at the Theatre Royal in Dublin. It 'depicted an invasion [of England] by the troops of the Northern Emperor, and the failure of the volunteers of Territorial forces to deal with them', according to the *Annual Register 1909*, p.8. It reflected one of the invasion scares sporadically current in Britain during this period.

31 The playwright Lennox Robinson (1886–1958) was director and literary manager of the Abbey Theatre from 1909 to 1914 and again from 1919 until his death. *The Cross-Roads*, one of his early plays, is set in rural Cork.

32 Cecil Chesterton, 'For the Reassurance of G.K.C.', and letter by H.T. Muggeridge, *New Age*, 6 May 1909.

33 The Chancellor of the Exchequer, David Lloyd George (1863–1945), had just introduced a budget that proposed tax increases on alcohol, tobacco and petrol, as well as a supertax on incomes above £5,000 per annum.

34 The theme of *The Embers* is young Ireland versus old Ireland, radical nationalism versus parliamentary politics. According to the *Cork Examiner* (7 May 1909), 'the play is peculiarly unconventional, and of that quality the author might feel fortified, if not proud'. It was written by Daniel Corkery (1878–1964), an influential writer and teacher. He was also the author of *The Hidden Ireland* (1924), and of *Synge and Anglo-Irish Literature* (1931). He was subsequently Professor of English at UCC from 1931 to 1947, and a senator of the Irish Republic from 1951 to 1954.

35 *New Age*, 13 May 1909.

36 This was the nickname, which originated in *The Leader*, published by D.P. Moran (1869–1936), for the section of the Irish Party associated with publicans and licensed vintners. The meeting was described in the *Irish Independent* on 13 May as 'An All Ireland Protest' against Lloyd George's budget.

37 There had been strikes in Cork involving tramway workers and builders' labourers. The following month there began a general strike that lasted for several weeks and paralysed the commercial life of Cork. Eventually the Cork Employers' Federation wore down the strikers, although, as the Cork Parnellite John J. Horgan recalled, 'like all such victories it created a false sense of power in the employers and bitterness in the employees': *Parnell to Pearse* (Dublin, 1948), pp.175ff.

38 This intriguing reference relates to an item in 'On the People's Service' in the *IN&P*, 13 March 1909. As Michael wrote, Archbishop Healy had criticised certain Dublin papers for undermining morals. Although he did not specifically cite the *IN&P*, it was widely believed to have been one of his targets. In a combative response 'On the People's Service' commented that Healy 'ought to be particularly careful in a matter like this ... there ought to be a special sense of sanctity and asceticism about his immediate surroundings. Yet in those surroundings some time ago two events took place within a week of each other which showed the weakness of human nature even in an archiepiscopal environment ... We suggest to him [Healy] that it will be well for him in future to be scrupulously careful in his references to national journals and the questions of morality...' It is not known to what events the *IN&P* was referring.

39 The novelist George Meredith had died on 18 May.

40 G.R.S. Taylor, 'H.G.Wells: Early Victorian Politician', *New Age*, 20 May 1909. The sketch by Bernard Shaw (1856–1950) was reprinted in the *New Age*, 27 May 1909.

41 James Keir Hardie (1856–1915) was MP for Merthyr Tydfil from 1900 to 1915, and was leader of the Labour Party from its foundation in 1906 until 1908 and again in 1910. Robert Blatchford (1851–1943) was a radical journalist and editor of the socialist weekly *The Clarion*. Victor Grayson (1881–1920?) was a journalist and lecturer who served as Independent Labour Party MP for Colne Valley from 1907 to 1910, and whose disappearance in 1920 remains unexplained.

42 Synge had died on 24 March 1909.

43 There was a spate of airship sightings over various parts of southern England at this time, but not over Ireland. On 31 May the Zeppelin II made a forced landing after spending a record thirty-seven hours in the air. Michael was also joking about the current atmosphere of invasion scares, provoked in part by Guy du Maurier's play *An Englishman's Home*. There was another 'airship scare' in February and March 1913.

44 Jacob Tonson, 'Books and Persons', *New Age*, 27 May 1909.

45 An essay by Karl Heckel on Nietzsche's thought, ibid.

46 *Michael Davitt, Revolutionary Agitator and Labour Leader* by Francis Sheehy-Skeffington (1878–1916) had been published the previous year.

47 Frederick Ryan (1873–1913) was a socialist journalist and writer; secretary of the Irish National Theatre Society; founder of the Dublin Philosphical Society (in 1906); co-founder of *Dana* with John Eglinton (pseudonym of William Kirkpatrick Magee, 1868–1961), and of *National Democrat* with Francis Sheehy-Skeffington; and editor of the *Egyptian Standard* from 1907 to 1909. Ryan used various pen names in the many periodicals to which he contributed, the best-known of which were Eoin, Finian and Irial. See also Introduction to this volume, pp.xxviii–xxix.

48 According to the *IN&P*, 19 June 1909, 'A very largely attended meeting was held in the Trades Hall, Capel Street, on Sunday evening, in response to an appeal issued to Irish Socialists willing to establish a Socialist organisation for Ireland. About 150 persons, including several ladies, were present.' The trade unionist William O'Brien was 'moved to the chair' and Frederick Ryan was appointed one of the honorary secretaries. Michael's membership card survives among his papers.

49 This letter and those following reflect the debate taking place in the *New Age* and other periodicals about the perceived physical decline and decadence of the population of the United Kingdom (then, of course, including Ireland). For example, at a luncheon given in honour of the Antarctic explorer Ernest Shackleton (1874–1922), Lord Halsbury (1823–1921) had declared that Shackleton's exploits in the Antarctic were proof that the 'supposed deterioration of the British race' was a myth. In a letter to *The Times* on 18 June 1909 Francis Galton (1822–1911), one of the leading proponents of eugenics, disagreed with Halsbury: 'The bulk of the community is deteriorating ... judging from the inquiries into the teeth, hearing, eyesight and malformations of children in Board schools, and from the apparently continuous increase of insanity and feeble-mindedness...'

50 Michael is here reiterating some of the points made by Francis Grierson in 'Towards Anglo-American Solidarity', *New Age*, 24 June 1909.

51 The O'Hickey controversy was about to reach its climax. On 22 June the Trustees of Maynooth passed a resolution calling on O'Hickey to resign his position as Professor of Irish. In its editorial of 26 June, the *IN&P* called his dismissal 'an act of gross injustice and ingratitude'.

52 *Irish Independent* 25 and 26 June 1909.

53 Sydney Brooks, *The New Ireland* (Dublin and London, 1907). Brooks (1872–1937) was a frequent contributor to British and American journals, and later wrote *Aspects of the Irish Question* (1912).

54 James McCann (1850–1904), MP for College Green, Dublin, had invited W.P. Ryan to edit the *Irish Peasant*. Following McCann's death his family came under ecclesiastical pressure to stop their financial support for the paper.

55 The article appeared in the issue of 3 July. It described O'Hickey's dismissal as 'really a miserable and intolerant business. It is high time to let Castle bishops and other bishops know, not violently, but squarely and unmistakably, that the days when they held the nation in the hollow of their hands, or could knock independent-minded men on the head with impunity, are as dead as the Middle Ages.' O'Hickey was never reinstated. He spent much of the following years engaged in a long and fruitless appeal to Rome against his dismissal. He died in 1916.

56 *The Ordeal of Richard Feverel* (1859) is a novel by George Meredith.

Notes on Chapter Two

1 Gustave Flaubert, *Madame Bovary* (1857); Alphonse Daudet, *Sapho* (1884).

2 In these elections William O'Brien (1852–1928) was, as Michael predicted, elected for Cork North-East. He was also correct in his prediction that Maurice Healy (1859–1923), brother of T.M. Healy (1855–1931), MP for Louth North, would take over this seat when, in the second general election of 1910 (in December), O'Brien opted to sit for Cork City. James Gilhooly (1847–1916) and D.D. Sheehan (1873–1948), two of O'Brien's supporters, were elected for Cork West and Mid-Cork respectively; Laurence Ginnell (1854–1923), an Independent Nationalist, was elected for Westmeath North, as was another O'Brienite, Patrick Guiney (1862–1913), for Cork North. John O'Donnell (1856–?), also an O'Brienite, was elected for Mayo South; John McKean (1868–?), Independent Nationalist, was elected for Monaghan South; P.J. O'Shaughnessy (1872–1920), of the Irish Party, was elected unopposed for Limerick West; Neville Stack (Independent Nationalist) was defeated in Kerry North by the sitting MP, M.J. Flavin (1861–1944), also of the Irish Party. Thomas O'Donnell (1872–1943) of the Irish Party was elected unopposed in Kerry West, the Moynihans' constituency. One of the hardest-fought electoral battles took place in Kerry East, where Maurice Moynihan, Michael and John's father, played an active role supporting the Independent candidate, Eugene O'Sullivan (1879–1942), who defeated the sitting MP, John Murphy. This result was overturned by an electoral court the following June because of irregularities on the part of O'Sullivan. In December 1910 O'Sullivan's cousin, Timothy O'Sullivan (d. 1950), stood in the constituency and won. In retrospect, John J. Horgan (1881–1967), a leading Cork Redmondite, saw these revolts against the leadership of John Redmond (1856–1918) in 1910 as 'the first step in the process which led to the eventual *débacle* of the constitutional movement': *Parnell to Pearse*, p.177.

3 Mary Moynihan's younger brother, Patrick Power, and his wife lived at Ballyvelly near Tralee.

4 The *Irish Independent's* 'Our London Letter' reported on 11 May that John Power was to edit the new journal of the London Gaelic League, *An tEireannach*. He held this post for only a year; it was then taken over by W.P. Ryan, who returned to London after the closure of the *IN&P* in December 1910.

5 Michael's surviving papers do not include any certificates for shares in West African companies. Most of his shares were in rubber companies.

6 'Mamma' or 'Grandmama' was Mary Moynihan's mother, Mary Power.

7 This was the London home of Michael's uncle John Power and his wife Lizzie.

8　Edward VII had died on 6 May. In Kerry the accession of his successor, George V, was proclaimed from the steps of the Courthouse in Tralee on 14 May: Peter Malone (ed.), *Images and Chronicles from the Archives of* The Kerryman *Newspaper: A Portrait of Kerry in the 20th Century* (Tralee, 2001), pp.32, 34.

9　Following elections in May 1910 conflict arose between the Catholic Church and the Spanish government over the reform programme of José Canalejas y Mendes, the democratic liberal Prime Minister. Canalejas revived earlier decrees that required the civil registration of religious orders. In the ensuing unrest a conservative leader was assassinated by an anarchist and there were strikes.

10　*The Celtic Twilight* was first published in 1893.

11　Cecil Chesterton (see also note 29 in Chapter 1) was writing a series of articles for the *New Age*, July to August 1910, entitled 'How the Rich Rule Us'.

12　The Parliamentary Franchise (Women) Bill was debated in the House of Commons on 11–12 July. To the fury of the suffragettes and their supporters, the Liberal Prime Minister, H.H. Asquith (1852–1928), and the Home Secretary, Winston Churchill (1874–1965), refused to support the bill, although it was supported by the Conservative leaders A.J. Balfour (1848–1930) and Andrew Bonar Law (1858–1923).

13　Michael is referring to the Dublin Horse Show.

14　Editor's translation:

Forgive me for not replying sooner to your letters.

I assume that you are working hard at your studies and that you are finding some interesting books?

I missed the CTS conferences completely. Also the proceedings of Mr F. Ryan and his comrades. As for his articles in *The Nation*, they would take too long to read. In my opinion, the main, almost the only, virtue of the Vatican is its opposition to democracy, and I regard efforts to eliminate that opposition as criminal and dangerous.

In this respect, I don't believe that the Conservative Party will collapse, as you seem to think. That would be too great a calamity. There is always hope!

Were you at the Theatre Royal recently? I read in the *News* that there was a good concert that was well-received, but alas! the audience did not live up to expectations.

Please excuse the mistakes...

15　There had been a poorly attended concert at the Theatre Royal in Tralee, featuring principals from the Limerick Operatic Society's production of *The Yeoman of the Guard*.

16　Editor's translation:

The political situation is very serious. The radical government, with a cynical indifference to the commercial interests of the nation, wants to preciptitate an election on an issue on which depends the whole future of the Empire. The prospect is so gloomy that, if the patriotic party loses this election, we will see...

The quotation in English comes from the closing pages of Well's *Tono-Bungay* (1909): 'England and the Kingdom, Britain and the Empire, the old prides and the old devotions, glide abeam, astern, sink down upon the horizon, pass – pass. The river passes – London passes, England passes ...'

17　The All For Ireland League (AFIL) had been founded by William O'Brien MP, who also owned the AFIL's newspaper, the *Cork Free Press*. Cronin was defeated by the sitting MP, John P. Boland (1870–1958).

18 M.J. Flavin (1861–1944) was returned unopposed for Kerry North and Thomas O'Donnell for Kerry West. In Kerry East, contrary to John's prediction, there were only two candidates, Timothy O'Sullivan (d. 1950) of the Irish Party and Patrick Guiney, an O'Brienite. O'Sullivan won.

19 The election resulted in a dead heat between the Liberals and the Conservatives, with 272 seats each. The Liberals remained in power, however, with the backing of the Irish Party and the Labour Party. The Veto Bill was aimed at restricting the veto of the House of Lords over legislation initiated by the House of Commons. The new king, George V, agreed to create the necessary number of new peers to ensure the passing of the bill, but the Lords avoided this by reluctantly passing it in August 1911. This paved the way for the introduction of the Third Home Rule Bill in April 1912.

20 Charles Hobhouse (1862–1941) was Financial Secretary to the Treasury from 1908 to 1911.

21 The coronation of George V had taken place on 22 June.

22 Father Charles Brennan was a curate at St John's in Tralee and was a supporter of Thomas O'Donnell MP. Boland was John P. Boland, MP for Kerry South. Father Brennan later became chaplain to the Tralee Volunteers in 1913–14.

23 The coronation visit of King George and Queen Mary to Ireland had taken place from 7 to 11 July.

24 The College of Science on Merrion Street became Government Buildings after 1922.

25 Mary had received the money from the estate of her father, who had died in 1907. Between 1909 and 1913 Michael regularly bought shares mainly in rubber and mining companies.

26 There appears to have been no reference to this incident in the newspapers.

27 Pat Power ('Pat the Rock') was a great-uncle of Michael and John, and father of John and Tess Power, mentioned in the following letter.

28 The brothers' cousin John Power was about to join the Dominican Order, whose provincial headquarters were at Tallaght in south Dublin.

29 *A Butterfly on the Wheel*, a drama, and *The Girl on the Train*, a musical, were being performed at the Theatre Royal, Dublin.

30 James McElligott had sat for the same civil service examinations that Michael had but was unplaced; he had apparently taken great exception to the unionist views expressed by the examiner at the French oral exam. He passed the Indian Civil Service examinations the following year but did not go to India, opting instead for an appointment with the Local Government Board in Dublin: Leon Ó Broin, *No Man's Man* (Dublin, 1982), pp.11, 66.

31 The title and author of this book are not known.

32 A.J. Balfour had resigned as leader of the Conservative Party on 8 November. He was succeeded by Andrew Bonar Law.

Notes to Chapter Three

1 Austen Chamberlain (1863–1937) had been defeated by Bonar Law for the Conservative leadership.

2 'Moss' is obviously a code word for a young woman, possibly the Delia Rorke mentioned in Document 54. On the back of this letter from John there is a draft

letter written by Michael to 'Miss D':

I hope I have not been slow in redeeming my promise to write. Ask how you have been since leaving the old country on Tuesday. I heard your journey over was a pleasant one, though it must have been rather fatiguing.

Doubtless London is like a Heaven to you after the terrible old town. It cannot be denied that we are a bit slow [word unclear] at least. You are lucky to get out of the place so soon, as they are talking now of stopping the mail boat to Holyhead, and I am sure if the strike continues much longer there will be no getting over to your side.

By the way, did you know any people named Loftus in your little town. There is a medical student of that name in here from Ballina.

I am in hopes of running over to London for a few days at Easter, and if so I shall not fail to look you up. Be a good child until then.

With much love to Leicester Sq. and all around & hope to hear from you soon. I am yours sincerely MJM.

3   'Without the alternative of a fine'. This comment seems to indicate that 'Moss' was involved in the suffragettes' window-breaking campaign in London, which started on 1 March. There is no mention of a Delia Rorke among those charged, although some of the names given in court were clearly false. The Irish suffragette paper, the *Irish Citizen,* reported in its first issue, dated 25 May 1912, that delegates from the Irish Women's Franchise League and other Irish women 'joined in these protests on their individual responsibility and were imprisoned'. The romance with 'Moss' does not seem to have survived these events.

4   Leo Casey was a Tralee friend of Michael and John's.

5   Lord Hugh Cecil (1869–1956), *Conservatism* (London, 1912).

6   This quotation comes from *Conservatism*, Chapter 4, 'Religion and Politics'.

7   Member of the Irish Parliament. It is not known to which cousin John was refer-ring as his letter has not survived.

8   The British Prime Minister, H.H. Asquith, was paying a visit to Dublin from 18 to 20 July. He spoke at the Theatre Royal on 19 July.

9   Edward Ponderevo is a character in H.G.Wells's novel *Tono-Bungay* (1909).

10 There had been some rowdy incidents during the Prime Minister's visit, most notably when the suffragette Miss Leigh threw a hatchet at Asquith's carriage and wounded John Redmond, the leader of the Irish Parliamentary Party. She was arrested with an accomplice who had tried to set fire to the Theatre Royal. At the meeting in the Theatre Royal a bearded clergyman sprang up as soon as Asquith started speaking and cried 'What about votes for women?' It was Francis Sheehy-Skeffington in disguise. The incident is described in Horgan, *Parnell to Pearse,* p.219.

11 The 'Mollies' were the Ancient Order of Hibernians (AOH). Box was a colleague of Michael's at the Surveyor of Taxes Office.

12 The Moynihans usually spent part of the summer at Fenit on Tralee Bay, about ten miles from Tralee.

13 Mr Hardcastle is a character in Oliver Goldsmith's play *She Stoops To Conquer* (1773).

14 Lord Halsbury was one of the 'ditchers' pledged to resist the removal of the House of Lords' veto to the last ditch.

15 *Daily Sketch* 20 July 1912. The photograph that John refers to is captioned: 'Clergy welcoming the Premier with flags as the boat approaches the quay at Kingstown.'

It is unclear which particular cleric attracted John's ire.

16 The sentiment is expressed by Ovid (43 BCE–18 CE), although not in these exact words, in *Ars Amatoria* iii, 21.

17 Michael Power, Mary Moynihan's uncle, lived in Cork.

18 Daly's was a firm of Cork butter merchants.

19 The nature of this 'folly' is unknown.

20 Michel de Montaigne (1533–92) *Essais*.

21 The clauses of the Third Home Rule Bill dealing with the proposed Irish Senate had been debated by the House of Commons at the end of October. Asquith stated that after an initial term of five years, when it would be nominated, the Senate would be elected by the four provinces using a system of proportional representation, which Asquith defended as a safeguard for the minority: *Annual Register 1912*, pp.227–8.

22 Czar Ferdinand of Bulgaria (1861–1948). War had broken out in the Balkans on 31 October with attacks on the Ottoman empire by Bulgaria and Serbia. Over the following month Ottoman forces suffered major reverses.

23 Nazim was the Ottoman Minister for War.

24 The 'Trinity amendment' was an amendment proposed by Walter Guinness MP (later 1st Baron Moyne, 1880–1944) that sought to place Trinity College Dublin on the reserved list of subjects for which the proposed Irish Parliament would not be able to legislate.

25 Major John MacBride (1865–1916), one of the leaders of the pro-Boer Irish Brigade, also spoke at this commemoration.

26 Mary was expecting her youngest child, Thomas, who was born in May 1913.

27 Jo Power was Mary's cousin, daughter of her uncle Pat Power, and sister of John and Tess.

28 Maisie Brosnan was the daughter of a Tralee hotel owner and Eily was the daughter of Larry Quinlan. The Quinlans were relatives and close friends of the Moynihan family.

29 Montenegrin forces had captured Mount Tarabosh from the Ottoman forces on 2 April.

30 H.G. Wells, *The New Machiavelli* (1911).

31 Immanuel Kant, *Critique of Practical Reason* (1788).

32 According to the report, the Kerry County Secretary, P.M. Quinlan, who had defeated Maurice Moynihan for the post in 1899, was resigning for health reasons. His son Michael Quinlan, already working for the County Council, was a candidate for the post. The only other name mentioned in connection with the appointment was 'Michael Moynihan, son of Maurice Moynihan, Tralee'. On 3 May the *Kerry Sentinel* reported that 'Mr Michael Moynihan writes from Dublin to say that he is not a candidate for the position of Secretary to the Kerry County Council, and that never at any time had he the slightest ambition for the post. He adds further that he has no personal interest in the matter, and is completely indifferent as to who is or is not elected.'

33 P.M. Quinlan was succeeded as County Secretary by his son Michael. When the latter died in November 1918, he was succeeded by his brother W.F. Quinlan.

34 J.B. Quinnell was the owner of the *Kerry News*; Maurice P. Ryle was the owner of the *Kerry People* and the *Kerry Evening Star*.

35 *Richard Carvel* (1899) and *Coniston* (1906) are novels by the American writer Winston Churchill (1871–1947). John was a great admirer of Churchill's books.

36 George Chapman (translator), *The Iliads of Homer* (1611); *The Iliad, Done into English Prose by Andrew Lang, Walter Leaf and Ernest Myers* (London, 1909).

37 The speech by Michael Aherne at which Michael scoffs was reported in the *Kerry Sentinel* on 7 May: 'We are glad that that Mr Quinlan's son is to succeed him, a Nationalist succeeding a Nationalist, and the fact that he is his father's son and that he has for some years past been specially trained into the County Council work by his able and experienced father is the best guarantee that the interests of the ratepayers will be faithfully and efficiently protected in the future ... After all there is nothing like breeding and training, and we have both combined in young Mr Quinlan.'

38 George Raymond was the editor of the unionist *Kerry Evening Post*.

39 *Richard Carvel* is an historical novel describing the eponymous hero's adventures in America and Britain in the period of the American Revolution, during which he meets the English Whig leader Charles James Fox (an incident that Michael refers to in the following letter).

40 The manager of the Provincial Bank in Listowel had been held up and robbed of £780 on the way to the Abbeyfeale branch. Six men were subsequently arrested and charged.

41 Samuel Taylor Coleridge (1772–1834), *Aids to Reflection* (London, 1854).

42 Ralph Waldo Emerson (1803–82), *English Traits: Representative Men and Other Essays* (London, 1908).

43 Larry Quinlan was the father of the Eily mentioned in note 28 above.

44 Thomas, Michael and John's youngest sibling, had been born on 19 May.

45 This is the first reference in the correspondence to Maurice Moynihan's ill health. He contracted tuberculosis and from this time his health steadily deteriorated.

Notes to Chapter Four

1 Ivy Greene was a local belle whom Mary Moynihan suspects of trying to ensnare Michael.

2 Uncle John Power's London home was on this street.

3 Box and Vale were both colleagues of Michael's. See also Document 67.

4 James Larkin (1876–1947), leader of the Irish Transport and General Workers Union, had recently been convicted on a charge of using 'seditious language'. In August 1913 William Martin Murphy (1844–1919), owner of the *Irish Independent* and leader of the Dublin Employers' Federation, had given workers an ultimatum: to resign from Larkin's union or be dismissed. This led to a bitterly fought lock-out of workers by many Dublin employers, which lasted until the beginning of 1914.

5 This is a reference to Ivy Greene.

6 Morley Roberts (1857–1942), *Salt of the Sea* (Edinburgh, 1912), a collection of sailing adventure stories.

7 'Poor Thing' refers to Ivy's husband. See also note 9 below.

8 In 1914 Hannah became a boarder at Loreto College on St Stephen's Green, Dublin.

9 Ivy had married F.J.D. Twigg, a medical graduate of University College Cork, who became a doctor in the Royal Navy. The *Kerry Sentinel* reported on 4 March 1916 that while Ivy was on her way to Gibraltar to join her husband, she survived the mining of her ship off Dover with nothing more than shock and bruises.

10   Leo Casey passed his engineering exams in 1914.
11   The Liberals held Linlithgow, but with a reduced majority. At Reading the Unionist candidate was returned with a majority of more than 1,000, with the Labour candidate doing particularly well. In both constituencies, according to the *Annual Register*, the recent conviction of James Larkin for using 'seditious language' had caused a Labour revolt against Liberalism: *Annual Register 1913*, p.227.
12   This refers to Michael's reading of *Salt of the Sea* by Morley Roberts (see Document 92).
13   Rowland George Allanson-Winn, 5th Baron Headley (1855–1935), of Aghadoe House, Killarney, was the owner of the Glenbeigh estate. He was an engineer, not an architect, and had contested the Kerry South seat as a Unionist in 1892, winning just 96 votes. He was later President of the British Muslim Society.
14   *The Alternatives to Civil War* (London, 1913) was written by F.S. Oliver (1864–1934), one of the leading exponents of federalism and of a federal solution to the problem of Irish Home Rule. He was a director of the London department store Debenham & Freebody.
15   The book titles refer to a series of novels depicting the life of an Italian noble family, written by the American expatriate Francis Marion Crawford (1854–1909): *Saracinesca* (1887); *Sant 'Ilario* (1889); *Don Orsino* (1892) and *Corleone* (1896). Crawford, a Catholic convert, was born in Italy and spent most of his life there.
16   Hilaire Belloc (1870–1953), *The Path to Rome* (London, 1902).
17   Michael is probably referring to Duckworth's series *Studies in Theology*, which included some biographies of saints.
18   See Document 80 (in Chapter 3).
19   Mary is referring to her uncle Denis Power.
20   On 2 March, without telling his family, Michael had enlisted in the Prince of Wales' Own Civil Service Rifles, a Territorial Force unit of the London Regiment. Cullington, a fellow Surveyor of Taxes at the Putney office of the Inland Revenue, had witnessed Michael's attestation when he enlisted.
21   The new session of Parliament had opened on 20 February, a session during which the Home Rule Bill became law under the Parliament Act 1911. The second reading of the bill had started on 9 March, when, as a concession, Asquith had proposed the provisional exclusion of any Ulster county from the provisions of the Bill for six years. This had been rejected by the Unionists. In a speech at Bradford on 14 March Churchill, First Lord of the Admiralty, had declared that the government would stand firm; this was endorsed by Asquith in the House of Commons on 16 March. There were increasing references in the debates to unrest over Ulster in the Army and Navy, and this came to a head during the following days in the 'Curragh Mutiny'.
22   *Public Opinion*, 21 March 1914. This James Douglas was an Irish journalist, not the man of the same name who subsequently became an Irish senator.
23   Possibly M.J. O'Mullane, *Craobh Ruadh or The Red Branch Knights* (Dublin, 1910).
24   George Tyrrell, *Christianity at the Crossroads* (London, 1909). See also the Introduction to this volume.
25   Marguerite Audoux (1863–1937), *Marie-Claire* (London, 1911).
26   In the course of meetings held on 20–21 March, Brigadier General Sir Hubert de la Poer Gough (1870–1963), commander of the 3rd Cavalry Brigade, had asked the Irish GOC, Sir Arthur Paget (1851–1928), to make clear whether, if the

Home Rule Bill became law, officers would be called upon to enforce it in Ulster. A minute was written in reply, signed by the War Minister, John Seely (1868–1947), and Sir John French (later 1st Earl of Ypres, 1852–1925), Chief of the Imperial General Staff, to the effect that the government did not intend to crush political opposition to Home Rule. This was sent to Gough on 23 March, the same day on which Michael was writing this letter.

27   Under the Territorial and Reserve Forces Act 1907 'any part of the Territorial Force shall be liable to serve in any part of the United Kingdom'. However, no Territorial Force units were established in Ireland and, whatever Michael hoped or expected, sensitive political considerations made it unlikely that they would be used in Ulster. In fact, senior army officers and politicians close to Gough and the 'mutineers' actually discussed the possibility of using the Territorials as a pawn in their intrigues. The Conservative politician Leo Amery (1873–1955) and Brigadier General Henry Wilson (Director of Military Operations at the War Office, 1864–1922) considered 'the possibility of the Territorials . . . transferring themselves to a Union Defence Force. [Field Marshal] Lord Roberts . . . was tremendously keen and was prepared to go to any length if the situation demanded.' In his study of the Curragh Incident, Ian Beckett writes that 'nothing better illustrates the essential cynicism of Roberts and his circle than their attitude to the Territorial Force, which was now to be pressed into the political service of those who had spent six years denigrating it . . . ': Ian F.W. Beckett (ed.), *The Army and the Curragh Incident, 1914* (London, 1986), pp.6, 52–3.

28   Brooks Adams (1848–1927), *The Law of Civilisation and Decay: An Essay on History* (London, 1895).

29   This is another reference to the novels by F. Marion Crawford mentioned in Document 97.

30   This was a theme that Sir Roger Casement (1864–1916), who was closely involved with the newly formed Irish Volunteers, was expounding in several pamphlets written at this time, such as *The Elsewhere Empire* (1914) and *John Bull's Other Empire* (1914).

31   The Irish Councils Bill of 1907 was an unsuccessful attempt by the Liberal government to introduce a modest form of Home Rule based on a council that would be partly nominated and partly elected. The council would control eight departments of the Irish administration, with the Lord Lieutenant having the ultimate veto. Unionists opposed it as a covert form of Home Rule, while Nationalists refused to consider anything less than full Home Rule.

32   Michael is referring to William O'Brien MP.

33   *Sunday Chronicle*, 29 March 1914.

34   Henry James (1843–1916), 'The Younger Generation' – on the current state of the English novel – in the *Times Literary Supplement*, 20 March and 3 April 1914.

35   John's letter has not survived.

36   Michael and his uncle kept in touch after this, although relations were strained.

37   The Irish Volunteers (IV) had been growing rapidly since their foundation the previous November in Dublin. The first Tralee corps was established at the beginning of April 1914 and soon enrolled 800 men (according to the *Irish Volunteer*, 18 April 1914). The *Irish Volunteer* of 2 May 1914 – the issue sent by John and referred to here – contained an article entitled 'Wanted! 500,000 Volunteers. Safeguard Against Mutiny and Treason. Duty of the Irish in Great Britain.' The article declared: 'By all means let the Irish Nationalists in Great Britain be up and doing.

There are plenty of Territorials amongst them, plenty of ex-army men, who will enable them to drill and organise, and they may rely upon it that they will not be left alone to carry out their programme.' In June two large Volunteer parades were held in Tralee. The second, held on 28 June, was inspected by Patrick Pearse (1879–1916).

38   Colonel Maurice Moore (1854–1939) was one of the leading organisers of the Irish Volunteers. Michael is punning on Moore's surname and the Irish word *Mór*, 'the Great'.

39   The editorial in *The Universe* of 24 April 1914, 'The Pope and the King', discussed a recent incident in Canada when the Lieutenant Governor of Manitoba had refused to attend a Catholic banquet in Winnipeg because the Pope's name preceded that of the King in the Loyal Toast.

40   Joseph Devlin (1871–1934), Nationalist MP for Belfast West, was national president of the Ancient Order of Hibernians.

41   Maurice Barrès (1862–1923) had a considerable influence on young French writers in the years before the First World War. He campaigned for the return of Alsace-Lorraine from Germany to France and defended the Catholic Church against the anticlerical policies of the Third Republic. He regarded the Church as a force for order, even though he himelf was an agnostic. In his trilogy *Les Deracinés, L'appel du soldat* and *Leur figures* (1897–1902) he developed his philosophy of *la terre et les morts* ('land and the dead').

42   Naval patrols around the Irish coast had been increased in order to prevent more attempts at gun-running, but, so far as is known, no naval ships arrived at Fenit.

43   The elections for Kerry County Council had taken place on 28 May. During the campaign there was a flurry of correspondence in the *Kerry Weekly Reporter* over the election of the previous County Secretary, P.M. Quinlan, in 1899 (see Documents 83–85, in Chapter 3). The *Reporter* claimed on 23 May that Quinlan 'was put into the position by the Unionists who refused to vote for Mr Moynihan his Nationalist opponent'. In a letter to the *Reporter* on 30 May Maurice Moynihan observed caustically that 'Mr P.M. Quinlan and myself were both candidates for the Secretaryship of the Kerry County Council, and as Nationalists had about the same standing. It so happened that you took sides with him against me, and I have always given you the credit of influencing the entire Unionist vote in his favour.'

44   Bridie Quinlan was a daughter of Larry, a sister of Eily and a friend of Hannah. See Documents 80 and 87 (in Chapter 3).

45   'The Brahman of Concord', *Times Literary Supplement*, 16 July 1914.

46   Following the Howth gun-running on Sunday 26 July three people were killed and scores injured when British soldiers opened fire on a crowd at Bachelor's Walk in central Dublin.

47   This is a reference to Redmond's speech to the House of Commons on 27 July, in which he called for a full judicial and military enquiry into the Bachelor's Walk incident: 'Let the House clearly understand that four-fifths of the Irish people will not submit any longer to be bullied, or punished, or penalised, or shot for conduct which is permitted to go scot free in the open light of day in every county in Ulster...' – as reported in the *Freeman's Journal*, 28 July 1914.

48   Father R.B. Duggan, a Dominican priest, was a family friend.

49   The Revingtons owned a large drapery store and woollen mills in Tralee.

50   One of Michael's fellow soldiers in the CSR, Ralph Thompson, wrote in his diary that the response to the Adjutant's appeal 'was not generous. The majority of the men were in well paid jobs; not a few of them being in Government

employ did not feel prepared to damage their prospects by entangling themselves in complicated military ventures ... A few days later we were again harangued by the Colonel who told us that ... soldiers who were in Government employment would receive full salary less the amount of their Army pay. Moreover they would not forfeit any seniority while on active service. As a result of this information approximately 50 per cent declared their readiness to sign for foreign service.' Quoted in Peter Simkins, *Kitchener's Army: The Raising of the New Armies, 1914–1916* (Manchester, 1988), p.45.

51 Michael was officially transferred to the Home Service Battalion of the Civil Service Rifles on 28 November 1914.

52 Hannah did not settle in at Loreto and was subsequently expelled. She returned to an active social life in Tralee and became a leading light in the Tralee Gaelic League. She and John became particularly close.

53 Bedmond is near Abbots Langley in Hertfordshire.

Notes on Chapter Five

1 For the first half of 1915 Michael's unit of the Civil Service Rifles was attached to the 1/15th Battalion, London Regiment. In July more than 600 men were drafted to the 1/15th for service overseas. As one of the Home Service men Michael stayed behind and became a member of the 105th Provisional Battalion, which was attached to the 2/15th Battalion, London Regiment. For much of the year his unit moved around the Home Counties, between Dorking, London, Watford, Saffron Walden, Braintree and Ware. They practised trench fighting, bayonet fighting, drilling, route marches and rifle training. However, as casualties mounted on the Western Front and the clamour for conscription grew, Michael became well-aware it was only a matter of time before he would have to serve overseas. It was a prospect, as the poem in Document 133 (in Chapter 4) indicates, that he privately welcomed, although he did not say so to his increasingly anxious mother. Information in this note is from PRO WO95/3030 War Diaries of 2/15th Battalion, London Regiment.

2 Owing to censorship Michael's cheerful account of this inspection omitted the real conditions that he experienced that day. Twelve thousand troops from a number of divisions had to wait for more than two hours in a downpour of sleet and snow until Kitchener's party arrived. Many men collapsed from cold and exposure, but there was only one ambulance on duty. Two men died. See Peter Simkins, *Kitchener's Army: The Raising of the New Armies, 1914–1916* (Manchester, 1988), pp.303–4.

3 Wilfrid Ward (1886–1916) was a prominent Catholic writer and apologist, an examiner for the former Royal University of Ireland, a member of the Royal Commission on Irish university education, a former editor of the *Dublin Review*, and a biographer of Cardinals Newman and Wiseman. Ward was criticised by the *IN&P* as one of a group of English Catholics hypocritically opposed to an Irish Catholic university 'unless in tone, trend and atmosphere it is thoroughly English': *IN&P*, 6 March 1909.

4 Lord Gormanston was Jenico Edward Joseph Preston, 15th Viscount Gormanston (1879–1925).

5 Winston Churchill, *The Inside of the Cup* (London, 1913). This novel, set in the American Middle West, describes the conflict between an idealistic young clergyman, John Hodder, and a powerful, unscrupulous financier, Eldon Parr.

6 Henry Seton Merriman (pseudonym of Hugh Stowell Scott, 1862–1903), *Barlasch of the Guard* (London, 1903).

7 This is the only incomplete letter in the collection: the closing pages appear to have been lost.

8 'Uncle Mick' was the brothers' great-uncle Michael Power (see also Introduction to this volume, pp.xv–xix). The *Kerry Sentinel* wrote that 'his generosity will be a loss to many. His nature was opposed to all things that savoured of hoarding the riches of the world. He loved the poor and the oppressed, and to them he gave what he earned in an unstinted and ungrudging manner. He was one of the Old Guard that fought so many battles for Ireland in the dark and evil days.' *Kerry Sentinel*, 6 March 1915.

9 John was possibly referring to George Perris, *A Short History of War and Peace* (London, 1911).

10 Michael underlined the word 'his' and wrote in the margin 'I don't recognise *his* Church at all'.

11 Following the death of the sitting MP, J.P. Nanetti (1857–1915), a by-election was held in June 1915 and won by the Irish Party's candidate, J.D. Nugent (d. 1940). Although Casement was mentioned as a possible candidate for this election, he was by this time in Germany, seeking help for an insurrection in Ireland.

12 Italy had left the Triple Entente with Germany and Austria–Hungary, and declared war on both these former allies.

13 The *Lusitania* was torpedoed off the Cork coast on 7 May 1915.

14 This professor has not been identified.

15 A coalition government had just been formed, consisting of thirteen Liberals, eight Conservatives and one Labour minister. John Redmond, the leader of the Irish Party, had refused to accept a post in the new government.

16 During the first week of June there had been heavy Zeppelin raids over the east coast of England.

17 Winston Churchill, *A Far Country* (London, 1915).

18 J.A. Cramb (1862–1913), *Germany and England* (London, 1914).

19 It is not known to which cousin Michael is referring here.

20 *Dichtung und Wahrheit* is the title of Goethe's four-part autobiography (1811–33).

21 The reference is to a review of A.M. Ludovici, *A Defence of Aristocracy: A Text Book for Tories* in the *Times Literary Supplement*, 12 August 1915.

22 Johann Wolfgang von Goethe, *Wilhelm Meisters Lehrjahre* (1795–96).

23 There had evidently been some anxiety in the family that Michael was being proselytised by the Young Men's Christian Association, which was associated with Protestantism.

24 In October 1915 Serbia was attacked by Germany and Bulgaria. In response, an Anglo-French expeditionary force landed at Salonika in Greece. Although Greece was allied to Serbia, the Greek government was reluctant to take the country into war and the Anglo-French landing led to the resignation of the Prime Minister, Eleutherios Venizelos (1864–1936), who favoured the Allies. However, the Anglo-French force was powerless to prevent Serbia from being overrun by German and Bulgarian forces by the end of November. During the retreat back to Salonika the brunt of the fighting was borne by the Dublin and Munster Fusiliers and the Connaught Rangers.

25 'Tino' was King Constantine I of the Hellenes (1868–1923).

26 John McGaley, a prominent Kerry GAA footballer and a member of the Tralee Corps of Volunteers, was sentenced to three months' hard labour for 'using language likely to cause disaffection to His Majesty, and to prejudice recruiting'. He was alleged to have said 'D... the King': *Kerryman*, 27 November 1915.

27 Dr Edward O'Dwyer (1842–1917), Bishop of Limerick, had written a letter, published in most Irish newspapers on 10 November 1915, criticising the treatment that he believed 'poor Irish emigrant lads' had received in Liverpool. 'They do not want to be forced into the English army, and sent to fight English battles in some part of the world. It is very probable that these poor Connaught peasants know little or nothing of the meaning of the war. Their blood is not stirred by the memory of Kossovo [*sic*], and they have no burning desire to die for Serbia ... Small nationalities, and the wrongs of Belgium and Rheims Cathedral, and all the other cosmopolitan considerations that rouse the enthusiasm of the Irish Party, but do not get enough of recruits in England, are far too high-flying for uneducated peasants.' The letter appeared in the *Kerryman*, 13 November 1915. It is discussed by Jerome aan de Wiel in *The Catholic Church in Ireland, 1914–1918* (Dublin, 2003) pp.71–4.

28 Ruport Brooke had died in Greece, of blood poisoning, in April 1915.

Notes on Chapter Six

1 John is possibly referring to the companion volume to the translation of *The Iliad* that he had liked so much in 1913 (see Item 84, in Chapter 3), *The Odyssey of Homer Done into English by S.H. Butcher and A. Lang* (London, 1885).

2 Charles Kingsley (1819–75), *The Heroes, or Greek Fairy Tales* (1856).

3 The Military Service Act, introducing conscription for men aged between eighteen and forty, had been passed by the House of Commons in January and came into force at the beginning of March 1916. Ireland was excluded from the operation of the Act. As Michael had expected, the introduction of the Act left him with little choice but to sign up for foreign service and although, for the sake of his mother, he dutifully went through the motions of an appeal, he knew that it would not succeed.

4 Father Robert Kane, SJ, 'Worth', a series of six lectures, the *Irish Catholic*, 25 March to 22 April 1916.

5 It is an indication of Michael's preoccupation with his service problems that he did not appreciate the extent to which the mails had been disrupted in the wake of the Easter Rising.

6 Michael seems to have been unaware that eight officers and 300 men from the battalion had already embarked for Queenstown (Cobh) on 1 May. According to the battalion's war diary, they established camp at 'Fotay Park' (Fota) and moved on from there to Ballincollig, Coachford, Macroom, Ballyvoigue, Nutley and Millstreet, having made one arrest in Macroom, when about a hundred soldiers accompanied by RIC officers went out to a farm and arrested 'a few Irishmen ... These were the "rebels" which the Battalion had set out to quell.' They returned to Warminster via Rosslare on 13 May. See PRO WO95/3030, battalion war diaries; and *History of the Prince of Wales' Own Civil Service Rifles* (London, 1921), pp.232–5.

7   Pearse's visit to Tralee had been reported in the Kerry press. 'Commandant
     Pearse of the Headquarters Staff of the Irish Volunteers visited Tralee on
     Sunday [27 February] and inspected the Corps of the Tralee District ... the
     review being attended by a large number of the public ... Commandant Pearse
     afterwards addressed the Volunteers, and impressed on them the importance of
     activity and of gaining efficiency in soldier's work...At the lecture delivered in
     the Rink by Commandant Pearse on "The Nature of Freedom", there was a very
     large enthusiastic audience ... He gripped the attention of the audience who
     followed every word with the greatest interest often breaking into loud applause
     to show their delight and approval of the eloquent, intellectual and able manner
     in which he dealt with the subject. Especially was this noticeable when after illus-
     trating one of his points he finished it off with the dogmatic pronouncement:
     "We have neither personal nor national freedom in Ireland today". His refer-
     ences to Wolfe Tone, Davis, Fintan Lawlor [*sic*] and John Mitchel also aroused
     much enthusiasm. It may be truly said that the lecture was never surpassed, if
     ever equalled, in Tralee.' These are extracts from the *Kerry Sentinel*, 1 March 1916,
     and the *Kerryman*, 4 March 1916. Pearse's lecture was organised as a benefit for
     John McGaley (see Item 153, in Chapter 5). On the same page of *The Kerryman*
     as the report just quoted there is a reprint of a letter to *The Times* from Sir
     Morgan O'Connell of Killarney, expressing the view that 'every village in Kerry
     is rotten with it [Sinn Féinism]'. O'Connell had to get police protection because
     of his hostility to Sinn Féin. PRO CO904/100, Monthly Report, June 1916.
8   Frank Fahy (1879–1953) had taught Michael and John at the Christian Brothers'
     School in Tralee. He played a prominent part in the War of Independence and
     on the republican side in the Civil War. He was a Fianna Fáil TD for Galway
     constituencies from 1927 to 1953. He also served as Ceann Comhairle of the
     Dáil from 1933 to 1953. Edward Daly (1891–1916), who came from a prominent
     Limerick Fenian family, was executed on 4 May.
9   *Irish Independent*, 19 May 1916. Sir Mathew Nathan (1862–1939) was Under-
     Secretary at Dublin Castle. The government had appointed Charles Hardinge, 1st
     Baron Hardinge of Penshurst (1858–1944), who had been Viceroy of India from
     1910 until earlier in 1916, to chair the commission that investigated the Rising.
10   During the Rising, on 28–29 April, soldiers from the South Staffordshire
     Regiment attempted to capture a Volunteer post at the corner of Church Street
     and North King Street. Approximately fifteen civilians living on or near North
     King Street were shot and bayoneted by soldiers. The Bryce Commission inves-
     tigated the massacre of Armenians in the Ottoman Empire during 1915–16: its
     report was published later in 1916.
11   The enclosed document has not survived.
12   This was reported in the *Kerry Sentinel*, 31 May 1916.
13   Austin Stack (1879–1929) and Con Collins (1881–1937) were key members of
     the Volunteers' leadership in Kerry. Stack was IRB head centre for Kerry and
     was a close friend of the Moynihans. Collins was later TD for the Kerry–West
     Limerick constituency, 1918–22. Stack and Collins were arrested on Good Friday
     (21 April) and put on trial in mid-June. They were found guilty and sentenced to
     penal servitude for life. Maurice Moynihan corresponded with Stack while he
     was in prison. See Austin Stack Papers NLI MS 17,089.
14   The *Irish Catholic* was strongly in favour of the war and hostile to the Rising.
15   The battalion left for France on 22 June and was based at Maroeuil, northwest of

Arras. It was in action on the first day of the Battle of the Somme, 1 July. Over the next three months it alternated with the 2/14th Battalion rotating between the three lines of trenches – front, support and reserve – which had been dug at a distance of four to five miles from the front line, with a week in rest billets. See PRO WO95/3030, battalion war diaries; and *History of the Prince of Wales' Own Civil Service Rifles* (London, 1921), pp.238–42.

16   The enclosure is missing but was probably Michael's will, which he had made that day. Mary was the sole legatee.

17   William Waldegrave Palmer, 2nd Earl of Selborne (1859–1942) resigned as President of the Board of Agriculture; Walter Long (1854–1924), a former Chief Secretary for Ireland, was President of the Local Government Board; and Henry Charles Petty-Fitzmaurice, 5th Marquis of Lansdowne (1845–1927), a former Viceroy of India, was Foreign Secretary (and a considerable Kerry landlord). These three were the leading Conservative supporters of the southern unionists. In the aftermath of the Rising, Asquith had deputed Lloyd George to try and find a political settlement based on the immediate introduction of Home Rule, but his efforts failed in the face of both unionist and nationalist opposition once they discovered he had been making contradictory proposals to both sides about the exclusion of Ulster.

18   Casement was hanged on 3 August 1916.

19   Sir Frederick Edwin Smith (subsequently 1st Earl of Birkenhead, 1872–1930) was Attorney General from 1915 to 1918. Rufus Daniel Isaacs, 1st Marquis of Reading (1860–1935), had been appointed Attorney General in 1910 but had attracted controversy when it was discovered that he owned shares in the American Marconi Company at a time when the General Post Office had a contract with the British subsidiary of the company, of which Isaacs's brother was joint managing director. He had been cleared of impropriety in 1913 and later the same year had been appointed Lord Chief Justice, in which capacity he presided over Casement's trial.

20   The exact nature of Michael's clerical post is unclear. As this and subsequent letters make clear, he was still in the trenches, although not in the front line.

21   Ferdinand Brunetière, *Honoré de Balzac* (London, 1906).

22   Leo Casey was a lieutenant in the Royal Engineers. He was wounded in January 1916 and spent some months at home convalescing.

23   J.A. McQuade was Superintending Inspector at the Tax Office.

24   Michael J. Flavin was MP for Kerry North.

25   John Baily was a county councillor. At the first meeting of the Kerry County Council after the Easter Rising, he had proposed a resolution deploring the 'criminal folly in Dublin' but this was rejected by the chairman. Baily's son Denis was a lieutenant in the Royal Munster Fusiliers and was awarded the Military Cross.

26   Mary enclosed an Apostleship of Prayer badge with this letter.

27   It is not clear what the purpose of this note was, since Michael was already at the front. It may have been connected with Mary's efforts to get him a clerical post. Chute came from a well-known military family in Tralee.

28   J.P. Crowley was one of the commissioners of the Board of Inland Revenue. He was from Bandon, County Cork, and is mentioned in Leon Ó Broin, *The Prime Informer: A Suppressed Scandal* (London, 1971), pp.112–16.

29   Ian Macpherson (1880–1937), a Liberal MP, was Under-Secretary of State for War. In 1919–20 he was Chief Secretary for Ireland.

30 Joseph de Maistre (1755–1821) was a Catholic royalist and influential writer on the Counter-Reformation. *Du Pape* (1819) offers a defence of papal infallibility.

31 Samuel Butler (1835–1902) was the author of *The Way of All Flesh* and *Erewhon*.

32 Blaise Pascal, *Lettres provinciales* (1656–57).

33 Count de Montalembert, *Monks of the West*, a translation of Comte de Malembert (d. 1870), *Les moines d'occident*, seven volumes (Edinburgh and London, 1860–77).

34 Honoré de Balzac, *La peau de chagrin* (1830); *Le curé de Tours* (1832); *Le colonel Chabert* (1832); *Eugénie Grandet* (1833).

35 In a letter of 25 July, published in the Irish press, William Walsh, Catholic Archbishop of Dublin (1841–1921), expressed bitter criticism of the Irish Party and its recent negotiations with Lloyd George: 'For years past I never had a moment's doubt that the Irish Home Rule cause in Parliament was being led along a line that could only bring it to disaster ... The Home Rule Act is still on the Statute Book. Will Irish Nationalists be any longer befooled by a repetition of the party cries, that this fact makes them masters of the situation; that the Act cannot be modified without Nationalist consent; and that Ireland awaits only the end of the war to find the portals of the Old House in College Green automatically opened for the entry of the members greater than Grattan?'

36 *Irish Opinion* was a short-lived weekly that started publication in June 1916. Initially supportive of Sinn Féin, it subsequently took up a militant pro-labour position, and was suppressed during the conscription crisis in 1918. General Sir John Maxwell (1859–1929) was appointed commander in chief in Ireland in the aftermath of the Easter Rising and served in that post until November 1916. John Graham Hope de la Poer Horsley-Beresford, 5th Baron Decies (1866–1944) was Press Censor for Ireland from 1916 to 1919.

37 John Power's movements in 1916 are cloaked in mystery. He left London hurriedly, perhaps because he feared conscription. Although conscription applied only to men aged between eighteen and forty, there were many rumours that it would be extended to men up to fifty years old.

38 'Uncle Pat' and Mrs Power were Mary's younger brother and sister-in-law, who lived at Ballyvelly.

39 James Murphy was the son of a Tralee solicitor and was serving with the Royal Munster Fusiliers. He was wounded in September 1916 but survived the war.

40 Honoré de Balzac, *Les Chouans* (1828).

41 John's letter has not survived. He had been in poor health for more than a year and his illness, the exact nature of which is unknown, left him with a crippled shoulder for the rest of his life.

42 *Nullique ea tristis imago*: 'this sad image of nothingness'; *atra pallida mors*: 'gloomy pale death'.

43 It is not known who this 'young person' was.

44 Dunne is also yet to be identified.

45 On 29 October Michael had been admitted to No. 6 Stationary Hospital at Frévent suffering from pyrexia of unknown origin (PUO), a form of trench fever that had become a common complaint. He was transferred to No. 3 Canadian General Hospital on 31 October, and went from there to No. 7 Convalescent Hospital and Rest Camp at Boulogne. He returned to duty on 13 November. Since the 2/15th was about to leave for Salonika he was transferred to the 1/15th at the No. 8 Infantry Base Depot, Le Havre.

46 Michael and John's cousin John Power had recently been ordained, as Father

Hyacinth Power, at the Dominican House, San Clemente, in Rome. It was actually five years since Michael had last seen him.

47 See Document 87 (in Chapter 3).
48 'French jollity, serious and light-hearted at the same time'.
49 H.H. Asquith had resigned from the prime ministership on 7 December and had been succeeded by David Lloyd George. Romania had declared war on Germany and Austria–Hungary in August. In mid-November German forces under General von Falkenhayn and Field Marshal Mackensen attacked Romania from the north and south, leading within weeks to the surrender of the capital, Bucharest. By giving the Germans access to Romanian corn and oil, this victory helped them to prolong the war after the reverses of 1916.
50 J. Holland Rose (1855–1942), *The Development of the European Nations 1870–1914* (London, 1915).
51 Francis Thompson (1859–1907), 'The Hound of Heaven', first published in his *Poems* (1893); Canon Patrick Augustine Sheehan (1852–1913), *The Triumph of Failure* (1899), a novel in which Sheehan describes the vicissitudes of a failed student, Geoffrey Austin, and his religious doubts, which are resolved in his decision to become a Carmelite brother.
52 This letter, which has been considerably abridged, comprises twenty pages, mainly taken up with discussion of the role of the Church in the modern world and its relations with secular powers.

Notes on Chapter Seven

1 Father Caulfield was a Catholic chaplain serving with Michael's regiment.
2 R.H. Benson (1871–1914), *The Dawn of All* (London, 1911).
3 Denis Baily was killed in February 1917. He was very popular with his men and his Requiem Mass in Tralee was 'thronged', according to Thomas P. Dooley, *Irishmen or English Soldiers?* (Liverpool, 1995), p.193.
4 Michael applied for a commission the previous month. He was approved as 'in every respect suitable for a temporary commission' and on 20 February he went to the Officer Cadet Brigade (OCB) at Newmarket. The OCBs, which had been formed in February 1916, granted temporary commissions to those who had served in the ranks. Candidates' applications had to be approved by their commanding officers. The course lasted four months and was aimed at 'developing leadership and the cultivation of initiative and self-confidence'. See PRO WO374/49430; and Keith Simpson, 'The Officers', in I.F.W. Beckett and Keith Simpson (eds), *A Nation in Arms: A Social Study of the British Army in the First World War* (London, 1985), pp.80–1.
5 Jean Nesmy (pseudonym of Henry Surchamp), *A Parcel for Heaven and Other Stories* (London, 1917).
6 A recent by-election in Roscommon North had been won by Sinn Féin's candidate, Count Plunkett, who had received almost twice as many votes as the candidate of the 'Redmondite' Irish Party. George Plunkett (1851–1948), who had been given the title of Count by Pope Leo XIII in 1884, was the father of Joseph Plunkett, one of the leaders of the Easter Rising who were executed by the British.

7 On 9 May Joseph McGuinness (1875–1922), who had been in prison since the Rising, had been elected Sinn Féin MP for Longford South.

8 P.N. Milyukov (1859–1943) was Minister for Foreign Affairs in the first Russian Provisional Government after the abdication of Emperor Nicholas II. He had been forced to resign at the beginnning of May after sending a note to the other Allied governments stating that the Provisional Government would honour the diplomatic and military obligations of its predecessor.

9 The return of Austin Stack and Frank Fahy to Tralee after their release from prison was reported at length in the *Kerry Sentinel*, 23 June 1917.

10 The Irish Convention was the vehicle for another attempt by Lloyd George to achieve an Irish settlement. It sat from 25 July 1917 to 5 April 1918, but it was boycotted by Sinn Féin, while the Ulster Unionists used it as a forum to press their demand for exclusion of at least six, or preferably all nine, of the counties of Ulster from any settlement.

11 Michael was commissioned into the 2/8th (Irish) Battalion of the King's Liverpool Regiment. The 2/8th was one of the regiment's six second-line Territorial battalions and formed part of the 57th Division, which took part in the second Battle of Passchendaele (26 October to 10 November 1917). The 2/8th arrived at Provin on 19 October and on 25 October it moved forward to Eagle Trench, a support trench to the front line northeast of Langemarck. According to the regimental history, conditions were terrible. The whole area was waterlogged and the line consisted of consolidated shell-holes, which usually had about a foot of water in them, despite efforts to pump them out. Men and pack animals got lost in the sea of mud. 'By the 10th of November that terrible struggle between men and mud was over – the mud had won': Everard Wyrall, *The History of the King's Regiment (Liverpool) 1914–1919*, vol. 3, *1917–1919* (London, 1935), pp.537–40.

12 James McElligott had fought in the General Post Office garrison during the Easter Rising and had subsequently lost his job, despite Tom O'Donnell's efforts to have him reinstated. He had been deported to Great Britain and interned in various jails, including Stafford Jail, where he was in a cell next to the one occupied by Michael Collins (1890–1922). Legend had it that McElligott's experiences at the GPO included 'kicking his way through Clery's plateglass window to open an escape route to Marlboro' Street [and] seeking refuge behind a pillarbox there only to find Sean MacEntee installed and drawing unwelcome fire from all quarters'. McElligott said of his exploits at the GPO: 'I didn't feel a bit heroic. I was roaring like the bull of Bashan and simply mad, mad, mad.' Both quotations from the *Irish Times*, 26 and 30 January 1974. Sean MacEntee (1889–1984) served in Eamon de Valera's governments from 1932 and, as Minister for Finance, worked closely with McElligott and also with John Moynihan.

13 Lansdowne (see also Document 173, in Chapter 6) had written a letter to the *Daily Telegraph*, published on 29 November 1917, stating that the cause of peace in Germany could be helped by an assurance that 'we do not desire the annihilation of Germany as a Great Power' and that Britain did not 'seek to impose upon her people any form of Government other than that of their own choice'. Lansdowne's letter was strongly criticised for its alleged defeatism, although it later transpired that the British Foreign Office had known beforehand of its contents.

14 The 2/8th Liverpools were out of the line until mid-December. On 16

December they moved forward to the front line, as part of the 171st Brigade, and were ordered to take over a portion of the Houthulst Forest sector. The 2/8th relieved the 2/5th on the night of 20–21 December. The weather on 22 December was clear, which meant considerable activity by enemy aircraft. A heavy barrage started that afternoon, resulting in heavy casualties. On 27–28 December the snow melted, and the ground reverted to mud and slush. See KRM KR/1/12, 2/8th battalion war diaries.

15 Michael's battalion was now in the L'Epinette sector. The battalion war diary confirms that there was little activity by the Germans. For the next two months the work of the battalion was concentrated on the wiring of roads, the cleaning and reorganisation of companies, courses for officers, and drill. The 1/8th and 2/8th Liverpools were amalgamated on 31 January: KRM KR/1/12, battalion war diaries.

16 Maurice Moynihan died on the evening of 15 January. Michael was not able to attend the funeral, but was given compassionate leave shortly afterwards and used it to visit his family in Tralee.

17 This was the incident that occurred in 1888 and is described in Moynihan's Dublin Castle file (see Introduction to this volume, p.xvii). Cecil Roche, who lived at Mayglass House, Ballymacelligott, was one of the 'flying magistrates' (as opposed to the ordinary resident magistrates) who were employed by the government during the Plan of Campaign.

18 In the general election of 1892 the anti-Parnellite Sir Thomas Henry Grattan Esmonde (1862–1935) defeated Edward Harrington (1852–1902), a long-time friend and political associate of Maurice Moynihan, in the Kerry West constituency. Esmonde held the seat until 1900 when, in the general election of that year, Tom O'Donnell defeated the Healyite candidate J.E. Julian.

19 Father Hyacinth (John) Power was about to leave the Dominican House in Rome and return to Ireland.

20 On 9 April the Government announced that it was planning to introduce conscription in Ireland, which had been excluded from the terms of the Military Service Act 1916.

21 The German spring offensive had started on 21 March. The 8th Liverpools moved into the line on 29 March, but were not engaged in the main offensives. Over the next three months they moved around, mainly on training and reconnaissance duties, between Estaires, Le Souich, Warlincourt, Terramesnil, Pommera, Authie and Pas-en-Artois, holding the trenches in preparation for an expected enemy attack: KRM KR/1/12, battalion war diaries.

22 'John' was their brother, Father Hyacinth Power.

23 Austin Stack had been arrested in Tralee on 3 May and was sent to Belfast Jail. In June he was nominated as Sinn Féin's candidate for the West Kerry constituency.

24 Leo Casey was to survive the war.

25 By this time Michael's battalion was in the front line at Gommecourt, between Arras and Albert.

26 Michael died in the Canadian Stationary Hospital at Doullens, north of Amiens, on the morning of 3 June. He never saw Mary's letter. The envelope was stamped 'Present Location Unknown' and was sent back from the Field Post Office stamped 10 June 1918. Michael was buried in Doullens Cemetery.

27 Tralee had been declared a Special Military Area on 24 June, following an attack

on two RIC sergeants in the centre of the town. One of the sergeants had been wounded and onlookers had helped the attackers to escape. The RIC County Inspector described it as 'one of the most daring outrages ever committed in this County'. There were also disturbances after the victory of Arthur Griffith, the leader of Sinn Féin, in a by-election in East Cavan by-election. See PRO CO904/106, June 1918.

28   This document (**PRO WO 374/49430**) was discovered by the editor of the present volume in 1998, when she was doing research at the Public Record Office, Kew, on Michael Moynihan's military career. Misspelling of Michael's surname occurs in other publications, notably *Ireland's Memorial Records 1914–1918: Being the Names of Irishmen who Fell in the Great European War, 1914–1918, Compiled by the Committee of the Irish National War Memorial* (Dublin, 1923), in which he again appears as Michael 'Moyniham'. The same mistake occurs in S.B. and D.B. John (eds), *Officers who Died in the Service of British, Indian and East African Regiments and Corps 1914–19* (Reading, 1993). The anonymous compiler of the Kerry War Dead statistics in Kerry County Library incorrectly states that Michael was a 2nd Lieutenant in the Royal Munster Fusiliers and that he died in May 1918. He was listed among the Other Ranks in the regimental history of the Civil Service Rifles. Although he never took his degree, Michael's name appeared on UCD's War List Roll of Honour, but his unit is described vaguely as the 'London Rifles'. His headstone at Doullens gives an incorrect date of his death (3 July). His correct name, date of death and place of burial are inscribed on his father's headstone in Rath Cemetery, Tralee.

Notes on the Epilogue

1   T. Ryle Dwyer, *Tans, Terror and Troubles: Kerry's Real Fighting Story 1913–23* (Cork, 2001), pp.228–53.
2   Frank Forde, 'The Liverpool Irish Volunteers', *Irish Sword*, X (1971), p.123.

Bibliography

A Note on Sources

The late Maurice Moynihan recalled Michael's letters coming home in a trunk from France. They remained in the possession of Mary and John until the 1950s when, after Mary's death in 1949, John went to live with Maurice's family. They remained in Maurice's house after John moved to Glasgow to live with Hannah. Maurice read over them occasionally and there are notes in his handwriting on the letters dating from the 1970s. However, the full extent of the family correspondence between 1908 and 1918 was only realised in 1995 when Maurice was moving house into a retirement home and many more letters came to light. He had decided to give his own papers to University College Dublin Archives Department, and Michael's letters were part of the deposit. Seamus Helferty, the archivist in charge of listing the papers, considered that the family correspondence was sufficiently distinct in provenance, date and subject to be accessioned separately as the Michael J. Moynihan Papers, a decision which Maurice Moynihan welcomed warmly.

There are nearly 250 items in the collection. P57/1–5 concerns Michael's school career; P57/6–9 deals with his civil service career and P57/10–12 with his military career. Miscellaneous personal items, including pocketbooks, cashbooks, share certificates and his membership card of the Socialist Party of Ireland are included in P57/13–21. The rest of the papers consist of correspondence between Michael and his mother (P57/22–67) but the bulk of the collection is the correspondence between Michael and his younger brother John (P57/68–231). However, once Michael went to France in June 1916, noticeably fewer of John's letters to him survived. Some of the letters have not been dated but many of the postmarked envelopes have survived. Letter 136 is incomplete as the final pages are missing.

The letters presented little difficulty as the handwriting was very legible and both men wrote clearly and fluently. Some of Mary's letters were written hastily in pencil and were harder to decipher. There are very few letters from John and Michael's father, Maurice, although two letters from him written in November–December 1916 surfaced in Michael's War Office file at the Public Record Office (Letter 189) and in Thomas O'Donnell's Papers at the National Library of Ireland (Letter 196). Both have been included in this collection. Mrs Anne Hayden has retained additional family papers which she has generously let me include and these are identified in the Archives section below by the prefix MFP (Moynihan Family Papers). The family photographs which appear in this book also come from this source. The photograph of John Power on p.5 is reproduced courtesy of the National Library of Ireland. For the present volume, which amounts to approximately two-thirds of the complete letters, I have condensed some of the brothers' longer discussions on philosophy and religion. I have made some minor changes to the spelling of names and places in the interests of consistency. Where possible I have included birth and death dates of people mentioned in the text.

Most of the letters were written from the following addresses: 1 Bridge Place, Tralee, where the Moynihans lived until 1915 when they moved to Springmount, Ballyard on the outskirts of the town. In summertime letters were also sent to and from Fenit, the seaside village outside Tralee where the family regularly spent their holidays. Some of John's letters were written from Listowel, where he often visited on business. After his first Dublin lodgings at 37 Waterloo Place, Michael lived for the rest of his time in Dublin at: 4 Sybil Terrace, Claude Road, Drumcondra; 3 Cabra Villas, Clontarf; and 17 Hume Street, St Stephens Green. In Croydon he lived at 28 Lansdowne Road.

Archives

Kerry County Library, Tralee
Typescript: Geographic Origins of Kerry War Dead

Museum of Liverpool Life: King's Regiment Museum, Liverpool
Service Records
Battalion War Diaries KR/1/10,11,12

National Library of Ireland Dublin
Thomas O'Donnell Papers NLI MS 15,458(7)
Austin Stack Papers NLI MS 17,075, 17,089

Public Record Office London
CO904 : Colonial Office Records (Harvester Press microfilm series *The British in Ireland: Dublin Castle Records 1880-1921* in Mary Immaculate College Library): Police Reports
WO95/3030 War Diaries 1/15ᵗʰ, 2/15th London Regiment
WO374/49430 Michael J. Moynihan, War Office file

University College Dublin Archives Department
Michael J. Moynihan Papers
Desmond Ryan Papers
W.P. Ryan Papers (these include Martin J. Waters, 'W.P. Ryan and the Irish Ireland Movement', Ph.D thesis, St Joseph's College, University of Connecticut, 1970)

Private Collection
Moynihan Family Papers (MFP): Michael's school copybooks; Letters 125, 128, 133, 203, 207, 221, 226, 232, 233, 237, 238

Newspapers and Journals

Clongownian
Cork Examiner
Daily Sketch
Dublin Magazine
An tEireannach (Journal of the London Gaelic League 1910–13)
Freeman's Journal
Inis Fáil (Journal of the London Gaelic League 1904–10)
Irish Catholic
Irish Citizen
Irish Independent
Irish Nation & Peasant
Irish Review
Irish Times
Irish Volunteer
Kerry Advocate
Kerry Evening Post
Kerry Evening Star
Kerry People
Kerry Press

Kerry Sentinel
Kerry Weekly Reporter
Kerryman
Liberator (Tralee)
New Age
New Ireland
Sunday Chronicle
The Times
Times Literary Supplement
T.P.'s Weekly
Votes for Women

Reference Works

Annual Register
Army Register
Beathaisnéis 1882–1982 vols. 2, 4, (eds) Diarmuid Breathnach and Máire
    Ní Mhurchú (Dublin, 1990, 1994)
British Imperial Calendar and Civil Service List
Dictionary of Irish Biography, ed. Henry Boylan (rev. edn. Dublin, 1999)
Dictionary of Irish Literature, ed. R. Hogan (revised and expanded: London,
    1996)
Dictionary of National Biography
Guy's County & City of Cork Directory
*Ireland's Memorial Records 1914–1918: Being the Names of Irishmen who Fell in
    the Great European War, 1914–1918, Compiled by the Committee of the Irish
    National War Memorial* (Dublin, 1923)
Irish Catholic Directory
Irish Literary Magazines: An Outline History and Descriptive Bibliography ed. Tom
    Clyde (Dublin, 2003)
Military Atlas of the First World War, by Arthur Banks (commentary by Alan
    Palmer) (Barnsley, 1998)
New Catholic Encyclopedia (New York, 1966)
New Oxford Companion to Literature in French (Oxford, 1995)
*Officers who died in the Service of British, Indian and East African Regiments and
    Corps 1914–19*, eds S.B. and D.B. John (Reading, 1993)
Oxford Companion to Irish History, ed. Sean Connolly (Oxford, rev. edn. 2002)
Parliamentary Election Results in Ireland, 1801–1922, ed. Brian M. Walker
    (Dublin, 1978)

Slater's Directory
Thom's Directory
University College Cork Calendar
University College Dublin Calendar
Who Was Who

Secondary Works

Joost Augusteijn (ed.), *The Irish Revolution 1913–1923* (Basingstoke, 2002)

T.J. Barrington, *Discovering Kerry: Its History, Heritage & Topography* (Dublin, 1976)

I.F.W. Beckett (ed.), *The Army and the Curragh Incident, 1914* (London, 1986)

I.F.W. Beckett and K. Simpson (eds), *A Nation in Arms: A Social Study of the British Army in the First World War* (London, 1985)

Paul Bew, *Land and the National Question in Ireland 1858–1882* (Dublin, 1978)

Paul Bew, *Conflict and Conciliation in Ireland 1890–1910: Parnellites and Radical Agrarians* (Oxford, 1987)

Paul Bew, *Ideology and the Irish Question: Ulster Unionism and Irish Nationalism 1912–1916* (Oxford, 1994)

Paul Bew, 'Moderate Nationalism and the Irish Revolution, 1916–1923', *Historical Journal*, 42 (1999), pp.729–49.

John P. Boland K.S.G., *Some Memories* (privately printed, Dublin, 1928)

John P. Boland, *An Irishman's Day: A Day in the Life of an Irish M.P.* (London, 1944)

Timothy Bowman, 'Composing Irish Divisions: The Recruitment of Ulster and National Volunteers into the British Army in 1914', *Causeway*, 2, 1 (1995), pp.24–9

Timothy Bowman, 'The Irish at the Somme', *History Ireland*, 4, 4 (1996), pp.48–52

D. George Boyce, *The Sure Confusing Drum: Ireland and the First World War* (Swansea, 1993)

D. George Boyce, 'Ireland and the First World War', *History Ireland*, 2, 3 (1994), pp.48–53

Sydney Brooks, *The New Ireland* (Dublin and London, 1907)

Terence Brown, 'Canon Sheehan and the Catholic Intellectual', in *Ireland's Literature: Selected Essays* (Mullingar, 1988), pp.65–76

Philip Bull, 'The United Irish League and the Reunion of the Irish Parliamentary Party, 1898–1900', *Irish Historical Studies*, XXVI, 101 (1988) pp.51–78

J.J. Burke-Gaffney, *The Story of the King's Regiment (Liverpool) 1914–48* (Liverpool, 1954)

Patrick Callan, 'Ambivalence towards the Saxon Shilling: The Attitudes of the Catholic church in Ireland towards Enlistment during the First World War', *Archivium Hibernicum*, 41 (1986), pp.99–111

Patrick Callan, 'Voluntary recruiting for the British army in Ireland during the First World War', *Irish Sword* XVII (1987), pp.42–56

Frank Callanan, 'The "Appeal to the Hillsides": Parnell and the Fenians 1890–91', in *Parnell: The Politics of Power*, ed. Donal McCartney (Dublin, 1991), pp.148–69

Frank Callanan, *T.M. Healy* (Cork, 1996)

Catherine Candy, *Priestly Fictions: Popular Irish Novelists of the Early 20th Century* (Dublin, 1995)

Patrick Casey, 'Irish Casualties in the First World War', *Irish Sword*, XX (1997), pp.193–206

Lord Hugh Cecil, *Conservatism* (London, 1912)

Winston Churchill, *Richard Carvel* (London, 1899)

Winston Churchill, *The Inside of the Cup* (London, 1913)

Samuel Clark and James S. Donnelly, Jr (eds), *Irish Peasants: Violence and Political Unrest 1780–1914* (Manchester, 1983)

I.F. Clarke, *Voices Prophesying War 1763–1984* (Oxford, 1966)

Marie Coleman, 'Mobilisation: The South Longford By-election and its Impact on Political Mobilisation', in *The Irish Revolution, 1913–1923*, ed. Joost Augusteijn, (Basingstoke, 2002) pp.53–69

Marie Coleman, *County Longford and the Irish Revolution 1910–1923* (Dublin, 2003)

Thomas Neilan Crean, 'Labour and Politics in Kerry during the First World War', *Saothar*, 19 (1994), pp.27–39

George Dangerfield, *The Strange Death of Liberal England* (London, 1936)

Terence Denman, 'The Catholic Irish Soldier in the First World War: The "racial environment"', *Irish Historical Studies*, XXVII (1991), pp.352–65

Peter Dennis, *The Territorial Army 1906–1940* (London, 1987)

Paul Dillon, 'James Connolly and the Kerry Famine of 1898', *Saothar* 25 (2001), pp.29–42

J.S. Donnelly, Jr, 'Cork Market: Its Role in the Nineteenth Century Butter Trade', *Studia Hibernica*, 11 (1970), pp.130–63

James S. Donnelly Jr. 'The Kenmare Estates during the Nineteeenth Century', *JKAHS*, 21–23 (1988–90)

Thomas P.C. Dooley, *Irishmen or English Soldiers?: The Times and World of a Southern Catholic Irish Man (1876–1916) Enlisting in the British Army During the First World War* (Liverpool, 1995)

Thomas P. Dooley, 'Southern Ireland, Historians and the First World War', *Irish Studies Review*, 4 (1993), pp.5–9

Raymund Dowdall OP, *Memories of Still More Recent Irish Dominicans who Passed Away Between the Years 1950–1960* (Dublin, 1968)

Myles Dungan, *Irish Voices from the Great War* (Dublin, 1995)

Myles Dungan, *They Shall Not Grow Old: Irish Soldiers and the Great War* (Dublin, 1997)

Colonel John K. Dunlop, *The Development of the British Army 1899–1914: From the eve of the South African War to the eve of the Great War, with special reference to the Territorial Force* (London, 1938)

T. Ryle Dwyer, *Tans, Terror and Troubles: Kerry's Real Fighting Story 1913–23* (Cork, 2001)

Fathers of the Society of Jesus, *A Page of Irish History: The Story of University College, Dublin 1883–1909* (Dublin, 1930)

William L. Feingold, 'Land League Power: The Tralee Poor Law Election of 1881', in Samuel Clark and James S. Donnelly Jr (eds), *Irish Peasants* (Manchester, 1983) pp.285–310

William L. Feingold, *The Revolt of the Tenantry: The Transformation of Local Government in Ireland, 1872–1886* (Boston, 1984)

Hugh Fenning OP, 'Father Anselm Moynihan', *Obituary, Irish Dominican Province: 1996–2000*, pp.55–7

Diarmaid Ferriter, *'Lovers of Liberty?' Local Government in 20th Century Ireland* (Dublin, 2001)

Joseph Finnan, '"Let Irishmen come together in the Trenches": John Redmond and the Irish Party policy in the Great War, 1914–1918', *Irish Sword*, XXII (2000), pp.174–92

Gabriel Fitzmaurice (ed.), *The Kerry Anthology* (Dublin, 2000)

David Fitzpatrick, *Politics and Irish Life 1913–1921: Provincial Experience of War and Revolution* (Dublin, 1977)

David Fitzpatrick, 'Strikes in Ireland, 1914–1921', *Saothar*, 6 (1980), pp.26–39

David Fitzpatrick, 'The Overflow of the Deluge: Anglo-Irish Relationships, 1914–22', in Oliver MacDonagh and W.F. Mandle (eds.), *Ireland and Irish-Australia: Studies in Cultural and Political History* (London, 1986), pp.81–94

David Fitzpatrick (ed.), *Ireland the First World War* (Mullingar, rev. edn. 1988)

David Fitzpatrick (ed.), *Revolution? Ireland 1917–1923* (Dublin, 1990)

David Fitzpatrick, 'The Logic of Collective Sacrifice: Ireland and the

British Army, 1914–1918', *Historical Journal*, 38, 4 (1995), pp.1017–30

David Fitzpatrick, 'Militarism in Ireland, 1900–22', in Thomas Bartlett and Keith Jeffery (eds), *A Military History of Ireland* (Cambridge, 1996), pp.379–406

David Fitzpatrick, *The Two Irelands 1912–1939* (Oxford, 1998)

Patrick Foley, *History of the Natural, Civil, Military and Ecclesiastical State of the County of Kerry* (Dublin, 1907)

Frank Forde, 'The Liverpool Irish Volunteers', *Irish Sword* X (1971), pp.106–23

Anne Fremantle (ed.), *The Papal Encyclicals in their Historical Context* (New York, 1956)

Paul Fussell, *The Great War and Modern Memory* (Oxford, 1975 rep.1979)

Tom Garvin, *Nationalist Revolutionaries in Ireland 1858–1928* (Oxford, 1987)

J. Anthony Gaughan, *Listowel and its Vicinity* (Cork, 1973)

J. Anthony Gaughan, *Austin Stack: Portrait of a Separatist* (Dublin, 1977)

J. Anthony Gaughan, *A Political Odyssey: Thomas O'Donnell M.P. for West Kerry 1900–1918* (Dublin, 1983)

Laurence M. Geary, *The Plan of Campaign 1886–1891* (Cork, 1986)

Virginia E. Glandon, *Arthur Griffith and the Advanced Nationalist Press Ireland, 1900–22* (New York, 1985)

Adrian Gregory and Senia Pašeta (eds.), *Ireland and the Great War: 'A War to Unite Us All ?'* (Manchester, 2002)

Adrian Gregory, '"You might as well recruit Germans": British Public Opinion and the Decision to Conscript the Irish in 1918', in *Ireland and the Great War* eds Adrian Gregory and Senia Pašeta (Manchester, 2002) pp.113–32

Stephen Gwynn, *John Redmond's Last Years* (London, 1919)

Niall C. Harrington, *Kerry Landing: An Episode from the Civil War* (Dublin, 1992)

Thomas Hennessey, *Dividing Ireland: World War I and Partition* (London, 1998)

History of the Prince of Wales' Own Civil Service Rifles (London, 1921)

Robert Hogan and James Kilroy (eds), *Lost Plays of the Irish Renaissance* (Newark, Del.,1970)

John J. Horgan, *Parnell to Pearse: Some Recollections and Reflections* (Dublin, 1948)

David Howie and Josephine Howie, 'Irish Recruiting and the Home Rule Crisis of August–September 1914', in Michael Dockrill and David French (eds), *Strategy and Intelligence: British Policy during the First World War* (London, 1996), pp.1–22

S.M. Hussey, *The Reminiscences of an Irish Land Agent (being those of S.M. Hussey compiled by Home Gordon)* (London, 1905)

John Hutchinson, *The Dynamics of Cultural Nationalism: The Gaelic Revival and the Creation of the Irish Nation State* (London, 1987)

Samuel Hynes, 'Personal Narratives and Commemoration', in Jay Winter and Emmanuel Sivan (eds), *War and Remembrance in the Twentieth Century* (Cambridge, 1999), pp.205–20

Neil Jakob, 'Representation and Commemoration of the Great War: A Comparative Study of Philipp Witkop's *Kriegsbriefe gefallener Studenten* (1928) and Laurence Housman's *War letters of fallen Englishmen* (1930)', *Irish History: A Research Yearbook*, 1 (2002), pp.75–88

Patricia Jalland, *The Liberals and Ireland: The Ulster Question in British Politics to 1914* (New York, 1980)

Keith Jeffery, 'The Great War in Modern Irish Memory', in T.G. Fraser and Keith Jeffery (eds), *Men, Women and War (Historical Studies XVIII)* (Dublin, 1993), pp.136–57

Keith Jeffery, 'Irish Culture and the Great War', *Bullán*, 1, 2 (1994), pp.87–96

Keith Jeffery, 'The Irish military tradition and the British Empire', in Keith Jeffery (ed.), *'An Irish Empire'? Aspects of Ireland and the British Empire* (Manchester, 1996), pp.94–122

Keith Jeffery, *Ireland and the Great War* (Cambridge, 2000)

Tom Johnstone, *Orange, Green and Khaki: The Story of the Irish Regiments in the Great War, 1914–1918* (Dublin, 1992)

Tom Johnstone and James Hagerty, *The Cross on the Sword: Catholic Chaplains in the Forces* (London, 1996)

David S. Jones, 'The Cleavage between Graziers and Peasants in the Land Struggle, 1890–1910', in Samuel Clark and James S. Donnelly Jr (eds), *Irish Peasants* (Manchester, 1983), pp.374–417

Mannix Joyce, 'The Story of Limerick and Kerry in 1916', *Capuchin Annual* (1966), pp.327–70

P. Karsten, 'Irish soldiers in the British Army, 1792–1922: Suborned or Subordinate?' *Journal of Social History*, XVII (1983), pp.31–64

Jean Kelly (ed.) *Love Letters from the Front* (Dublin, 2000)

Liam Kennedy, 'Farmers, Traders, and Agricultural Politics in Pre-Independence Ireland', in Samuel Clark and James S. Donnelly Jr (eds.), *Irish Peasants*, pp.339–73

Kerry's Fighting Story 1916–21 (Tralee, n.d., c.1947)

Jeremiah King, *King's History of Kerry* (Wexford, 1912)

Michael Laffan, *The Resurrection of Ireland: The Sinn Fein Party 1916–1923*

(Cambridge, 1999)

Jack Lane (ed.), *Aspects of Life: Cork-Kerry Butter Road 1748–1998* (Aubane, 1998)

Jane Leonard, 'The Catholic Chaplaincy', in David Fitzpatrick (ed.), *Ireland and the First World War* (Mullingar, 1988), pp.1–14

Jane Leonard, 'The Twinge of Memory: Armistice Day in Ireland since 1919', in Richard English and Graham Walker (eds), *Unionism in Modern Ireland* (London, 1996)

Jane Leonard, 'The Reaction of Irish officers in the British Army to the Easter Rising of 1916', in Hugh Cecil and Peter H. Liddle (eds), *Facing Armageddon: the First World War Experienced* (London, 1996), pp.256–68

Pat Lynch, *They Hanged John Twiss* (Tralee, 1982)

Gerard J. Lyne, *The Lansdowne Estate in Kerry under the agency of William Steuart Trench, 1849–1872* (Dublin, 2001)

Donal McCartney (ed.), *Parnell: The Politics of Power* (Dublin, 1991)

Donal McCartney, *UCD: A National Idea* (Dublin, 1999)

Seamus McConville (ed.), *The Dominicans in Kerry 1243–1987* (Tralee, 1987)

Sinead McCoole, *Guns and Chiffon: Women Revolutionaries and Kilmainham Gaol 1916–1923* (Dublin, 1997)

Lucy McDiarmid, 'The Man Who Died for the Language: The Reverend Dr O'Hickey and the "Essential Irish" Language Controversy of 1909', *Eire-Ireland*, XXXV, 1–2 (2000), pp.188–218

Walter McDonald, *Reminiscences of a Maynooth Professor* (ed.) Denis Gwynn (London, 1925)

J.J. McElligott, obituaries of in *Irish Times* 26 January 1974 by TKW [T.K.Whitaker] and 30 January 1974 by PO'K [P. Ó Ceallaigh]

Deirdre McMahon, 'Maurice Moynihan (1902–1999) Irish Civil Servant: An Appreciation', *Studies*, 89, 353 (2000), pp.71–6

Francis MacManus, 'The Fate of Canon Sheehan', *The Bell*, XV, 2 (1947), pp.16–27

Dorothy Macardle, *Tragedies of Kerry 1922–23* (Dublin, 1924)

Peter Malone (ed.), *Images and Chronicles from the Archives of* The Kerryman *Newspaper: A Portrait of Kerry in the 20th Century* (Tralee, 2001)

Wallace Martin, *The New Age under Orage: Chapters in English Cultural History* (Manchester, 1967)

Patrick Maume, *D.P. Moran* (Dublin, 1995)

Patrick Maume, *The Long Gestation: Irish Nationalist Life 1891–1918* (Dublin, 1999)

James Meenan (ed.), *Centenary History of the Literary and Historical Society of University College Dublin 1855–1955* (Tralee, 1956)

Patrick Mileham, *'Difficulties Be Damned': The King's Regiment 8th 63rd 96th: A History of the City Regiment of Manchester and Liverpool* (Knutsford, 2000)

Arthur Mitchell, *Labour in Irish Politics 1890–1930: The Irish Labour Movement in an Age of Revolution* (Dublin, 1974)

Thomas F. Morrissey SJ, *Towards a National University: William Delany SJ (1835–1924)* (Dublin, 1983)

John Moynihan, obituaries of in *Kerryman*, 12 December 1964; *Irish Press* 11 December 1964

Maurice Moynihan, 'Charles Stewart Parnell: A Sketch of His Life', *Kerry Sentinel*, 7–28 October 1916

Maurice Moynihan, 'The Gaelic Athletic Association', *New Ireland*, 18 November 1916 (reprinted in *Kerry Sentinel*, 25 November 1918)

Billy Mullins, *Memoirs of Billy Mullins: Veteran of the War of Independence* (Tralee, 1983)

James Murphy, *Catholic Fiction and Social Reality in Ireland, 1872–1922* (Westport, Conn. 1997)

James Murphy, *Abject Loyalty: Nationalism and Monarchy in Ireland During the Reign of Queen Victoria* (CT, 2001)

J.E. Nelson, 'Some Irish soldiers in the Great War', *Irish Sword*, XI (1973–74), pp.9–15

Ben Novick, 'Advanced Nationalist Propaganda and Moralistic Revolution, 1914–1918', inJoost Augusteyn (ed.), *The Irish Revolution, 1913–23*, pp.34–52

Joseph O'Brien, *William O'Brien and the Course of Irish Politics 1881–1918* (Berkeley, 1976)

William O'Brien M.P. *The Irish Revolution and How It Came About* (Dublin, 1923)

Leon Ó Broin, *No Man's Man: A Biographical Memoir of Joseph Brennan - Civil Servant and First Governor of the Central Bank* (Dublin, 1982)

Margaret O'Callaghan, 'Denis Patrick Moran and the "Irish colonial condition", 1891–1921', in, (ed.) *Political Thought in Ireland Since the Seventeenth Century*, D. George Boyce (London, 1993), pp.146–60

Margaret O'Callaghan, *British High Politics and Nationalist Ireland: Criminality Land and the Law under Forster and Balfour* (Cork, 1994)

Eunan O'Halpin, *The Decline of the Union: British Government in Ireland, 1892–1920* (Dublin, 1987)

Eunan O'Halpin, 'The Civil Service and the Political System', *Administration*, 38 (1990–91), pp.283–302

Timothy J. O'Keefe, 'The 1898 Efforts to Celebrate the United Irishmen: The '98 Centennial', *Éire/Ireland*, 23 (1988), pp.51–73

Timothy O'Keefe, "'Who Fears to Speak '98 ?'': The Rhetoric and Rituals of the United Irishmen Centennial, 1898', *Éire/Ireland* 27 (1992), pp.67–91

Philip O'Leary, *The Prose Literature of the Gaelic Revival, 1891–1921* (Philadelphia, 1994)

Seán Ó Lúing, 'The Phoenix Society in Kerry, 1858–9', *JKAHS*, 2 (1969), pp.5–26

Seán Ó Lúing, 'Aspects of the Fenian Rising in Kerry', *JKAHS*, 3–7 (1970–74)

Seán Ó Lúing, *I Die in a Good Cause* (Tralee, 1970)

Donal O'Shea, *Tralee: Street by Street History* (Tralee, 1990)

Pádraig Ó Snodaigh, 'Neart Fórsaí Shasana i dTrá Lí ', *JKAHS*, 3 (1970), pp.171–2

Donal J. O'Sullivan, *Church of St John the Evangelist Ashe Street, Tralee* (Tralee, 2001)

Peter Parker, *The Old Lie: The Great War and the Public School Ethos* (London, 1987)

Senia Pašeta, '1798 in 1898: The Politics of Commemoration', *Irish Review* 22 (1998), pp.46–53

Senia Pašeta, *Before the Revolution: Nationalism, Social Change and Ireland's Catholic Elite 1879–1922* (Cork, 1999)

Senia Pašeta, 'Thomas Kettle: "An Irish Soldier in the Army of Europe"?', in *Ireland and the Great War*, Adrian Gregory and Senia Pašeta (eds), (Manchester, 2002) pp.8–27

G.K. Peatling, *From Unionism to Liberal Commonwealth: The Transformation of British Public Opinion towards Irish Self-Government* (Dublin, 2000)

Bob Peedle, *Encyclopaedia of the Modern Territorial Army* (Wellingborough, 1990)

Donal A. Reidy, *The Diocese of Kerry (formerly of Ardfert)* (Tralee, 1937)

Andrew Roberts, *Salisbury: Victorian Titan* (London, 1999)

Desmond Ryan, *Remembering Sion: A Chronicle of Storm and Quiet* (London, 1934)

W.P. Ryan (William Patrick O'Ryan), *The Plough and the Cross: A Story of New Ireland* (Dublin, 1910)

W.P. Ryan, 'The Meaning of the Irish Language Movement', in Basil Williams (ed.) *Home Rule Problems* (London, 1911), pp.23–34

W.P. Ryan, *The Pope's Green Island* (London, 1912)

W.P. Ryan, *The Irish Labour Movement: From the 'Twenties to our own day* (Dublin, 1919)

Colin Rynne, *At the Sign of the Cow: the Cork Butter Market 1770–1924* (Dublin, 1988)

Johnathan Schneer, *London 1900: Imperial metropolis* (Yale, 1999)

Canon [Patrick Augustine] Sheehan, *The Triumph of Failure* (London, 1898)

Canon Sheehan, *My New Curate* (Boston, 1900)

Canon Sheehan, *Luke Delmege* (London, 1901)

Canon Sheehan, *Lisheen, or The Test of the Spirits* (London, 1907)

Canon Sheehan, *The Intellectuals: An Experiment in Irish Club-Life* (London, 1911)

Canon Sheehan, *The Graves at Kilmorna* (London, 1915)

Canon Sheehan, *The Literary Life and Other Essays* (Dublin, 1921)

F. Sheehy-Skeffington, 'Frederick Ryan', *Irish Review*, III, 27 (1913), pp.113–19

Peter Simkins, *Kitchener's Army: The Raising of the New Armies, 1914–1916* (Manchester, 1988)

Hew Strachan, *The First World War: Vol.1 To Arms* (Oxford, 2001)

John Terraine, *The Great War* (1965: rev. ed. London, 1997)

T.R. Threlfall, *The Story of the King's (Liverpool Regiment)* (Liverpool, 1916)

John Turner (ed.), *Britain and the First World War* (London, 1988)

Philip Warner, *The First World War: A Narrative* (1995: new ed. London, 1998)

H.G. Wells, *Tono-Bungay* (London, 1909)

H.G. Wells, *The New Machiavelli* (London, 1911)

Ray Westlake, *The Territorial Battalions: A Pictorial History 1859–1985* (Tonbridge Wells, 1986)

Ray Westlake, *The Territorial Force 1914* (Newport, 1988)

Ray Westlake and Mike Chappell, *British Territorial Units 1914–1918* (London, 1991)

Jérôme aan de Wiel, *The Catholic Church in Ireland, 1914–1918: War and Politics* (Dublin, 2003)

Glenn R. Wilkinson, *Depictions and Images of War in Edwardian Newspapers, 1989–1914* (London, 2002)

Jay Winter, *The Great War and the British People* (Basingstoke, 1986)

Jay Winter, *The Experience of World War I* (London, 1989)

Jay Winter, *Sites of Memory, Sites of Mourning: the Great War in European Cultural History* (Cambridge, 1995)

Jay Winter and Emmanuel Sivan (eds), *War and Remembrance in the Twentieth Century* (Cambridge, 1999)

Robert Wohl, *The Generation of 1914* (London, 1980)

Everard Wyrall, *The History of the King's Regiment (Liverpool) 1914–1919*, 3 vols (London, 1930–35)

Index